"The book is a rich compendium of ideas you can try. David has synthesised many essential topics of management that will save you time in helping you structure your own approach. It is a great stimulus for both thought and action."

SIR MICK DAVIS
Former Chief Executive, Xstrata plc

"David Hodes distils years of trial-and-error experience into insights that combine science-based diagnostic methods for productivity improvement with a human-centred, dialogue-based mindset. This combination is the secret sauce to sustainable organisational productivity and adaptability—when it becomes more than just work."

TULLY CASHMAN
Manager Organisational Development, Cargill APAC

"In a very powerful way, *More Than Just Work* combines the elements of the Theory of Constraints and Systems Thinking with just the right blend of the best thinking around the people in the system. Potent fuel to help businesses take off like a rocket or roar out of recession."

JEFF JARRATT
Principal Consultant, Executive Central, Australia

"This is the collective evidence of what can be achieved by combining a lifelong dedication to learning with fearless leadership and application of innovation in productivity that is necessary and sufficient for making the world a better place. An amazing body of knowledge that's as practical as it is cerebral—a true reflection of the author."

STEPHEN CASEY
Chief Operating Officer

"The 'Theory of Constraints' is often dismissed as a 'theory' with no practical application, or belittled as just 'chasing the next bottleneck.' Few realize that it is a deep body of knowledge that distils the experiences and thoughts of the sharpest thinkers who aimed their attention and minds at developing a deeper understanding of business systems.

"Dr Goldratt certainly led the way, and used the expression 'standing on the shoulders of giants' when describing his own work with respect to the giants of the field, like Henry Ford and Taiichi Ohno. Dr Goldratt was also clear: the best way to honour these giants is not to admire them in awe—as they certainly deserve—but to stand on their shoulders to see further and continue their work and advance it even more. It is the essence of the Process of Ongoing Improvement. Never cease to improve; don't let inertia, convenience and complacency stop you. Going further and beyond is the best way to honour the giants that came before us.

"In this book, David does that as he honours Dr Goldratt's exhortation while he strives to explain the systems thinking perspective that is grounded in the Theory of Constraints—a perspective you will immensely benefit from in your business and maybe even in your personal life.

"Read this book. Let David be your giant. Then it will be your turn to stand on his shoulders and go even further."

STEVE TENDON
Inventor of the TameFlow Approach

"David Hodes brings revolutionary methods for increasing productivity together with a deep understanding of the human need for purposeful work. An engaging—and necessary—call to arms."

BILL DETTMER
Author, *The Logical Thinking Process*

"An amazing body of knowledge that's as practical as it is cerebral—a true reflection of the author."

SANJEEV GUPTA
TOC-ICO Lifetime Achievement Award Winner

More Than Just Work

Innovations in productivity to inspire your people and uplift performance

David V. Hodes

Copyright © David Hodes, 2017
All rights reserved

Published by Ensemble Publishing

No part of this book may be copied, reproduced, adapted, stored in a retrieval system, communicated or transmitted in any form or by any means without prior written permission from the author. All inquiries should be made to the author via the web address below.

Contact the author:
David.Hodes@EnsembleConsultingGroup.com
EnsembleConsultingGroup.com

Cover illustration by Brandfibre. Ensemble rocket and cockpit by Trevor Paul. Other illustrations by Mea Jordaan. Logic trees by David Hodes.

Typeset by Hourigan & Co.
in Linux Libertine

For Gill
and a better world for Rafe and Jake

About the author

David Hodes is a qualified System Thinker and Practitioner. He was awarded a National Engineering Scholarship in the UK and attended the Imperial College of Science and Technology in London, where he graduated with a degree in Mechanical Engineering. He is certified as a TOC expert with the TOC-ICO (TOC International Certification Organisation) and is a consulting member of SOL (Society of Organisational Learning). His passion lies in the creation of learning environments where new ideas can take root and deliver rapid, tangible benefits to the people and companies he deals with. He founded Ensemble Consulting Group in January 2000, and has been applying TOC for more than 20 years in Australia, Asia, the Americas and South Africa. He has led the implementation of work management systems for the successful execution of billions of dollars of engineering and business management projects in tier-1 Australian companies in the mining, banking, construction, manufacturing, retail and aviation industries.

To contact David, please email
David.Hodes@EnsembleConsultingGroup.com

Contents

FOREWORD *Sir Mick Davis* xv

THE ETHICS OF 'JUST WORK' *Rabbi Dr Dovid Slavin* . . xix

AUTHOR'S NOTE: How to Read This Book. 1

PREFACE: Working on Changing Work 3

INTRODUCTION: Turning Intention into Reality. 9

    The 'what', 'how' and 'why' work. 9

    A theory and practice of systems thinking 11

    Of goals, purpose and sounding together 14

    The courage to embark on a Hero's Journey 15

    The Just Work Manifesto. 17

PART 1   WHY CHANGE?   19

A Powerful Question is More than Half a Good Answer . 21

1. TECHNOLOGY: Enabling the Ensemble. 33

    Projectiles, projecting and projects 35

    Adopting and adapting for new opportunities. 38

  Lots of bits and bytes 40

  To be or not to be. 43

2. PEOPLE: Putting a Man on the Moon 47

  Avoiding becoming the tool of our tools 48

  Mythology and meaning-making 50

  Pausing between stimulus and response. 51

  On being too big for your boots 56

  Autonomy, mastery and purpose 57

  A Shakespearean moonshot. 59

3. PROCESS: How to Get it Together 63

  Just the way it's done around here 65

  The consequences of getting it wrong 67

  The challenge of getting it right 71

  Focus on how things flow from end to end. 75

PART 2 WHAT TO CHANGE   79

Winning Results: The Ensemble Way 81

4. INNOVATION: Those Who Innovate Fastest Win 85

  Failure or discovery? 86

  What's really at stake? 88

  Fold or hold?. 89

  Leaders must learn to let go. 92

Contents

    Turning up to your life 94

    Working on playful teams 96

    The state, the ivory tower and new ideas 98

5. STRATEGY: Thinking Tools to Reach Your Goal 103

    Setting goals to fulfil a purpose 106

    The business of business management systems 109

    Switching on to operating discipline 110

    What, to what, and how to change—within reason . . . 113

    A reason to be logical 118

    Turning common sense into common practice 122

    The quick way out usually leads back in 124

6. CULTURE: Building a Shared Vision 129

    Constructing culture 130

    Sharing stories 132

    Overcoming our learning anxiety 134

    Successfully entering future after future 136

    Internal cohesion and external adaptation 138

    Hiring Hercules to lift your vision 141

    Innovating fast means learning fast 144

    Seeing system archetypes 149

7. LANGUAGE: Step into their Shoes 153

    A grammar of the social field 154

Feeling what we're seeing 158

The stop at the top of the trajectory 161

8. ORGANISATION: The Strange Freedom of Hierarchies 169

The paradox of a hierarchy of freedom 171

As required by nature. 173

Start with end-to-end thinking. 175

Fully defining the work. 179

Crossing the silos. 182

Time to think of chronos, kairos and modes of work . 184

Team of Teams 190

9. RESOURCES: What's Reasonable and Possible 193

Human resources. 195

Material resources 197

Financial resources. 199

Information resources. 202

10. OPERATIONS: Playing on Cue Every Time 207

TOC: Theory of Constraints. 207

The 5-Step FOCUS 209

Project management. 216

Production management 218

Distribution and replenishment management 221

Contents

PART 3 WHAT TO CHANGE TO?   227

Playing in Time 229

    Invitation to a meditation 231

    What's what? 234

    Four pillars hold up the goal 235

    Looking through different lenses 236

    Innovating across all types of work. 237

11. DEFINITION: The How, What and Why 241

    Start with your own work. 242

    GOVERNANCE AND STANDARDS. 246

    Maturing from the start, one step at a time. 248

    CONTEXT, PURPOSE AND SCOPE 252

    VERSION CONTROL AND ICT MANAGEMENT . . . 255

12. PREPARATION: Getting Ready to Perform. 263

    LEARNING, LEADERSHIP AND CULTURE. 264

    MINDSET AND BEHAVIOUR ANALYTICS. 270

    Mind the gap. 275

    ACCOUNTABILITY HIERARCHIES. 277

    Architecting simplicity to navigate complexity 281

13. OPTIMISATION: Focusing your Efforts. 285

    Empowered means engaged. 288

PLANNING, SCHEDULING AND PROCESS MGMT . 290
First the flight plan, then the schedule. 293
Standard ways to schedule the dance. 297
Some questions on scheduling 299
RESOURCE MANAGEMENT 301
Being there isn't the same as doing it 304
Aggregation and the law of large numbers. 305
Practically capable of doing work 307
Finding constraints and collaborating to optimise . . . 310
SCENARIO TESTING 313
Agile and active is the way forward 315

14. PERFORMANCE: Hitting All the High Notes 317
WAYS OF WORKING. 322
Running better meetings. 325
REPORTING AND ANALYTICS. 329
REQUIREMENTS AND DELIVERABLES MGMT. . . . 337

PART 4   HOW TO CHANGE   341

New Problems, New Thinking. 343
From hell on earth to paradise city 344
The productivity tide to practically lift all ships. 345
Learning about fate and destiny 346

Contents

    The hero's journey—no highway option. 348

    A life vest, not a straitjacket. 352

15. EXPLORE: Mapping the Terrain. 355

    GENERATIVE INTERVIEWS 356

    Keeping records. 358

    Starting with ourselves. 360

    FOUNDATION WORKSHOP 361

    Fail often to succeed sooner. 368

16. DESIGN: Rewriting the Score. 373

    LEARNING JOURNEYS 375

    RETREAT AND REFLECT 380

    CRYSTALLISE INTENT 385

17. DELIVER: Tuning the Innovation Engine. 389

    The dance of change. 391

    INNOVATION WORKSHOP 394

    IMPLEMENTATION. 399

EPILOGUE: Transcending the Game 403

APPENDICES: The Thinking Process 409

    Appendix A: Sample Goal Tree. 410

    Appendix B: The Current Reality Tree. 412

    Appendix C: The Evaporating Cloud. 414

Appendix D: The Future Reality Tree 416

Appendix E: Logic Checks 418

Bibliography 421

Thanks and acknowledgements 427

Foreword

Sir Mick Davis
Former Chief Executive, Xstrata Plc

David Hodes builds this monumental work, on work, on the foundation of the powerful proposition of Holocaust survivor Viktor Frankl that man is always free to search for meaning. How we respond to the vicissitudes of life, its optionality and its constraints defines the life we live, the value we add and our place in society. This process gives us meaning and worth and allows us to be in harmony with the rhythms that shape our society.

So much of our lives is taken up with work that the odyssey of discovering who we are and what value we can add is, for most of us, found or lost in the workplace. It is thus axiomatic that the business of work is not just about activities and actions which serve a defined need. Rather, work is core to the existential wellbeing of mankind. It is a noble undertaking and those who work deserve the accoutrements of nobility—to be lionised by employers, to have their needs properly attended to, to be inspired and challenged and to be held to account to the highest standards of chivalry. If management creates such an environment, those in their employ can develop and grow. Their contributions enrich society.

The title of this book suggests that a fundamental contribution of the employer is to create an ethical workplace, supported by certain immutable values that come together in work, which does justice to employees, employers and the myriad of stakeholders who have legitimate interest in their endeavours.

I have run large international enterprises where the interface with communities, governments, employees and consumers has been complex and at times fraught. My industry, mining, disturbs the environment, uproots communities, generally finds itself in contested space and lays claim to resources locked in the land of others. Yet its outputs are essential to life as we know it. My colleagues and I took Xstrata plc from fledgling beginnings to one of the largest mining companies in the world over a 12-year period. I think our employees found meaning in their work and added value across the range of Xstrata's stakeholders. They did this because fundamentally they owned the central propositions that made Xstrata an extraordinary company to work for. My experience resonates with the principles of 'just work' that David lays out in the chapters that follow.

Xstrata's driving value was the creation of value. But the value we sought to create was a value to society—the value of doing good. Just as we found that safety and productivity went hand in hand in our hundred-plus operations, so did doing good in society and for shareholder returns. Our employees' search for meaning was turbocharged because they worked in a company where being meaningful was our central value driver.

The value of constant innovation, of always trying to be

FOREWORD *Sir Mick Davis*

different, fostered spontaneity and an inquisitive mind. This was even more powerful as we religiously delegated not only responsibility and accountability (which all employers do), but also authority and attendant decision rights as well (which most employers do not) so that our employees were inspired by the empowerment to act that we gave them. This meant we had to licence realistic risk-taking and act as wicketkeeper when the risk did not pay off. We treated bad outcomes as learning experiences upon which we could build future success. For this type of accountability, I encourage you to read carefully Chapter 8, 'Organisation'.

At the heart of David's work is the Golden Rule: 'treat others as you would wish to be treated'. To seed a culture that grows an organisation which cares for its employees, for the environment in which it operates and for the communities who host it is the highest calling for an executive. The theme throughout this book is courage: the courage to do what's needed to create justice at work, helping all to achieve their potential and find meaning.

The chapters that follow contain some key ideas whose adoption can lead to what David calls 'better ways to do better work'. The book is a rich compendium of ideas you can try. He has synthesised many essential topics of management that will save you time in helping you structure your own approach. It is a great stimulus for both thought and action.

David sets the stage with a powerful question: 'Why change?' He then views it through three lenses: people, process and technology. Our post-pandemic world is still coming to terms with the changing nature of work in this technological age. Seeking new solutions to how these elements combine is essential if today's marginalised can be confident of the value of the work they do and can derive value from it. Unless we can regain that equilibrium, social mobility will remain stalled and the liberal democracies will continue embattled and impotent to respond to the challenges that ordinary people face today.

This book is an important contribution to that endeavour. If David had written it 20 years ago, I would certainly have distributed it to my senior managers and beyond.

The Ethics of 'Just Work'

RABBI DR DOVID SLAVIN
EXECUTIVE DIRECTOR,
RABBINICAL COLLEGE OF SYDNEY
FOUNDER, OUR BIG KITCHEN

I have sat with David Hodes on many occasions and sought his input across a variety of responsibilities I've had, from community matters to the charitable organisation I founded. These were complicated matters which I would normally have to explain at length. With David everything was very clear, very quickly. He understands the essence of things extremely well, down to the minutia, yet always finds simpler, more effective ways to do things.

David's book *More Than Just Work* is an incredible resource for anybody who wants to work smarter rather than just working hard, and who wants to inspire staff to achieve their utmost. His decades of personal experiences are woven through the pages, including challenges with make-or-break moments and how he overcame them. This makes it an engaging personal story, even as these real-world experiences highlight how he understands others facing similar situations.

If you want to attempt all this yourself from scratch, good luck. But it's highly recommended to stand on the shoulders of giants who preceded us. David draws on concepts from the European, American, and Japanese masters of the work environment who have all contributed to what David calls, 'better ways to do better work'. He has condensed their wisdom for the reader's benefit. In particular, his use of the rocket ship metaphor provides very clear signposts, taking each aspect and breaking it into bite-sized pieces so they can be better understood and are practically usable for whatever business you are in.

I'm sure everybody will find their favourite part of the book. One of mine is the concept of the ensemble and the conductor. David writes that the maestro must learn to lead the whole group, or else play every single note of every single instrument. This is a powerful metaphor for leaders in large organisations, and the chapters offer the tools to lead in this way.

Advice is the one thing that people love giving but not taking. David has been extremely good at being able to give advice in a way where the recipient, in this case me, was extremely happy to receive it. This book will give readers a glimpse of what it's like to interact with David. For executives who have been waiting for a step-change in responsibility—and, now the big break has arrived, are seeking some guidance—this is the ideal handbook.

Finally, I would add that David's ideas about what it means to provide 'just work' resonate strongly with the ideals I strive to uphold in the organisations I oversee.

AUTHOR'S NOTE
How to Read This Book

I like to think that this book works as well for anyone wanting to dip in and out of specific topics as for those who want to explore more fully the arc of the narrative. I have thus organised it into four major parts, with a preface and introduction at the beginning and an epilogue and appendixes at the end. Depending on what type of reader you are and the reason you're reading it, here are a few tips that I hope will help you get the most out of it.

Preface and Introduction. I have included these for those of you who would like to know a little more about how the book came about and why I wrote it.

Part 1: Why Change? This part addresses the fundamental triad of people, process and technology and how these elements fit into the most basic framework of systems thinking from an operational, learning and organisational design perspective.

Part 2: What to change? This part introduces the Ensemble Way framework for understanding your value creation engine. I've used the metaphor of a spaceship, and you might imagine that each of the chapter headings is an exploratory space-walk of discovery into the critical domains before returning to the mother ship for the next adventure.

Part 3: What to change to? This part describes the workings of the command and control unit of your value creation engine – the Value Management Office, and is full of the practical application of the ideas contained in part 2 to the task of planning the work, then working the plan.

Part 4: How to change? This part addresses the process by which you can undertake transformational change using the Ensemble Way and a description of each of the phases contained in such a journey.

Epilogue. Many of the readers who reviewed this book before publication told me that they thought it might appeal to certain types to read the epilogue first. There is nothing lost if you want to begin with the end in mind and commence your adventure with the epilogue.

The appendixes. The appendixes give examples and explain how to read the trees from the Logical Thinking Process contained in Chapter 5 on Strategy.

PREFACE
Working on Changing Work

Far and away the best prize that life has to offer is the chance to work hard at work worth doing.

Theodore Roosevelt

I WAS 13 YEARS OLD and about to make a fateful choice about what I would study in Year 8. I had already opted to do physics, chemistry and maths. English language and literature were a given, and I'd decided I would rather do French than Afrikaans—native languages not being a choice. But the education system in Rhodesia required I make a fourth choice: history or biology.

I absolutely loved history. In my first year of high school, a gifted teacher had made Mesopotamia and Hammurabi come alive. When the time came to choose, I was ready to engage with the French Revolution, Napoleon's whiff of grapeshot, Metternich's Congress of Vienna, Bismarck's unification of Germany and Garibaldi's heroic exploits in unifying Italy. I never stopped for a moment to think how odd it was to be studying the history of Europe and not that of the Imperialism and Colonialism of my native land.

Having to pick history over biology seemed perverse. I was more than a little annoyed I couldn't study all my subjects. At that age, we had not yet done anything in biology besides dissect a frog and come to understand the difference between domains, kingdoms, phylum, class, order, family, genus and species. It would be decades before I would come to properly understand the revolution Darwin produced, and its far-reaching implications.

Physics, though, had always been my first love. The nickname for my home town of Bulawayo is 'Skies', and I was forever wondering outside at night to stare into the profound mystery of the Milky Way, wondering just what that unfathomable space could possibly contain. I was ten years old and watching live on television when Neil Armstrong made that 'giant leap for mankind'. With my beginner's mind, I asked: What came before time? How big is the universe? What happens when you reach the end of it? Some big questions to muse on when not playing soccer with friends or trying my luck at catching the girl.

I finished school in England and went to university in London at what was then the Imperial College of Science and Technology. When I graduated with a Mechanical Engineering degree, I felt deeply that an opportunity for my real education had been wasted. I was surrounded by an unbelievable feast of institutions within one square mile: The Royal College of Music, the Royal College of Art, the Natural History Museum, The Victoria and Albert Museum, the Science Museum, the Royal Albert Hall.

PREFACE: *Working on Changing Work*

Yet from the lecture halls of my Mechanical Engineering faculty, that inspiring pocket of South Kensington had no apparent connection to a young undergraduate trying to learn about the world and make his way in it. Worse still, no one seemed to care much about the availability of this cornucopia of human endeavour—so powerfully curated, displayed, taught and performed within each of those glorious buildings, but hidden from view, each from the other.

I could not find a way to engage with all the experience of what it was to be human in the last decades of the millennium, despite it being so richly represented in that square mile. How awful it felt to be just a sausage in the machine, filled from top to tail with the physics and mathematics of the minimum necessary achievement to be awarded a bachelor's degree in engineering.

I was profoundly disappointed that I was never once asked the question, 'Well, David, to what mighty purpose will your studies towards your degree be put?' It was assumed that securing an entry-level job with an early start to building a pension was about as good as it gets. I was back in the same dilemma I had in Year 7, wondering why I had to study scientific reasoning with disembodied precision, stripping it of the vast richness of human experience contained in the arts. Why should the two cultures be alienated, one from the other?

The uniqueness of our age

In the more than 30 years of work that has followed, I have come to know a little better the answer to that question, and recently chose to write this book about it. For I believe my missed opportunity of all that time ago points to the plague of our age—our alienation from ourselves, other people and the world at large.

Every age is tempted to claim that the challenges it faces are unique. At this point in the second decade of the 21st century, we can, however, acknowledge that some things truly make our situation one without precedent. Our world presents us with new realities requiring genuinely innovative ways of thinking about how we organise ourselves to achieve the good, the true and the beautiful.

Over a period of some 6,000 years of civilisation, for example, it's only around 50 years ago that a human being was able, for the first time, to view all our good earth standing on another heavenly body. Meanwhile, the phenomenon of globalisation has emerged as an effect of (among other things) the ability to move people, materials, money and data ever faster and more inexpensively around the world.

As all this has happened, we find that some of the biggest crises we collectively face with regards to social, economic and environmental challenges cannot be solved by the nation states and institutions responsible for creating them.

One avenue to explore in addressing our future challenges and opportunities is to examine how we work. The underlying

PREFACE: *Working on Changing Work*

fundamentals of today's ways of managing work are deeply grounded in the late 19th century, which needed a system for training obedient workers to turn up, check out and do what automata do. This antiquated system hurts any organisation looking to carve out a sustainable future. Which, let's face it, is all of them.

An underlying organising principle of the 19th century was to break complex systems into so many parts, then try to manage each disembodied, inanimate part to maximise its efficiency. Not much has changed.

There is seldom a question asked about how the system can work as an organic and organised whole, comprising people, process and technology. Rather, blind hope, unexamined assumptions and the exhaustion of the treadmill reinforce the falsehood that the sum of the parts can be marshalled to deliver an optimal systemic outcome.

The assumptions of local optimisation have led to extraordinary waste, both of human potential and material resources. Compounding this fact is the sad truth that in most organisations I've worked with, you don't have to outrun the lion, you need only be faster than the guy next to you. This prevailing paradigm, the 'good enough' mindset, may please shareholders (in the short term, at least) but it leaves enormous human and material value on the table, and has people feel they are labouring in a Dilbert cartoon.

In our brand new global world, the negative consequence of this error in thinking can only be amplified as we increasingly stretch the boundaries of our systems. We integrate products and services from global ecosystems of supply, and then seek to market them through increasingly discerning, empowered customers. It has become so very easy to compare from around the world one product or service offering to the other without ever having to leave your desk. Winning the right to keep playing in this environment demands mastery of systems thinking. It gives you the opportunity to create a decisive competitive advantage and the ability to increasingly outpace your customer's seemingly unreasonable expectations.

Successfully navigating this new world of commerce demands the best from your people. These days, they overwhelmingly demand meaning from their work. So, how do you remain an attractive employer when any abuse or unfair trade is relayed around the organisation, and the world, in a matter of seconds? How do you win the war for talent if your reputation sucks? How do you inspire the use of discretionary effort if creativity is actively suppressed?

We live in the age of digital disruption, and thus, leaving unexamined the steam-age assumptions about how to plan and perform work will surely send you broke. We need to think deeply about abandoning the machine metaphor for something far more organic, connected, whole and trusted.

To achieve this end, what is needed more than anything else—more than a killer product, more than the greatest new app or service—is a revolution in the way we go about planning and performing work. Not just how we use our new and radically different internet technology platform, but also what we choose to do with it. And, at the deepest level, why we choose to do what we do.

INTRODUCTION
Turning Intention into Reality

In nature we never see anything isolated, but everything in connection with something else which is before it, beside it, under it and over it.

Johann Wolfgang von Goethe

The 'what', 'how' and 'why' work

LET'S TAKE a close look at work.

Manufacturers know they need to reliably design, build, test, produce, sell and distribute their products with ever-shorter notice from their customers and markets. Banks know they need to build trust with their customers, squaring the circle of high levels of service, often across multiple products (and divisions) at ever lower cost. Airlines know their job is not simply to transport passengers from one airport to another, but to delight them with the suite of services those customers consume: online booking, check-in, security, boarding, in-flight service, disembarking, baggage collection and a safe on-time arrival at the destination.

Let's call this the 'what work' companies do—or should do. Those organisations willing to invest in their core competency and develop a unique and differentiated offer are the ones you'd expect to survive and prosper. But a desire to deliver is not the same as having the capability to do so.

Even for those who have defined their 'knitting'—by deciding not only what to do, but also, arguably just as importantly, what not to do—entropy is, sooner or later, inevitable. Standards fall, processes become out of date, things fall apart. When performance is affected, returns decrease and the organisation so easily enters a downward spiral of cost-cutting and layoffs. One key reason? Not enough attention to the work going into managing the work behind the work. The 'how' work.

This 'how' work goes by many names: process management, project management, resource management. It's how we sequence events and allocate resources to deliver a desired result. Too few companies realise the gains to be had from applying the rigour of science to managing this well. Beyond whatever it is organisations produce—from widgets to services—they need to consciously address this meta-work with an intense level of reasoning if they expect to thrive in the long run. This is what I mean by the 'how work'.

At the deepest level is the 'why' work. What's the meaning of what you're setting out to do? What is your intention when you get up of a morning and apply head, heart and hand to the 'how' and the 'what'? What difference would it make if you were not there? Would anyone miss you or what you're attempting to bring into the world? How does what you do help

INTRODUCTION: *Turning Intention into Reality*

you and others to learn and grow? Why work at all?

More Than Just Work applies to anyone who works for or with an organisation. My aim is to highlight better ways to do better work through a deeper understanding of how people, processes and technology can combine in powerful ways to make a meaningful contribution to the world we all share. Whether you are a member of a large organisation or a sole trader, we all interface with large-scale bureaucracies, even when only as a customer or supplier. I hope *More Than Just Work* can offer you a compass to navigate the complexity inevitably arising around organisations.

A theory and practice of systems thinking

The core of my approach to the planning and performance of work is 'systems thinking', informed by three rather different schools of thought. The first is the Theory of Constraints, invented by the iconoclastic physicist-turned-management-consultant Eliyahu Goldratt.

The second is what I think of as 'the MIT group' and includes three academics: Edgar Schein, who spent decades observing organisations and reported his findings in works such as *Organisational Culture and Leadership*; Peter Senge, whose classic *The Fifth Discipline* suggested new ways of developing 'learning organisations'; and Otto Scharmer who has done pioneering work in the development of Theory U and the social field.

The third is Stratified Systems Theory, the often awkward truths uncovered by Elliot Jaques in his exploration of organisational design.

These three bodies of knowledge didn't pop up all at once. In the late 1990s, I was the Managing Director of South Africa's largest commercial refrigeration contractor. After suffering a famine of work, we were suddenly inundated when a major customer embarked on their long-delayed store renewal program. We managed the first tranche of stores by running ourselves ragged. It was clear we needed a different approach if we were going to preserve our workforce and our values. I went to see the National Productivity Institute in Pretoria and came away with two books—*The Fifth Discipline* by Peter Senge and *The Goal* by Eli Goldratt.

Although I read and enjoyed both books, it was *The Goal*—which entertainingly laid out the Theory of Constraints—that proved more useful in the first instance. There was something very appealing and resonant in the story, written as a novel, whose fictional protagonist was an in-over-his-head boss of a failing factory. It had powerful answers to perennial operations questions, and included within the body of knowledge a Strategic Thinking Process and a valuable alternative framework to traditional notions of management accounting.

Conversely, I didn't fully appreciate Senge's cohesive five disciplines until a decade later, when I started to ask deeper questions about how to create self-sustaining change. It was the beginning of a very deep dive into the whole field of organisational learning, trying to get to the bottom of one of W. Edwards Deming's prerequisites of transformation—the psychology of people, society and change. Among many others, I studied what Schein had to say about culture and leadership as

INTRODUCTION: Turning Intention into Reality

well as Otto Scharmer's interpretation of *Theory U*, its process of transformation, grammar of the social field and capacity to catalyse deep personal learning and growth.

I went on to experience firsthand the power of digging down—together with colleagues, clients, family, friends and mentors—to access this space of individual and group learning. Now, when I talk about 'winning results' in general, I mean both the measurable-by-throughput results for your organisation as well as the personal development and career benefits to be gained for yourself.

By late 2008 my work was leading me to bigger and bigger engagements. Once again, I felt something missing. The missing piece turned out to be my poor understanding of organisational design and the critical role it plays in my field of specialisation—the planning and performance of work. It was then, through a friend who had a previous history in the military, I was pointed to the work of Elliott Jaques, his stratified systems theory and the idea of the requisite organisation.

Understanding organisational design through the correlation of cognitive capacity, time horizon of work and complexity opened me up to an entirely new way of seeing. Before discovering the work of Jaques, what I had thought of as being necessary and sufficient to reliably deliver successful transformational outcomes had missed this critical component of organisational structure. Not only did it provide an empirically proven account of how mental processing ability governs the appropriate level of work for any given individual, it also provided a thorough framework for defining management accountability hierarchies—both functional and cross-functional.

Of goals, purpose and sounding together

Business executives will often talk about the goal of the company being to continuously increase returns on shareholder funds. This goal obviously keeps shareholders interested in reinvesting, provides the cash to pay for staff and their development, and allows for investment in the products and services to keep customers coming back for more. And, let's not forget the contribution made to society at large by paying taxes. This appears all very rational. But I don't see too many people leap out of bed of a morning, whistling 'heigh-ho, heigh-ho, it's off to work we go', thinking how thrilled they are to be increasing return on shareholder funds.

People are motivated by many things; making other people more money is surely way down on the list. Don't we all want to feel we are making a difference? That we are connected to something bigger than ourselves? Don't we want to learn, to love what we do, and to live connected to what we value most?

Isn't it time we inverted the pyramid of money first and people second? Shouldn't we be thinking more carefully about how to create motivated people and teams? Isn't it the case that the greatest companies in the world—the ones where the best people want to go and work—are primarily about doing meaningful work? My observation is that these companies make the most money as an effect of mighty purpose, not because they are chasing the last dollar.

In this book, then, I would like to broaden the conversation and encompass what it means to be fully human at work—and not shy away from the ancient Greek virtues of truth, beauty and good. To transcend the limiting beliefs and habits of mind perpetuating the machinery of mediocrity, leading to a dead end of no possibility.

The courage to embark on a Hero's Journey

I read a great deal and, other than my professional reading, my favourite writer is the late Joseph Campbell, whose work in the realm of mythology has helped me answer some of the deepest questions I have about life, its purpose and the many ways we as sojourners on this good earth have come to explain its mystery, form our societies, and learn to lead the good and beautiful life.

Campbell coined the phrase 'follow your bliss', which comes from the third component of the Sanskrit Sat-Chi-Ananda or existence, consciousness and bliss. While I don't know whether we are all 'called' to the work we do, I do know that if we're open to the possibility, our vocation may find us. As Campbell said, 'We must be willing to get rid of the life we've planned, so as to have the life that is waiting for us.' I certainly feel strongly about the opportunity I have—to share the learnings of my three-decade search for 'innovations in productivity', and make my contribution to setting the world to rights.

Campbell's first book, *The Hero with a Thousand Faces*, introduced the idea that all cultures the world over share a story: a hero ventures forth from the world of common day into a region of supernatural wonder, encounters fabulous forces and wins a decisive victory. Upon returning from this mysterious adventure, the hero has the power to bestow boons on a grateful people.

It's that journey I would invite you to join me on. *More Than Just Work* is written for people at all stages of their careers, and who are ambitious about making their work count. I hope to take you through each step of the way so you can see how to gain the highest leverage you can for your organisation and in so doing, create audacious and sustainable change.

Importantly, I'm asking you to get the sense that if your organisation is not giving you the opportunity you deserve, there are ways to change that—from seeking a new role in your current organisation to finding a new one outside of it. Or, indeed, to create an organisation with its own audacious ambition.

I hope *More Than Just Work* will be a reliable companion on your hero's journey.

With that, let's begin with my Just Work manifesto.

INTRODUCTION: Turning Intention into Reality

The Just Work Manifesto

Just Work includes my belief that it is possible to be 'just' at work—to do unto others as you would have them do unto you. Everyone has the right to be well managed.

What might such a radical proposition as 'everyone has the right to be well managed' mean? I figure it means that the people you lead through your management hierarchy properly understand the context of the work they're doing. They feel connected to the overall purpose of the enterprise and are aligned to its vision and values. They work to arrive rather than arrive to work. They are empowered with the requisite authority over the resources required to acquit all of that for which you hold them accountable.

You know what you have called for is both reasonable and possible, given the human and material resources you place at their disposal. They have a deep sense of the significance of what they are doing and experience the world as a better place for them being in it. They feel safe to make mistakes while exploring new ways of being and doing—they're excited by the prospect of continuous learning and growth.

Part 1
Why Change?

A Powerful Question is More than Half a Good Answer

It is not your duty to finish the work, but nor are you free to desist from it.

                Rabbi Tarfon, *Ethics of the Fathers* (2:16)

Figure 1: Systems Thinking

MORE THAN JUST WORK

THE AIRBUS A380 is the largest commercial airliner in the world—the icon of our jet age. What a potent symbol of the progress we humans have made in harnessing technology to shrink the planet. And I was on board, hurtling comfortably from Sydney to Singapore where I would lead my team in the early phase of a very large project I'd won for my company. Having quickly racked up miles to platinum status, I was delighted on this trip when the attendants called me aside at the departure gate and quietly upgraded me to first class.

So there I was, all creature comforts taken care of, pampered by the very best of hospitality the flying kangaroo crew had to offer. Singapore was the centre of the universe for that project; the centre of all that was being designed and built to transform our client's company and vault it from a mere industry benchmark, into the pantheon of the commercial gods. Their ambition was to be thought of in the same exalted terms as those global names who at different times inspired whole economies: Toyota, Sony, IBM, 3M, Microsoft, Boeing and Apple. All of them eventually lose their sheen, but what a privilege it felt, here in first class, contemplating how I could make my contribution to doing something of such scale and grand vision.

Many years before that moment, I had graduated as a mechanical engineer, with a final-year project looking at the performance of turbines on jet engines. I leaned back in the soft nap of the seat, closed my eyes and listened in to the gentle undercurrent roar of the mighty turbofans turning flawlessly, thousands of times, minute after minute, hour upon hour.

I marvelled at the power and fury of the combustion of Jet

Fuel burning in the engines, so humanly brought under control to be put to productive use without breaking our flying machine in the process. How profoundly had we all changed through technology! How far since we first tamed fire.

Just over 100 years after the Wright brothers flew at Kitty Hawk, here I was on a flight that would take me more than 6,000km from home, and all I had to do was sit back and enjoy. In the blink of a historical eye, the human race had gone from incredulity that anything heavier than air could fly to taking for granted a global aviation industry. That transformation made it a reality that even the most remote locations on our shared earth can be reached within 24 hours, and most of that by regular commercial airlines. To the primitives I was a God enthroned in the heavens above. But for the modern world, of which I was a part, I was no more than a corpuscle of commerce, flowing through the veins and arteries of our interconnected world.

And then I stared out the window, round about when our flight was directly over the middle of the Australian continent that is now my adopted country. Below I could see the clouds, and it instantly brought to mind the Africa of my upbringing.

I was born and grew up in Bulawayo, a city of about one million people in what was then Southern Rhodesia. Every year the main rains would be carried on the winds that gave rise to the 'inter-tropical convergence zone', marked by giant cumulonimbus clouds. They brought with them the smell of a soaking, the sight of violent flashes of lightning and moments later the sounds of cacophonous blasts of thunder. What sheer joy it was in the unfettered freedom that was the gift of my youth to hold tight to an inflated tractor tyre as the storm waters rose in increasing swells on the Matsheumhlope River. In the dry heat of summer, that unheralded stream was no more than a sand bed. But with those drenching rains, it was a highway to excited adventure for my mates and me. A symbol of life itself.

But Bulawayo had a much grander claim on history than my youthful adventures on the Matsheumhlope River. It is the final resting place of that icon of the British Empire, the man who gave the country its name, Cecil John Rhodes. And Rhodes had a vision—to build a railway line from 'Cape to Cairo'—to paint the map of Africa British Colonial red.

So here I was, the product of an Imperial dream, safely ensconced in a brand new A380, reflecting how in that age the world had been similarly transformed through technology. For my generation, it was the age of mass aviation; for theirs, the coming of the railroad. No technology, no progress.

There was, however, a problem with this perfect world of mine, and as I got to an age when I could better understand how things actually were, it became increasingly obvious that a great injustice had been perpetrated on the people native to my home. The boon that Rhodes brought with his colonial train was not equally shared by all those who had a claim on it.

If you were white in my country of birth, you had highly privileged access to education, healthcare and land. If you were black, you were disenfranchised, stripped of your best land, and lived under the curse of having to earn a livelihood almost exclusively through the sale of your labour in the factories, mines, fields and houses of the white man.

A Powerful Question is More than Half a Good Answer

It wasn't as if all was harmony before the white man colonised that corner of Africa. The two major tribes, the Shona and the Ndebele, were often at war with each other, and made a habit of stealing each other's cattle and enslaving their women. This, though, was on my watch, and the Jewish faith in which I was raised was unequivocal when it declared in the book of Deuteronomy, 'Justice, justice shall you pursue, that you may thrive and occupy the land your Lord is giving you.'

By the time I got to my 17th birthday, I faced a stark choice—be drafted into the army of Prime Minister Ian Smith and fight a war to preserve white privilege, or leave the country, complete my schooling in England and come to know what fate that path had in store for me. I chose the latter.

Now I'm on this magnificent aircraft, 40,000 feet above sea level and cruising at more than 1,000km per hour. I am on my way to a very big workshop, the success of which would be vital to the broader success of the project. I'd been asked to design and facilitate the event with the help of my colleagues, but I knew that it was going to take something much more from me than I had ever delivered before. Though I was being given a shot at a play in the major leagues, I felt clueless as to who I needed to be and what I needed to do to succeed in that setting.

After all, there would be 70 people in the room for two days, including all the top leadership of the project. That room would be filled with really smart people designing a complete system of management to run one of the world's largest companies. This was going to have to go way beyond an exercise in left-brain thinking. I needed a new model. What had served me so well for so long just wasn't up to the task I had ahead of me.

From my reclined position, I start doodling on a cocktail napkin, drawing three intersecting circles. These, I realise, put my ideas about people, process and structure into sharper focus. I push the button to bring the chair upright, and pull out the table and my notebook. The circles represent the great systems of thought I had incorporated into my consulting practice.

The top-left circle was the realm of operations management—projects and production, hard measures and the science of getting work done. The top-right circle was the realm of organisational learning, addressing what Deming called the 'psychology of people, society and change'. And in the bottom circle were all the elements of organisational design and how management is exercised through an accountability hierarchy.

I'd had this model in mind for some time, each circle representing a progressive evolution of my philosophy around how to make a meaningful difference to the experience people have of planning and performing their work. In my early years as a mechanical engineer, the science of designing and implementing better ways to do better work had an obsessive rational focus. But I soon discovered that people are not convinced by reason alone—we are emotional creatures, carried further by how we feel than what we think.

So while I felt both good about, and committed to, the implementation of high-performance processes as necessary for creating repeatable results, I realised process alone is not sufficient. We need structure. To be effective, we need to know what we are accountable for, and we need to be given authority over the resources required to acquit the work with which we've been charged. We also need to do work that is the right size for our capabilities. I liked the three circles both for their symmetry and simplicity. With this framework in mind, I paused for thought on a couple of questions.

'More than half of a good answer,' said one of my first mentors, 'is a powerful question.' What remarkable difference will I make in the world if I give myself over to successfully plaiting the strands of each individual concept into an organised whole? What if I approached the challenge on a grander scale than a mental concept represented by a doodle on a cocktail napkin? Could this produce an innovation in productivity that could fulfil my desire to make a significant difference in setting the world to rights?

I was a voracious reader of articles from the global associations that represented the three circles I was working with. I'd attended conferences and workshops about each of them: the Theory of Constraints International Certification Organisation (TOC-ICO), the Society for Organisational Learning (SOL) and the Global Organisational Design Society. But the conferences had dealt only with the single topic. I was convinced that if I could synthesise each individually powerful idea, the whole could be far more than the sum of its parts.

I felt the whine of the jets drop a couple of notes and the aircraft's nose start its descent to Changi Airport. Over the sound of the announcement to fasten seatbelts and get ready for landing, I came to from my reverie. I was lost in the tantalising possibility raised by my questions. How, now, do I ground my

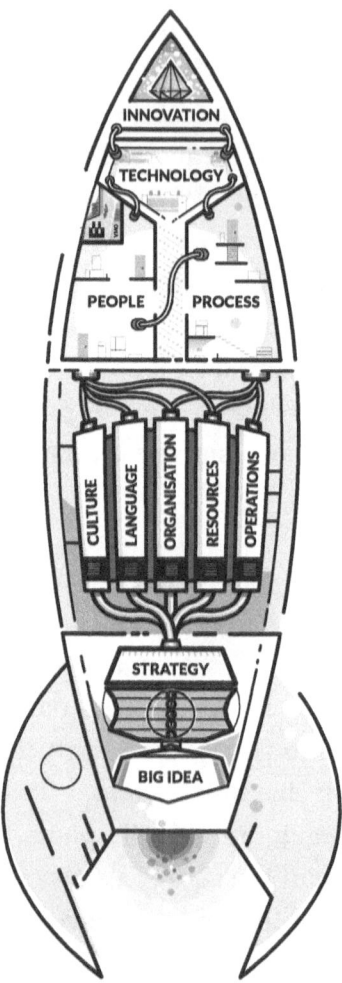

Figure 2: The Ensemble Way

ideas in this landing strip of the future?

Over the many years since that transformative experience, I have managed to distil most of what I have learned into a framework I call the Ensemble Way, represented in Figure 2. It's primarily an aid to deep listening. Listening with the Ensemble Way in mind is a key to coming to understand how progressive ideas flow through an organisation, and what bottlenecks block the way of repeatedly and reliably turning those ideas into additional value and wealth.

The Ensemble Way is a model for engaging in a structured conversation about how to sustainably increase the flow of innovation. It helps clarify, through dialogue, an understanding of the complex interplay of all the domains described in the graphic. No organisation exists without these domains at play, regardless of whether they have been examined as separate parts, or as an interlinked whole.

We know that technology is changing faster than ever. By this, I don't mean only information technology, but anything that applies scientific knowledge to practical purposes. There is no field of human endeavour untouched by the massive increase of scientific knowledge being generated in these early decades of the 21st century: health, education, agriculture, mining, manufacturing, engineering, finance, communications, transport and more. To win results, then, we must be willing to profoundly transform through technology, for no progress occurs without change in both technology and the way people engage with it.

Systemic innovation is the core achievement, but it cannot be realised to its fullest strength without developing the amazing in people, supported by the engineering of seamless processes. It is at the confluence of people and processes that art meets science, where the subjective informs the objective, and where the humanities meet technology. These three components at the top of the spaceship—**people**, **process** and **technology**—are universal engines of progress and growth.

Powering it all is the rocket fuel of winning ideas. Without innovation, organisations die. Getting the most out of the best ideas depends on how well you understand and can exploit your knowledge of the other domains of strategy, culture, language, organisation, resources and operations. How they interact in your value-creation engine—and what to do about the bottlenecks that inevitably arise—is the central question when looking to achieve your goal and win results.

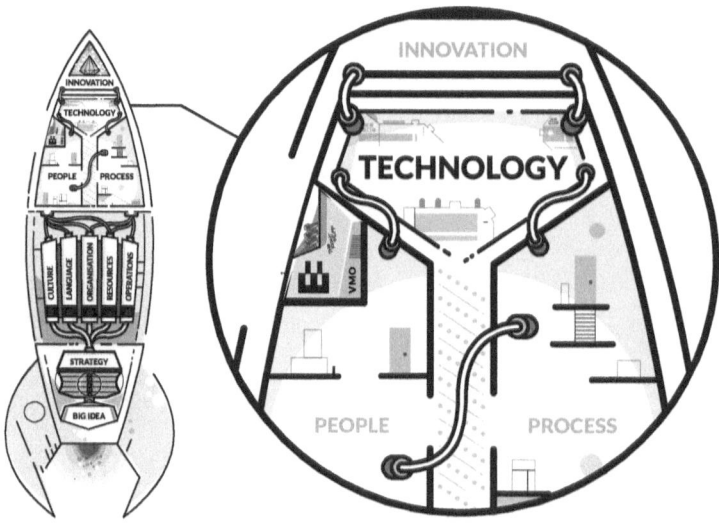

Figure 3: Technology

Chapter 1

TECHNOLOGY: *Enabling the Ensemble*

There is nothing either good or bad but thinking makes it so.
William Shakespeare

'TECHNOLOGY,' wrote American sociologist Read Bain, 'includes all tools, machines, utensils, weapons, instruments, housing, clothing, communicating and transporting devices and the skills by which we produce and use them.' The word technology, from the Greek *techne*, 'art, skill, cunning of hand', and *logia*, 'the study of', is really the science of craft.

Until relatively recently, it was believed the development of technology was restricted to human beings. But recent studies indicate that other primates and certain dolphin communities have developed simple tools and passed their knowledge to other generations. Barring these exceptions, what marks us out as humans is our ability to apply reason to the work of our head and hands and in so doing fulfil a human purpose.

From the wisdom of the ancients through to the heroes of our present day, what makes us most human is our inescapable connectedness—our ability to form tribes, from the strongest blood ties to communities based on village, region, nation, religion, race, interests and myriad other identities. And, of course, the tribes we belong to in order to do the work filling our days. Our most noble and timeless virtues revolve around the idea that we are at our best when we serve a purpose that is bigger than ourselves.

When one is not lost to the outer edges of the normal range of human temperament, we long to do something significant with our lives. To know that the world we leave behind is a better place for us having lived in it and that our endeavour has made a contribution to growth and progress. We will likely never all agree on the question of what kind of progress constitutes a better world, but it seems to me that the virtuous impulse I mention has its deepest roots in that moment our species first became conscious.

In the powerful opening scenes of *2001: A Space Odyssey*, director Stanley Kubrick cycles through a number of situations faced by our earliest hominid ancestors. In the last scene, the alpha male ape-like creature defeats his opponent by violently crushing his skull, using a bone as a newly discovered weapon. Then, he throws the bone into the air and, after floating against a blue sky, it morphs into the space station at the centre of the space odyssey of the title.

How far have we come in our use of technology from those early hominids in Kubrick's story? And what was your response to the image conjured by an ape-like man crushing the skull of his rival? And what are your thoughts about the evolution of technology from that time on, particularly the big-ticket items

1. TECHNOLOGY: Enabling the Ensemble

like fire, the wheel, iron and gunpowder?

What profound changes were brought about by the printing press, the telescope, the steam engine, the internal combustion engine, electricity, penicillin, the pill, the telephone and the internet? We take for granted that ships that are heavier than water can float and that planes that are heavier than air can fly. We hurl rockets into space, have walked on another heavenly body and sent a vehicle beyond the reaches of our solar system. And with the advent of functional magnetic resonance imaging, we can see the brain at work and come to understand the outer reaches of our innermost spaces.

Each of these events has heralded a profound change in how we humans live in our societies, and yet when such massive technological change happens around us, we often fail to truly apprehend the consequences.

Projectiles, projecting and projects

Not too long ago, I took some time off work and retired to the architectural beauty of the Mitchell Reading Room of the Library of New South Wales. The stained-glass window commemorating William Caxton, the first English printer, sits at one end of this remarkable room. In my revelry that day I played a little thought experiment.

The first book Caxton printed was completed in 1473, over 500 years ago. What might our world look like 500 years from today? It was a very strange thought. We are well used to looking back through the telescope of history, equipped as we are with all of the evidence of what came before us. Depending on the power of the lens, we can gaze deep into the very beginnings of time itself, the formation of the cosmos, the geological epochs and the eras of civilisation. But, looking forward, how far into the horizon, how deep into the frontier could I go?

If I could meet someone looking back at the early decades of the 21st century from the vantage point of 2573, as far away in time from me as I was from Caxton, what would they have to say about our technological prowess? Indeed, would there be anyone alive to tell the tale? It seemed to me that questions of this kind could form a useful basis for understanding just how profoundly we change with technology.

And what of those individuals who dare to bring these human discoveries and inventions into the world? Galileo, the father of all science, when forced to retract his heliocentric view of the earth we live on said, 'And yet it moves'. His declaration was powerful; the doctrine might be quite to the contrary, but the facts are still the facts, even when their discoverer is silenced.

One can read about and imagine the terror that Darwin must have felt when he contemplated how his discovery of natural selection would upend the privileged position we humans imagined we occupied. It is not a universally accepted idea; to this day, only 40% of the population of the United States answers 'true' to the proposition that 'human beings, as we know them, developed from earlier species of animals'.

The first time I walked into the Smithsonian's National Air and Space Museum on the mall in Washington, DC, I was an

1. TECHNOLOGY: *Enabling the Ensemble*

adult yet felt like an excited child. The huge Saturn V rockets and inter-continental ballistic missiles at the entrance were keeping guard over the Gemini space capsule that carried our type beyond the clutches of earth's gravity. But the hall that really caught me was the one upstairs that housed the feats of the Wright brothers. In my simplistic way, I had thought that these bicycle mechanics had simply slung together their famous flying machine from bits and pieces of what anyone would find in a cycle shop, bolted a motor and propeller to the front of it and had a go. I was quite taken aback by the finely curated story, with objects, artefacts and pictures that told of their rigorous experimentation, perseverance against technical and commercial odds, and their will to succeed against far-better-resourced rivals.

A mere two years after the Wright brothers launched their powered flying machine, Albert Einstein published his special theory of relativity. Building on what Michelson and Morley had uncovered in their famous experiments to measure the speed of light—often called the beginning of the second scientific revolution—Einstein's theoretical framework provided a model for how light, energy and matter work. You can't go faster than the speed of light, he claimed. As you approach the speed of light, your mass will tend to infinity and time will come to a standstill. Matter and energy are in fact the same thing.

Almost at the same point in human progress that we started our small hops off the surface of our good earth, we learned new secrets about the deepest reaches of the cosmos. Everything we thought we knew about the nature of nature had been upended.

Within 20 more years, through the work of the likes of Bohr, Heisenberg and Schrodinger, the phantasmagorical world of quantum mechanics was postulated. How very peculiar that depending on what you were looking for, energy and matter could be demonstrated to be both particle and wave. When I first understood the implication of such a phenomenon, it had the most profound effect.

How revolutionary the thought that, at the most fundamental level, the nature of the question I asked about what's in front of me yields the nature of what's in front of me. I have agency in how the universe behaves!

What we think, gives rise to what we make. What we make, gives rise to new ways of doing. What we do, gives rise to new ways of thinking. And so the wheel keeps on turning. From that first bone used as a weapon by the *Space Odyssey* hominid, this continuous cycle has given us everything you can see, feel, touch, hear, smell or taste that is not directly sprung from the natural world. Think of the words on the page of this book, the texture of its cover (or the pixels on your screen), the roar of the engine flying overhead, the smell of the coffee brewing and the taste of the biscuit that goes with it.

Adopting and adapting for new opportunities

My work, however, steps back from the realm of physics—the large-scale of Einstein and the very small of Bohr. I leave it to

1. TECHNOLOGY: *Enabling the Ensemble*

our generation of geniuses, beavering away in their academies and labs to discover the truth of the holy grail—the true nature of nature—to find the grand unifying theory that ties into a single integrated whole the cosmic with the subatomic.

We cannot avoid the fact that our genetic inheritance gave us a prefrontal cortex and an opposable thumb. That inheritance allows us to think, exercise judgement and to use our head, heart and hands to bring new worlds into being.

Those of us privileged enough to live in the developed world lead longer, more comfortable, healthier lives than those of only a few generations ago could have imagined. In countries that encourage free enterprise, we have never been more at liberty to go about our business, pursuing our own versions of freedom and happiness.

Never before, by a long shot, have so many people or so much data, money and stuff been moved around in such an incessant whirl, dancing across the daily cycle of our planet, turning on its axis. And all this hi-tech action traces its roots back to the first scientific revolution, sparked by Galileo. And yet it moves, indeed.

But are we really aware of what's going on in our hi-tech culture as it envelops our every action? I enjoy spending time alone in nature—sleeping under the stars to be at one with the awesome mystery of the cosmos, in a way our farthest ancestors knew, but which most of us have long since forgotten. The internet is not there, nor mobile telephony, and I'll even take off my watch to slip the shackles of clock time in favour of nature's rhythms.

In nature, there is nothing of human culture besides, above or below me. It's a place where I lay my ego down for a rest. In this field of all-oneness, nature couldn't give a hoot about who I think I am when I'm away doing my dance in the world of people.

It's from this place outside of human culture that we wake up to see our world afresh and come to understand how profoundly technology has—and continues to—transform us. And with this understanding comes a choice. Do we consciously embrace the new and innovative? Or do we stumble, half asleep, through the dance of change, a victim of its predations, agnostic to its moral consequence?

Lots of bits and bytes

Whatever we choose, we can't escape the digital nature of our age. It was in 1926 that Julius Lilienfeld first conceived of the transistor, the precursor of everything associated with our digital age. Computers, telephones, appliances, the internet—all powered by the descendants of transistors, increasingly smaller and more powerful.

A friend of mine works on a global research project building the Square Kilometre Array telescope in the Australian deserts. She and her astrophysicist friends point this device to the heavens and let it represent what's out there in a daily trawl of petabytes of data. Who can tell what we might learn? Are we alone? Never before have we been able to gather such a vast trove of bits and bytes to represent in ever greater detail what lies beyond the power

1. TECHNOLOGY: *Enabling the Ensemble*

of our existing machines to fathom the cosmic mystery.

Once again, just as Galileo did, we peer through the 'lens' and use historically unimaginable computing power to analyse vast tracts of the unknown cosmos. What belief system will we overturn? What will be our equivalent of 'and yet it moves'? How far have we come that the whole apparatus of the state is now involved in a multinational endeavour, involving thousands of people and many millions of dollars to use the technology of our times to actively ask the questions from an open mind?

Data collection, sorting and interrogation is at the heart of so much of what we do in our modern world. As an example, my son works in an advertising agency, specialising in digital marketing. It astounds me when he explains how much data they have at their fingertips about who I am, what demographic I belong to, what my shopping preferences are, and how to serve up just the right ad in a nanosecond bid by the merchants of the product and service, who often seem to know what I am looking for before I do.

More and more, we see how technological advances developed for one purpose can be adopted for quite different uses. The global positioning system (GPS) was developed for, and is still run by, the military. First, commercial shipping took it up, then recreational sailors. Today, dozens of apps use it on the phone in my pocket.

Combine GPS, barcode scanners and online networks, and you can transform an industry's productivity. A recent assignment for my company involved a very large supermarket chain.

They imagined a supply chain in which any product from any source around the globe could flow through any of its multitude of warehouses and stores into the hands of any consumer.

Through advances in machine learning and artificial intelligence, they can instantly understand the supply and demand constraints of every one of the tens of thousands of products ranged in their stores, and will have just the right amount of the right inventory in just the right place, at just the right time. The ability to monitor, in real time, where a pallet needs to be moved from a supplier to a distribution centre, or from a store to an online shopper, lets them double the utilisation of their transport fleet at minimal additional cost.

And that's not all. The next generation of warehouses will use robotics to unload containers, pack pallets into storage locations, retrieve items against an order, consolidate a load and send the merchandise to a store or direct to a customer.

Meanwhile, a service technician maintaining the robots gets a notification from a sensor connected to the internet of things (IoT). He dons his augmented reality (AR) glasses to 'see' the equipment being maintained, then automatically pulls up the relevant repair manual on his tablet, and allows a supervisor half a world away to red-line, in real time, the piece of equipment as viewed through the AR lens. Instantaneously, the parts, equipment and people needed for the maintenance work are requisitioned and scheduled. The digital twin of the equipment is updated and can be queried at any time with regard to its historic operating metrics and maintenance events. Machine learning algorithms continuously crunch all of this data to get better and better at optimising safe, reliable production.

All the while, the packaged-up goods head out of the warehouse on driverless trucks.

To be or not to be

These are only a few examples among thousands telling the story of the revolution afoot in every single industry and government agency—a profound change that is occurring, once again because of technology. The transformation has most assuredly come further since I wrote these words and is happening even as you read them. So, a potent question to ask yourself is, 'What part will I play? What will I do to give shape to how this next wave of technology transforms our world?'

Wherever you find innovation, in any area of human endeavour, the very qualities exhibited by the likes of Galileo, Darwin or the Wright brothers are there, on display or embedded. It takes a certain courage to stand apart from the safety of certainty and venture into the realms of the unknown. A willingness to explore the frontier of your own existence in a journey beyond the borders of what's familiar.

You must possess a willingness to let go of the mental models that have served you well in the past, to allow a richer, more diverse and inclusive understanding of a new world which calls on you to bring it into being.

So, where do you see yourself in this revolution of our times? Have you thought about how it might affect you, your team and your organisation and whether or not you will be its victim or champion? Do you hear the spirit of the courageous pioneers like Galileo, Darwin and the Wright brothers calling you to be the hero of your own life, living on its frontier, at the intersection of that life and the technology of our digital age racing through it? What political decisions and controls do we need to make with regard to jobs, the distribution of wealth and power, cyber-war and crime? How do we curb the totalitarian potential of Artificial Intelligence whilst harvesting its possibility and what to do about the multi-faceted revolution wrought by social media?

Questions for TECHNOLOGY

1. How has technology transformed your world in your lifetime?

2. Which technologies do you see having the most impact ten and twenty years from now? How do we optimise the economic benefits whilst mitigating the social risks?

3. How could technology change the game your organisation plays in? Could it be completely transformed? What role might you play in making it happen? What if it displaces you and your colleagues from your jobs?

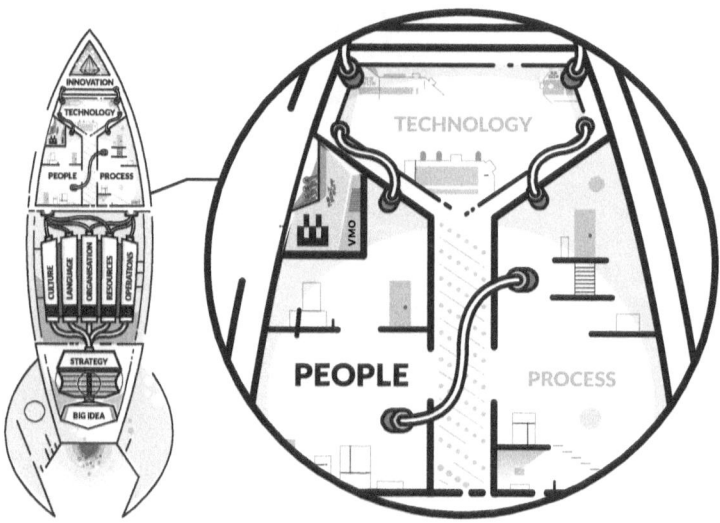

Figure 4: People

Chapter 2
PEOPLE: *Putting a Man on the Moon*

> *Life is like arriving late for a movie, having to figure out what was going on without bothering everybody with a lot of questions, and then being unexpectedly called away before you find out how it ends.*
>
> Joseph Campbell

A CONSULTANT WALKS INTO A BAR. After ordering a whisky, she turns to her friend who's just asked her what she's been up to. She has recently returned from a six-week assignment, travelling half the globe to do an exploratory piece of work for the CEO of a global player in the world of electronics manufacture. She recounts how at the beginning of the assignment she'd met the CEO in his corner suite and listened to his admiration for the work of Dr Goldratt and his Theory of Constraints—the field of her expertise. What, he wondered, would an expert in the field make of his global operation when it came to the first question about where to find the constraint?

Many conversations, much analysis and tens of thousands of frequent-flyer miles later, she was back in his executive suite. As she drains her glass and orders another, she tells of the exchange just a couple of hours earlier:

'So,' he asks me, putting his arm around my shoulder, 'you're the expert in this field of bottlenecks. Where's ours?'

I take a deep breath to give me the courage to talk my truth to power, then say, 'where it always is, at the top of the bottle.'

Avoiding becoming the tool of our tools

Life is so rich for having people in it, but sometimes I would think it a lot easier to bring new systems of management into being if it weren't for staff, or for that matter customers and suppliers. How much simpler would it be to program our machines and let them loose to deliver value.

Outside of what nature does in its own sweet way, nothing happens without involving people. Even when we talk about the new world of digital transformation and the rise of machine learning and artificial intelligence, we must conclude that behind every machine outcome is a deep human cause. Someone, a human being, programmed the algorithm; someone, a human being, can reprogram it.

I am often left in grave doubt as to whether we will survive our species evolution of both an opposable thumb and a prefrontal cortex. What makes us stronger might, in fact, kill us. Yet despite the unimaginably gargantuan odds against all of this 'people' business ever having happened in the first place, we're all still here. So perhaps we can get through these uncertain times and make our great-grandchildren proud.

2. PEOPLE: *Putting a Man on the Moon*

As I mentioned earlier, my formal studies took me down the path of the exact sciences. Not for me much study of the humanities—what philosophy, literature, painting, sculpture, theatre, dance and music can tell me about the human condition. No, my learning was predominantly in the realm of falsifiable hypotheses and the one right answer which could be double-underlined and concluded QED—a Latin abbreviation for 'which was to be demonstrated'.

But I am a curious bloke and have never ceased trying to understand what this deep mystery of life is all about. There more I know, the more I want to know and the less I know that I know. I accept that we are all hamstrung by the fact that life itself cannot be run as a controlled experiment. Once we have lived out a given choice, we can't rewind the clock and rerun an alternative option to see if it turns out for the better. We have to live with our choices.

Trying to understand the people dimension in any given system has other challenges. We all must learn from scratch when we are born, and our legacy is left open to the interpretation of others once we've slipped this mortal coil. Goodness, I don't need to hold others to account for changing my mind and its thoughts—I change it regularly enough of my own accord!

So, when we walk into a room, a bar or otherwise, what can we go with? What frames of reference could be helpful?

Mythology and meaning-making

In my deepest inquiry into the topic of human nature, my bedrock is the world of mythology, so elegantly written about by the late Joseph Campbell. All of my wanderings through the social sciences of psychology, sociology and anthropology constantly point back to mythology. And Campbell, when asked, has such an endearing definition of mythology as 'other people's religion'.

Hidden below the surface of what we do during our daily lives are the assumptions and, at an even deeper level, the myths that inform how we perceive the world around us. These assumptions and myths serve the function of answering our deepest questions about our life, its origin and purpose, the nature of suffering and malevolence, what happens when we die, what rules bind us into our communities and society at large, and how we can lead a good and beautiful life. For the most part, these myths remain almost completely unexamined as we go about our daily business—except when we occasionally talk, usually in quite vague terms, about 'the culture' of the joint.

It turns out that the myths we live by make a big difference to our worldview. If we grow up with the Occidental mythology from west of the Euphrates and not the Oriental from its East, we do not see the same world in front of us. Mythology shapes what we describe as characteristics of national culture and how these might have developed from, for example, the Judeo-Christian heritage which has most shaped my outlook.

In our globalised world, where these differences of culture

are in a constant dance of change, we need to develop a sense that what we mean when we communicate some aspect of our work is not necessarily what is understood by our colleagues. To paraphrase Mark Twain, it can often seem that our conversations always involve two people separated by a common language.

Given that we are all arriving at the movie of our life from different places at different times, I have found some useful 'thinking frames' which help develop understanding, build connection and deepen trust.

Pausing between stimulus and response

We would all be well served if we paused for a moment to take the advice of psychiatrist and Holocaust survivor Viktor Frankl: 'Live as if you were living for the second time and had acted as wrongly the first time as you are about to act now.'

For those of us within the range of normal temperament, Frankl's advice is wise. Creating a gap between the stimulus of what someone has said, and the response it immediately evokes, allows for the more thinking and feeling part of the brain to catch up. As we are in most cases unlikely to be taken out by a sabre-toothed tiger or its modern equivalent, we can and should train our 'lizard brain' to pause for a moment before responding with fight, flight or freeze.

And in that momentary pause, we should be trying to discern the kind of thinker we're in conversation with. I find the work of William 'Ned' Herrmann, who led management education at GE, to be a particularly useful starting point. He found that some people prefer to think analytically, while others are more process oriented. Some are big-picture strategic thinkers and others far better equipped in the realm of emotional intelligence. This is not to say that any given person cannot think in each of these modes. But if we understand preferences, we can make a conscious effort to frame the change we are looking to bring about in terms that resonate for a given individual. When connecting to a wide audience, it often pays to approach the audience with a smorgasbord of different presentational styles to ensure you bring them along, regardless of their given preference.

Howard Gardner, a professor of psychology at Harvard, went further than Herrmann in his research and identified seven distinct intelligences:

> Students possess different kinds of minds and therefore learn, remember, perform, and understand in different ways. We are all able to know the world through language, logical-mathematical analysis, spatial representation, musical thinking, the use of the body to solve problems or to make things, an understanding of other individuals, and an understanding of ourselves. Where individuals differ is in the strength of these intelligences—the so-called profile of intelligences—and in the ways in which such intelligences are invoked and combined to carry out different tasks, solve diverse problems, and progress in various domains.

In a short, powerful book called *Changing Minds*, Gardner talks about the forces at play when people change their minds, and how these can be used as levers to effect change. Each (perhaps not coincidentally) begins with RE:

Reason: What is the science behind the change you are calling on me to undertake?

Research: What empirical evidence do you have to show that the reasoning works?

Representational redescription: Give it to me in different ways, as there are a multitude of different 'intelligences' by which I can access the ideas and concepts you are trying to communicate to me—such as verbal or numeric reasoning, or through kinaesthetic sense or visual language.

Resonance: Does what you tell me resonate with my specific context? What experience do you have of applying your solution to my discipline, my industry or my cultural context?

Real-world events: What is going on in the real world that would compel me to give up the safety of the status quo to undertake the risk and pain associated with change?

Rewards: What's in it for me?

Resistance: Why am I feeling resistance to what you have on offer? What assumptions are either of us making which lead me to feeling this way?

But understanding thinking preferences, knowing of different intelligences and being comfortable with the levers needed to change our minds is not enough. Nobel laureate Daniel Kahneman, pioneer of behavioural economics, gives us deep clues about the raft of biases which challenge the idea that we are always the rational actors we might think we are. What his research unearthed, popularised in his best-selling book *Thinking, Fast and Slow*, gives us heuristics to understand human biases.

Anchoring, for example, shows how prone we are to gravitate to any value we've been given as an 'anchor' before we answer a question. So, if you want to sell your wine for more, bump up the price of the cheapest one on the menu—or add an unreasonably high-priced bottle you know no one will buy—and you will observe people making decisions based on the relative position on the price list rather than the absolute quantum of the price.

One of my favourites is the availability heuristic, which puts forward the notion that 'if you can think of it, it must be important'. That is, the easier it is to recall the consequences of something, the greater we perceive these consequences to be. The statistical evidence for a particular outcome may be entirely different to the perception, and yet, all the same, we proceed with our bias.

Take for example the attacks on the World Trade Centre in September 2001. Many at the time made the point that this was the worst attack ever on American soil, and that all of civilisation was coming to an end. Worse than the London blitz? Worse than the bombing of Dresden? Worse than the dawning of the nuclear age with the bombing of Hiroshima and Nagasaki? By

2. PEOPLE: *Putting a Man on the Moon*

any objective means, of course it wasn't. But, the horror of the events of 9/11 were immediately available to us, and thus occupied a much larger space in our psyche than those long-ago events in faraway places.

Kahneman has determined that we are at the same time over-optimistic and loss averse. The over-optimism arises from our inability to see, with our subconscious 'fast thinking', beyond the known knowns, which he calls WYSIATI—what you see is all there is.

Furthermore, we value what we have and fear losing it by a factor of twice as much as what we might gain from any given decision. It turns out that how we frame a decision is as important as the decision itself. If you say you have a 90% chance of success, you are more likely to chance your arm than if you say you have a 10% chance of failure.

And are we ever blind to the idea of sunk cost. So much value has been squandered by not considering the odds of further investment in a dud project delivering an unlikely positive result. It would seem we have a prewired disposition to throw good money after bad.

Given all these and other findings by Kahneman and his late fellow researcher, Amos Tversky, it becomes evident that our view of ourselves as rational actors in the field of planning and performing work is, at the very least, highly suspect. What would it take to have people apply the rigour of reason and the power of logic to their decisions and actions?

Chapter Five talks to the application of a logical thinking process to construct, test and communicate the logic of thinking.

But how many busy executives are willing to slow down and do the hard work of rigorously testing assumptions, looking for causal connections and actively seek out disconfirming data? We 'feel' far more than we like to think—and think far less than we feel we do.

On being too big for your boots

We will look at the work of Elliott Jaques and his stratified systems theory in more detail in Chapter 8, but while we are on the topic of trying to penetrate the fog of what it is to lead and manage people, we should make brief mention of his central idea. Based on a life of research, Jaques discovered that there is a correlation between cognitive capacity, the the time-horizon of work and the inherent complexity of that work. A supervisor can handle a longer horizon than a frontline worker in the same way an executive can handle the complexity of a three- to five-year transformation project which a mere manager cannot.

The trouble is, people often don't know anything about this correlation and end up in jobs which are either too big or too small for their cognitive ability. This leaves the teams around such people wondering how they landed up with an incompetent boss who fulfils the Peter Principle (people rise to their level of incompetence); or they feel the agitation of team members who are bored mischievous by being given work demanding so little of their mental horsepower.

Even when you're aware of the general principles—perhaps you've formally studied psychology—you still don't know whom you are facing into on any given day. I have been married now for more than 30 years. Even though my wife and I know each other at least as well as could be expected after such a long time of living and loving together, there are days when we can be a complete mystery to each other. You know the feeling of just having a bad day, and being out of sorts. Yes, we could practise becoming enlightened, and I'd recommend it, but as someone once told me, don't think you're in range of such a lofty goal until you've spent a week living with your mother-in-law.

These ideas above are hardly comprehensive in determining what will prove successful in leading and managing people towards a worthy goal, but they at least illustrate the point that it is no small thing to influence what sits at the base of every system: people. And, to be sure, when you walk into that bar, you have no idea what is going on behind the face you look at. That unlikely ragtag bunch of aliens in the *Star Wars* cantina? That's us.

So how can we navigate something as complex as the human condition? What can we say about the weird and wonderful creatures we are? And how can we help people develop courage in the face of adversity when taking on meaningful change?

Autonomy, mastery and purpose

In his popular book *Drive*, Dan Pink synthesised an approach to understanding what motivates people to do great things, based on much research (including from Kahneman and Tversky, among others). If we ensure the necessary condition of people feeling their pay is fair for the level of work they do, then what motivates us, according to Pink, are three things: personal mastery, autonomy and transcendent purpose. In my own work, I have found this to be true and enormously useful.

For example, it turns out we will spend hours in the cellar practising the cello even if we never have the opportunity to play in an orchestra. We get an enormous lift from getting really good at something we love. This desire to develop personal mastery flies in the face of those who think in terms of carrots and sticks. The trick to sound leadership is to talk to your people and discover what they might want to master, then help them do it.

Within the bounds of the structure required to achieve a collective goal, we rarely work with much more energy and commitment than when we are given a degree of autonomy in how we go about solving problems. We are creative beings and like to be appreciated for doing more than the work of a machine. We should be hired to exercise our judgement and discretion. If that's not needed, get a machine to do it. (The very real probability of many jobs disappearing in this way is something I'll address briefly in this book's Epilogue.)

Finally, it turns out we want to be working on something that makes a difference—what Pink calls transcendent purpose—which brings us all the way back to Joseph Campbell and his most famous work on the universal myth of *The Hero's Journey*:

2. PEOPLE: *Putting a Man on the Moon*

> When we quit thinking primarily about ourselves and our own self-preservation, we undergo a truly heroic transformation of consciousness [...] One way or another, we all have to find what best fosters the flowering of our humanity in this contemporary life, and dedicate ourselves to that.

Writing a short chapter on people seems woefully inadequate when I consider the complete libraries full of great thinkers on the topic. I haven't touched on the Big 5 personality traits nor theories of human development from the likes of Ken Wilber's Spiral Dynamics to Robert Kegan's idea of the evolving self to name but a couple. Ultimately, though, this whole book is about people and constantly learning how to develop the amazing in each of us. With practice, we all have the capacity to open our hearts and minds to joining hands in making the impossible possible. And given the opportunity, even the most hardened cynic can be converted to being the hero of their life by turning purposefully towards that which is bigger than themselves.

A Shakespearean moonshot

Finally, before consigning the people dimension to such a potentially formulaic vision of optimism, noble as it might be, I'd like to recall a talk I heard by the renowned poet David Whyte. Whyte has carved a niche as a business consultant yet mixes just as readily in academia. On this occasion, he related how one of his university colleagues once snootily asked what he could possibly find in the world of business that was worthy of the poet's pen.

Was it not all rather dry and tedious—spreadsheets, processes, accounts, hierarchies—and all the while oozing that faintly odious smell that comes from the grubby world of commerce? No, Whyte replied, most emphatically. Business is a realm that's Shakespearean in range. Love, power, lust, passion, failure, treachery, nobility, tragedy, perseverance, resilience, capitulation, heroism, comedy, victory—it's all there. The drama plays out in organisations around the world, every day.

In arguably the greatest epic of the ascent of man and our incessant reaching for the stars, there is a famous story told of the floor-sweeper at Cape Canaveral. This man was employed by NASA in the heyday of the race to fulfil Kennedy's vision of getting to the moon within the decade. So connected was he to his colleagues and his work, that when he was asked what his job was, his answer came back, 'I'm putting a man on the moon'.

What fascinates me about people and the human condition is our potential to reach deep into ourselves and find meaning and strength in our work. Whether you're a floor-sweeper or a rocket scientist, apprentice or president, how do we collectively 'put a man on the moon'?

2. PEOPLE: Putting a Man on the Moon

Questions for PEOPLE

1. Who are you? Why do you do what you do? What is your work?

2. How do you discern the differences people bring to their work in terms of personality, thinking preferences, learning styles, cognitive ability and critical thinking skills?

3. How would you develop a team capable of 'putting a man on the moon?'

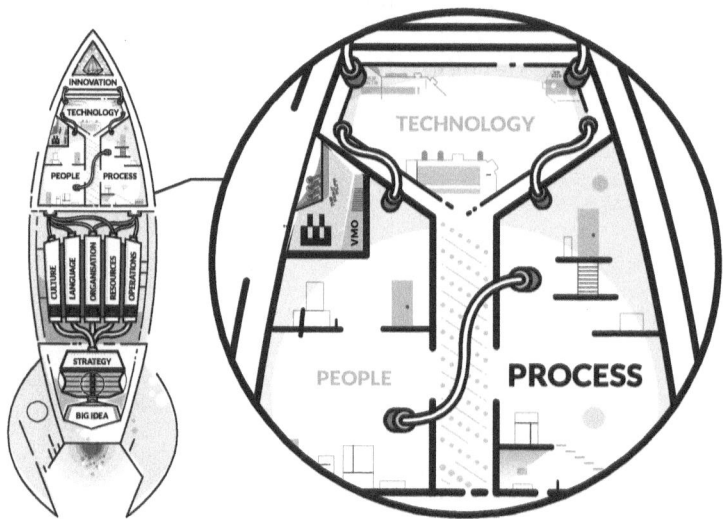

Figure 5: Process

Chapter 3
PROCESS: *How to Get it Together*

I know that two and two make four—and should be glad to prove it too if I could—though I must say if by any sort of process I could convert two and two into five, it would give me much greater pleasure.

Lord Byron

WHATEVER WALK OF LIFE we come from, and in whatever field of work we make our contribution, we are surrounded by process. Those of us fortunate enough to live in the free world enjoy the benefits of the democratic process, which in the words of Churchill is the worst kind of political process except for all the others. Besides government, we have legal, educational, business, medical, agricultural, political and other processes, too.

If we define a process as simply the steps required to achieve an outcome, then nothing escapes process. Some processes may be heavily prescribed, like quality assurance for the manufacture of pharmaceuticals or safety for the aviation industry. Other processes may be far more subjective—how the artist creates a painting, the author writes a book or the musician composes an opera.

Since this book is about the world of work, I'll keep my focus on the processes that help us manage projects, production and distribution. Perhaps surprisingly, these three processes capture all the 'work behind the work' that goes into any specific domain you could name. Construction and engineering are about projects, but so is software development. Manufacturing is production, but a sales process also has repeatable elements we can address the same way. Your supply chain is about distribution, but so is an emergency response system of fire and rescue units, ambulance crews and police teams.

Without defined processes, every one of the above domains—as well as legal, medical, engineering and architecture practices; schools, hospitals and government ministries and departments, or museums and orchestras—will inevitably fall short of the high levels of team performance that will get them to their goal.

Designing, implementing and continuously improving processes, however, is hard. People are creative by nature, and a standard process, in many cases, is designed to remove individual creativity and get people to do the same job, the same way, every time. So does this necessarily mean creativity is suppressed?

Let me offer a metaphor from music, specifically the process by which we come to gain mastery of an instrument. The starting point is learning all our scales, modes and arpeggios, then practising them in all 12 keys. Even the most accomplished musician will spend time reviewing these fundamentals. While the drills are not the music, practising them consolidates the basic building blocks that show up time and again in actual compositions, in endless variation.

Mastery of these generic elements, coupled with deliberate practice of the unique notes of a specific piece, is what allows the musician to achieve a flawless performance of even the most complex work. Let's remember, though, that the goal is not merely to impress the listener with technical virtuosity, but to move them with a personal interpretation of the piece's meaning. Nonetheless, without a proper process for practising, the musician can never move beyond the piece's technical demands and imbue it with truly creative expression.

Process is thus necessary but not sufficient for higher purpose. A combination of proficiency and creative expression should inform the design of process management in every domain. Endeavours that are worthy of our talents require technical mastery in the service of making a full contribution to something bigger than we can achieve on our own.

Just the way it's done around here

The sad fact is that processes are too rarely designed with such noble intent. The big questions of why we do something in a given way are simply not asked. Processes are imposed from the outside in, creating order but limiting possibility. Their designers do not see people longing to contribute, but automata who need to be controlled.

Often, processes are old and unexamined, with large variation between the written procedures which contain them and the way work is actually completed. So much of how work gets done is left to tacit understanding gained from the osmosis of knowledge; stick around long enough and you'll come to learn how people have been working around the procedures, and then become a master in doing the same yourself.

On one occasion, I was working on an assignment which looked at putting the whole of the sales process for the Yellow Pages online. I mentally stapled myself to a sales order, imagining its route through the organisation. There was a step to print the order, put it into a manila folder, add a signature and a date and send it off to the accounting department. This seemed mighty strange to me. All the information on the sales order had, many years prior, been captured on the enterprise system of record, so why would they need this printed copy? The accounts department had equal access to the sales order as we did, and if they really did need a hard copy, they could simply print it out themselves.

I asked the clerk assisting me. She could only offer the thought that it was done because someone needed it. I decided to test that proposition by cutting out the step altogether. I figured if anyone missed the manila folder I would find out soon enough. After a couple of days, no one came calling for the folders, so I went to accounts, and asked who usually received the folder. At the back of the office was a filing cabinet full of old manila folders with the printed orders and signatures. I asked the clerk in charge if they missed receiving the ones I had instructed to stop sending. 'No,' she replied, 'no one ever looks at them, but this is what we've been doing for years, and no one could be bothered to change it.'

3. PROCESS: How to Get it Together

While process is very important to establish how work is done—especially how it articulates how work is transferred from one person to another and one part of the organisation to another—it also serves a second function. From what we know about the principle of entropy, things naturally fall apart. It's why a room will not by itself get tidier, a cup of tea will get cooler and the sun will eventually disappear. To stop this degradation, we must apply energy. We must tidy the room and boil the kettle. (We needn't worry too much about the sun flaming out, as we won't be around when it happens.) A process can be seen as a set of instructions which prevents, or at least slows, the slide down the slippery slope of entropy by articulating the minimum standards necessary to deliver an outcome on time and to quality.

The consequences of getting it wrong

So how do we go about designing a good process? How to achieve the correct balance between satisfying the legitimate needs of all the stakeholders touched by a process without being unnecessarily bureaucratic? This is a real challenge, as different people have different preferences to their way of thinking. Some are more big-picture, more relational. Others have a natural affinity for seeing how the parts are engineered together to make a coherent whole. And it's clearly not everyone's strength or inclination to either design or comply with the process.

Of course, the consequence of a given process not working or not being adhered to can be very different. If one is doing a clinical trial on a new drug, you would think there would be tighter controls on process than if all you were trying to achieve was the cashing-up routine for the branch of a retailer. But consequence is not always measured by either the quality of a process or the discipline with which it is applied. Recently a quack doctor was uncovered in my home state of New South Wales after having posed as a physician for a decade. The reasonable person may well ask how on earth that can happen.

On a grander scale, systems can hide faulty processes even when many qualified experts have oversight. In the Gulf of Mexico, the Deepwater Horizon drilling rig exploded due to faulty cement, valve failures and misread test results. And the root cause of the Challenger Space Shuttle blowing up was a couple of faulty O-rings. Even though some technicians voiced their concern before lift-off, the process didn't allow for a no-go decision at that level.

I have done work in a bank where the relationship bankers for institutional lending stated categorically that they have no need of process, as every deal is unique and standardisation would be a hindrance. The fact that their job title includes the word 'relationship' says something about their preferences when it comes to how they go about their business.

Then along come the risk folk to apply their strict risk assessment and governance processes, giving the lie to the preferences of the relationship bankers. The product people, meanwhile, abound in processes to engineer the specifics of the complex loan types required to meet the needs of the borrower, making a grander joke of the thought that there is no process required.

3. PROCESS: How to Get it Together

Difficulties are compounded as each of the major functions—client coverage, risk, product—have their own processes worked out in their functional silos. Usually, these relationship bankers are unaware of (or simply don't care about) the legitimate needs of their colleagues, and resent having to comply with a process from which they—by virtue of how their own performance is measured—derive little or no value.

So, how to go about designing a good end-to-end process that satisfies the legitimate needs of all stakeholders—including the ultimate customers? It turns out there is a whole body of knowledge on process contained in the business analysis body of knowledge, or BABOK (now in its third version). Although this is designed for complex programs of work in large enterprises, the common-sense approach can apply equally to smaller projects:

- Enterprise analysis
    - Define business need
    - Determine gap in capabilities
    - Determine solution approach
    - Define solution scope

- Requirements elicitation
    - Prepare for elicitation
    - Conduct elicitation
    - Confirm results
    - Document results

- Requirements analysis
    - Prioritise requirements
    - Organise requirements
    - Specify and model requirements
    - Validate requirements
    - Verify requirements
    - Determine assumptions and constraints
- Solution assessment and validation
    - Assess proposed solution
    - Allocate requirements
    - Assess organisational readiness
    - Validate solution
    - Determine transition requirements
- Resources
    - Subject-matter experts
    - Business users
    - Business process owners
    - IT managers
    - End users
    - Support
- Tools
    - Workshops
    - Focus groups
    - Interviews

- Feature lists
- Prototyping
- Surveys

Technically, then, a very solid body of knowledge around process management already exists. But how enthusiastically will people adopt a new process if there isn't a compelling case as to why it has been introduced?

The challenge of getting it right

After the first release of a global Enterprise Resource Planning (ERP) implementation, I sat in on a workshop with one of the business units that had been through release one—the pilot for the far larger scope of release two. The whole implementation was enormous in its ambition to standardise and simplify the processes of the entire organisation. The vision was to have the business run off one set of processes and a common set of data, regardless of where the work was undertaken—in any of the five continents where they owned assets and ran operations. The explicit premise of this use of technology to rewrite the encyclopaedia of processes for the entire enterprise was to perfect those 20% of the processes which determine 80% of the outcomes—and more or less let the rest take care of themselves.

I asked the attendees at the workshop how the vision of simplifying the business was going for them. A torrent of expletives poured out, the gist of which was: 'Simple for who—us or the executive?' Whatever they had previously done as an autonomous unit was now very difficult to achieve within one global set of processes and rules. Just getting a new part-number listed took forever.

Changing a process to accommodate local conditions meant having to run the gauntlet of the global process-owners who had their own process for adoption of new or changed processes. This involved submission to a representative panel and endless rounds of questioning and second-guessing of the need for the requested change.

This part of the business, participating in release one, had a reputation within their IT department of being extraordinarily adept at making the existing ERP system do anything anyone asked of it. They quipped they could even have it produce a cappuccino on demand. When the manager of the department told his story at the workshop, his head hung low and his voice was almost breaking as he said, 'They've taken all my functionality away.'

The flip side of the argument was that breaking this habit of relentless customisation was a key goal of the project. Simple standard processes would mitigate business risk in a period of high growth. Staff could be trained in one facility and easily move to another and be instantly productive without having to learn a whole new set of processes.

A particular advantage of having a single way of working across the enterprise was that every function in the business could be internally benchmarked against its peer function in other business units. If you wanted to see how well you were doing in being able to close out month-end accounts against the accounting departments in all 12 strategic business units, the information was readily available—and credible for having been collected in the same way. If you wanted to know how your 'delivery performance to promise' stacked up against your peers in the supply chain, the information was there for all to see.

What was interesting to note was how people were using this benchmarking information. For some, it was a rod with which to beat their people: 'How come we're still ranked at number 7 out of 12? If you don't do something to fix that, you'll be out of a job.' I find this approach to process management very unsatisfactory. At best, it produces a grudging compliance, with little incentive to experiment, collaborate and learn. Some enlightened executives, however, saw this internal benchmarking as an opportunity to learn: 'Why don't you ask the leader of the team who is benchmarked as being at the top of their game and see if we can learn from and replicate some of their insights?'

The truth is that sometimes one must use the coercive powers of management and the controls available in technology to break habits that undermine the evolution to a better way of doing better work.

I recall a case where the figures for completing maintenance activities, on time, on big expensive pieces of equipment were running at an appallingly low rate. The implication was clear. If equipment could not be returned to service on time, it would be more likely to break down when handed back to operations and would thus cause high levels of lost production due to unplanned outages.

None other than the CEO wrestled with the problem and he concluded the reason for this ongoing chain of undesirable events was due to poor planning. At first, this was a bit of a mystery, because in every maintenance department across the business there were enough people employed in the position of planner. However, when he observed what these planners did, he determined that for the most part, their job was more about being the supervisor's expeditor than conducting the job of planning.

This CEO was a notable simplifier. 'There are only three kinds of work,' he once famously said to all his staff. 'Planning, doing and improving.' In a note he sent out to the solution architects, he instructed them to configure their system in such a way that the planners could only have access to those parts of the system which dealt with next week's work and beyond. They would, therefore, be unable to order parts, assign staff or mobilise contractors for any work orders valid in the current work week. In other words, planners had to plan.

This meant that even if the supervisor working on the current week's maintenance activities instructed the planner to do work on their behalf for that week's work, there was nothing the planner could do, as they were effectively frozen out of the system. In his note, the CEO conceded that it was taking a blunt instrument to solve the problem, but he explained that supervisors had to realise that part of good management is foresight. And that starts with planning.

Addressing the root cause of poor planning was where the leverage in improvement of system performance lay. No lasting beneficial change would occur without vigorously tackling the persistent cause of poor performance.

3. PROCESS: How to Get it Together

This is a classic case of how technology can be used to both change processes and enforce the discipline around new ways of working. It's often not pleasant, but just as often necessary if there's a big enough problem to solve. Your market of investors and customers won't wait for your company to respond to changing demands because your people's habits get in the way of getting your process act together.

Focus on how things flow from end to end

In the world of Toyota, they think of three different kinds of flow and have processes for managing all of them: material flow, information flow and innovation flow. If ever you want to have simple, standard end-to-end processes, you'll need to examine how materials flow, determine what information is required to represent the flow of those materials and what process needs to be in place to accommodate continuous improvement in those processes.

Going back to our musical metaphor, imagine an orchestra turning up to play a concert. The musicians are all of the highest calibre and musical intelligence. But what if every one of them had their own idea of what they were going to play and how they are going to play it? What kind of cacophony would that produce?

Instead, the composer has already placed melody, harmony and rhythm into a satisfying musical structure. The conductor's essential task is to interpret the score, and rehearse the ensemble to coax out her own musical vision. Then, in performance, she sets the tempo and dynamics in the moment to ensure each of the parts contributes to a beautiful whole. No one argues with the composer about which key or time signature they should play in. These are the givens. And while the players must infuse their own parts with technical skill and an emotional charge, it's clear that the conductor has the last word on how the orchestra should thrill and delight the audience.

What do we need to do to produce a similar sentiment of a cohesive ensemble in our business processes? And how might we do it in such a way that we don't suffocate the creative impulse of the musician, but rather cultivate the conditions in which they can make their fullest contribution to their own and their colleagues work of art?

3. PROCESS: How to Get it Together

Questions for PROCESS

1. What are the different kinds of project and production processes you have in your organisation? Who owns those processes and how are they enforced? How do you measure adherence to your processes and how are they maintained and changed?

2. Why do you run your processes the way they are currently run? What organising principles and standards underpin your processes? Which of your existing processes are still suited to the environment you now find yourself in?

3. How do you and your organisation go about changing and continuously improving processes, especially those that affect many different stakeholders?

Part 2
What to Change?

Winning Results: The Ensemble Way

It is the framework which changes with each new technology and not just the picture within the frame.

Marshall McLuhan

MY ASSUMPTION IS THAT YOU are reading this book because you want to be inspired by new thinking, uplift your people and repeatedly and reliably deliver better results. You're drawn to this book because you're bold and ambitious. Bold and ambitious at a personal level—to create a win for your own learning and growth—and bold and ambitious to fashion a great result for the organisation of which you are a part.

Over the last 35 years of my working life, I have increasingly sought a means to make sense of what I observe as we humans act to turn our intention into concrete accomplishment. I've looked at a wide array of situations in the world of managing work, and applied different frames to the inquiry to aid better understanding.

In my time, I have looked at the Theory of Constraints (TOC), Lean, Six Sigma, Deming's System of Profound Knowledge, PMBOK, Prince II, Agile, Theory U, The Fifth Discipline approach to organisational learning, the Requisite Organisation; ADKAR change management, the list goes on. At bottom, what these frames have in common is the desire to provide the enterprise with the ability to continuously improve results—be that as radical as transformation, or as gradual as small, continuous improvement.

In the following chapters, I'll share with you some of the theories, methods and tools I have found useful in framing the business challenges I've faced, and how they come together to facilitate the conversion of the biggest and best ideas into bankable innovation.

I have found the most succinct way to articulate this frame is in the use of one of the tools from TOC's Logical Thinking Process: the Goal Tree (Figure 6). The spaceship metaphor I have been using is underpinned by the logic of the Goal Tree and is a graphically more pleasing but less verbose expression of the same basic ideas.

The goal tree is read from top to bottom. Each statement in the box is a logical entity. The arrows define the relationships between the entities. It is read as follows: In order to [entity at the tip of the arrow], we must [entity at the base of the arrow]. Thus, starting at the top, we read: In order to win results, we must profoundly transform with technology. While the tree is read from top to bottom, the actions required are from the bottom to the top. Thus, we start our journey with the idea that we must 'inspire systemic innovation'.

In Part 1, we addressed the domains of technology, people and process. Let's turn our attention now to innovation, and how it feeds the rest of your value-creation engine.

Winning Results: The Ensemble Way

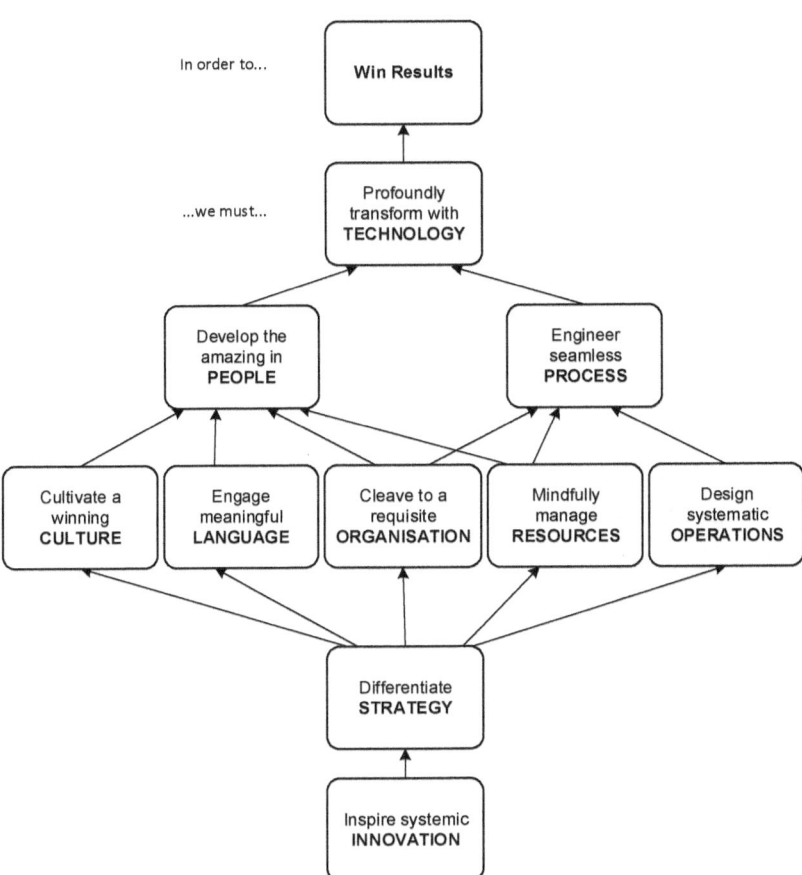

Figure 6: The Goal Tree

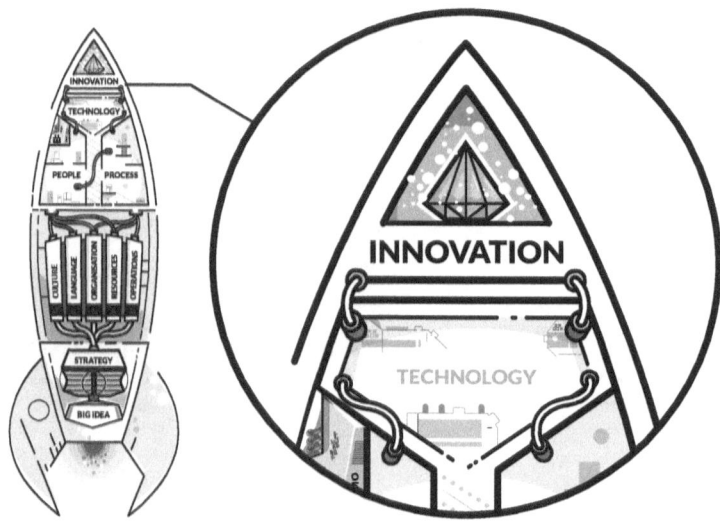

Figure 7: Innovation

Chapter 4
INNOVATION: *Those Who Innovate Fastest Win*

If you look at history, innovation doesn't come just from giving people incentives; it comes from creating environments where their ideas can connect.

Steven Johnson

INNOVATION IS VITAL in any organisation. It is, with marketing, the most important of all its activities. Without innovation, the organisation dies. We all know life is change and that evolution has made us what we are as a result of our ability to adapt to our universe's changes as they occur over the nanosecond and the aeons. Change is the imperative of life itself.

But let's be clear. Innovation is not the ability to have a good idea; nor is it the fancy new product. It is the ability to turn an idea into value, which means something someone is willing to pay for in time, money or taxes. Innovation is a risky business. For just as organisms evolved in circumstances that were unpredictable, what we now do ourselves to keep evolving must always be done in a world of uncertainty.

We can never know enough to be sure that our idea will take flight. The variables capable of derailing a great idea are enormous—categorised so elegantly in the concept of the 'known knowns', the 'unknown knowns', the 'known unknowns' and the 'unknown unknowns'. It's a little unnerving, no? How can we possibly be successful every time we try to bring an idea into the world if these ideas are governed—in part or whole—by factors about which we have no certainty, but which will affect the ultimate outcome? And it gets worse!

There are mathematical models demonstrating that even the best and most valuable ideas will, over time, succumb to the laws of diminishing returns. Thus, coming up with new ideas, and knowing how to repeatedly and reliably turn them into additional value and wealth is a prerequisite, above all others, of sustainable organisational growth and development.

Failure or discovery?

What, then, are the conditions in which innovation flourishes? How do the best ideas come to benefit people, their teams, the organisations they serve and the communities of which they are a part?

It seems to me that, at every level, humans have two powerfully competing impulses—one that drives us towards predictable outcomes and relief from the anxiety attendant on uncertainty, and the other that demands we give expression to our deepest creative impulses. Driven by the former, we dread the shame of failure; driven by the latter, we are on constant lookout

4. INNOVATION: *Those Who Innovate Fastest Win*

for ways to create a better life. In other words, we like a challenge, so long as at a minimum it avoids failure, but has within it the real possibility of success.

Once, when leading a workshop at which I'd introduced some thinking about the process of generating creative ideas, I made the claim that nothing great would ever come of all our ideas if we did not establish a culture that actually encouraged the notion that failure is a good thing. It received many murmurs of tacit agreement, and guffaws of ridicule, fuelling our further conversation.

We talked of how we admire those who have the courage to 'fail', mentioning the feats of Thomas Edison, who famously described his 10,000 experiments with light bulbs not as failure, but discovery. He had discovered the many ways that light bulbs could not be made. We concluded that ultimate success is born of the ability to stare down failure, not to lose heart from the opinions of others, but to continue resolutely, celebrating the sometimes incremental gains and other times monumental breakthroughs that come from trial and error.

Then, one of the participants put her hand up and asked, cheekily, if anyone in the room had any performance metrics in their job description rewarding them for failure? She laughed as she told us of her vision of walking her boss up to the chart on the wall measuring everything she had done that had not worked and, with glee saying while pointing to the high level of failure: 'Now, about that increase you offered for great performance…'.

What's really at stake?

So, whose job is it to create the environments and cultures where risk-taking is encouraged? At what level of the organisation is this set, and must we all wait for that person at that level to drop the flag before we innovate?

Many years ago, I first read Viktor Frankl's book *Man's Search for Meaning*. Frankl, an eminent psychiatrist and survivor of the Holocaust, had unique insight into the true nature of the human condition, in both its most depraved and heroic forms. I was completely taken by his idea that, even in the most testing of circumstances, 'everything can be taken from a man but one thing: the last of human freedoms—to choose one's attitude in any given set of circumstances, to choose one's own way'.

The truth of Frankl's idea—that we own our response to any given circumstance—is compelling. Thus, the first place where innovation starts is with you. For only you can choose your attitude to any given situation. You cannot outsource this decision to your partner, boss, community or political leader. You own your own life, and it's up to you to be courageous enough to be the best possible version of yourself. If you deny yourself that freedom, then you lose something essential and vital about being fully human. You forfeit your destiny and crucially hand over your freedom to someone else. Compared to what was at stake for Frankl and his fellow inmates of the death camps, I believe we could all be braver in our choices and our attitude to what life serves up to us.

4. INNOVATION: *Those Who Innovate Fastest Win*

Digging a bit deeper into this thought of personal 'response ability', I'm struck with the idea that to be an innovator at any level requires leadership—a willingness to take the road less travelled, to go where others have not, and forge a path that clears the way for followers. It demands we know who we are and have a clear sense of personal purpose. Without these two gyroscopes of the soul, it is impossible to navigate the known unknowns and accommodate the emergence of the unknown unknowns.

Tying oneself to the mast of the ship to avoid getting thrown about the deck during the tempest secures the sailor, but does nothing to diminish the likelihood of the vessel smashing against the rocks. We need a frame of mind that is pulled forward by the power of our vision, providing the focus and motivation to continue in the quest for a better way, despite all around inflicting the plague of their cynicism on the chances of the success of our big idea. Moreover, the bigger the idea and the more disruptive it is of the existing order, the deeper the reserves of courage and leadership are required.

Fold or hold?

In my journey, I've found it an exquisite dilemma to know when or if to quit, and to decide what needs to be thrown overboard because it is not essential to completing the voyage and what is worth holding on to, even under the most difficult circumstances? What is central to my being, and living a life on and of purpose?

My mind has proven to be a very effective trickster, capable of fooling me time and time again, telling me that nothing is really that important, that the expedient trumps principle and that there is no line worth drawing that cannot be rubbed out if something seemingly more enticing comes along. Then, in the nick of time, the words of the sages return: 'know thyself'. For deep down, I have to recognise that my expedient cowardice today could lead to my profound regret tomorrow. Heroic failure has dignity, whereas avoiding the tournament is an ignominious surrender of the gift of life.

Innovation is defined by the Business Council of Australia as 'the application of knowledge to the delivery of additional value and wealth'. I put to you, then, that the first application of knowledge must be the knowledge of self. As Joseph Campbell put it, 'Follow your bliss, and the universe will open doors where once there were only walls.'

My bliss resides in the idea of bringing more justice to work, building a world in which those who are organised for collective endeavour do so in such a way that their thoughts and actions follow the golden rule: 'Do unto others as you would have them do unto you.'

These twin pillars of 'know thy self' and the golden rule are the source inspiration of everything I do. They are the compass point to which I return whenever a new idea or initiative seems to be going off track. They have sustained me in failure and tempered my hubris when I have known success.

It's a difficult credo to live by without opening myself to charges of hypocrisy and the chant of how poorly I score in the

4. INNOVATION: *Those Who Innovate Fastest Win*

league table of those who similarly aspire to develop the good, the true and the beautiful. But without it, I have no centre, and would not have been able to pursue my own inquiry into the kind of innovations in productivity that are the focus of this book.

Allow me to assume that you have put some effort into asking yourself who you truly are. Not just what your name is, but a questioning of your sense of your true, best self. That you can imagine yourself in your highest liberated form. Let me also assume that you have asked yourself the question about what your work is—not your job, but what unique purpose you see for your life before you draw your last breath.

You may have determined that your purpose is to dwell in solitude in a cave. If that is the case, this next thought won't fit. But if you feel it's to be engaged in the world, then whatever you feel is your life's purpose, it is impossible to contemplate its fulfilment without engaging with others. In fact, I challenge you to contemplate your life without others and see what you can get done. Even solitary pursuits such as writing a book require editors, publishers, distributors, readers, and critics.

At one end of the spectrum, that engagement with the other might be characterised as a submission to the will of a tyrant or tyrannical idea, and at the other end to live liberated in the flow of your own creativity, leaving ample space for others within your orbit to find the full expression of their own creative impulses and gifts.

While most of us dwell somewhere in between these two opposite poles, not much at all that is innovative can occur where the solution to all problems and the exploitation of all opportunities resides in the mind of the tyrant. By definition, the tyrant arrests learning and seeks no more than to bend the world to their own unedifying ends.

Truthfully, the lifeblood of innovation is collaboration. And it has been my experience that if ever one is to create the conditions in which good creative ideas can repeatedly and reliably be turned into tangible value, then certain practices and principles need to be in place. The mantra 'fail often to succeed sooner' promotes a culture that rewards risk and acknowledges that, as you increase risk, so the likelihood of failure increases.

The sooner you go through that which doesn't work, the closer you get to refining what does. You cannot be learning if you are not failing—knowledge comes from experimentation, testing hypotheses, building prototypes and critically examining what to keep and what to let go.

Leaders must learn to let go

I once worked on an assignment in the local manufacturing subsidiary of a global player in the electric cables business. Copper rod would come in at the receiving bay and huge drums of multicore cables would be shipped out the other end. Five factory buildings dealt with each of the major process steps required to turn copper into cable. This output ranged from lightweight wires for instrumentation and appliances, to product capable of carrying electricity from its generation at power stations, across the national grid to all who need it.

4. INNOVATION: *Those Who Innovate Fastest Win*

The general manager of production was, by all accounts, a very smart man eager to show us around the plant and share how much he knew about every little detail of the facilities he managed. What he seemed to want to forget was the reason we were brought in to help—he wasn't hitting his production targets. He was making too much of some product and too little of others and his delivery-to-promised-date was very poor.

What emerged from all my interviews of his direct reports, his peers and his boss, was an overwhelming malaise around anyone's desire even to put forward any idea to do things better, more efficiently, let alone go through the hard work of implementing it. Some cunning individuals had worked out that if ever an idea capable of delivering an improvement in performance was to be adopted, it was best to propose it in a way that appeared as if the idea was their boss's own.

During the first occasion I sat in on a meeting with this man and his team, the atmospherics in the room immediately changed. It was as if someone had flicked off the energy switch of the participants. The very air itself seemed short on oxygen, stale and sleep-inducing. The man proceeded to talk for an hour straight, without brooking any interruptions, detailing what he saw as the problem, the idea he had to fix it, and the plan as to how that idea was going to be implemented—down to the detail of who in the room was assigned to do what and by when.

At the end, he invited everyone to comment on what he had just detailed. What he was actually calling for was an affirmation of his brilliance in identifying the problem and his solution for fixing it. One brave soul ventured to say, in that fearful, tentative but polite way that people have of addressing tyrants, how the problem was misidentified and thus would not deliver the desired result. She was shut down immediately, labelled as stupid because she couldn't possibly comprehend the complexity apparent to him as their leader. The meeting was summarily closed. Sadly, this kind of experience, to some degree or another, is repeated millions of times a day across almost every workplace in the land.

Turning up to your life

As I live by the creed of giving all a fair go, I decided to explore with this manager why he had turned up to that meeting—and, indeed, his life—in such a way as to completely stifle any kind of creative interchange. At first, he found the questions and the idea of composing any answer really difficult. But when he did begin to talk, falteringly and in short sentences, I got a sense that he was unhappy both within himself, as well as with the poor results he'd had with the business. With some active listening and then some careful coaching, together we managed to tease out his fears. They could be peeled back to three fundamental layers.

In the first instance, he was deeply afraid of being judged as not being good enough. This had been the source of his motivation for as long as he could remember. Even back to his school days, when despite having been adjudged dux of his year, he'd felt that it was just a matter of time before he would be caught out and someone better would come along to show him up.

4. INNOVATION: *Those Who Innovate Fastest Win*

This fear had deepened in its next layer, which was a highly practised cynicism. He had completely lost the ability to be vulnerable. The shield he'd developed to protect himself from any judgement—or, worse, criticism—was the emotional equivalent of the type that space capsules use to prevent burning up when re-entering the earth's atmosphere. It may have protected him from many bad feelings, but it also cauterised him from any feeling of joy, or being able to genuinely and generously connect to and form relationships with others.

The final layer showed up as a fear of death—not a physical death of the body, but the death of the ego construct he had so carefully built, over more years than he cared to remember. Here was the guy who, in his own mind, was really clever; he was the man who had all the answers, the one who could work out any problem, no matter how difficult. He just couldn't imagine what would be left of him if any of that was no longer true. Who would face the world if he had to admit his ignorance and no longer be that guy?

With further careful and sensitive probing, it emerged that he had a real and vivid dread of letting go of that person he had so assiduously crafted over the decades. Deep within, however, he knew that the seeds of the new man had no chance to grow unless he let the old constructs die and surrender to the deep mystery of the unknown. There could be no connection to his vision of his future self, nor a better relationship with any of his family, colleagues and friends unless and until he understood just how much he was standing in his own way. This was a breakthrough in our conversation and the nub of a theme we'll return to in Part 4.

Working on playful teams

Really good ideas are often the product of a process where one starts with crazy ones. The best place to get great ideas is by listening at the periphery of your organisational boundary to what the users of your products and services actually need, whether articulated by them or not. Thinking that an innovation manager is going to come up with the next big thing by virtue of his title is wishful thinking for the deluded.

As the renowned design business IDEO puts it in their philosophy of design thinking, 'Enlightened trial and error succeeds over lone genius.' It is of the essence that collaboration has a significant element of playfulness about it. Playfulness facilitates the reduction in anxiety attendant on trying ideas that will invariably fail the first time out.

Organising, coordinating and project-managing the development of an idea from its inception to a product or service that creates value is not the job of the most senior person on the team, but that of the person with the best skillset to get that aspect of the work done.

While on the topic of skillsets, my experience of the best and most fertile innovation fields are those that draw on a wide variety of perspectives, from disciplines as diverse as engineering, psychology, the arts, sport, finance, teaching, sociology, medicine, anthropology—indeed, any field of inquiry that examines our species in meaningful ways. We should also not forget to remedy our tendency to only include those who look, feel and believe as we do, but to be mindful as well to open the

4. INNOVATION: *Those Who Innovate Fastest Win*

innovation conversation to different genders, cultures and ages.

It is, of course, the case that trial and error cannot go on forever. There's always a commercial imperative, and a good leader of innovation processes knows when to call time, focus the conversation on the critical areas that are showing most promise and proceed to an outcome.

But how do we come to know what we know? Whether to fold or hold, call time or extend? W. Edwards Deming highlighted the Theory of Knowledge, or how we come to know what we know, as one of the four prerequisites of transformational change. Big ideas cannot reliably be transformed into value if we don't develop an approach to how we come to know what we know.

Knowledge can be simply defined as the ability to predict that a particular action will result in a specific outcome. Thus, we know that when water reaches boiling point, it will change state and turn into steam. Any organisation aspiring to improve the flow of value from ideas must create an infrastructure supportive of the use of knowledge developed about how to turn ideas into value.

With the advent of the internet, the ability to store and retrieve information sorted by relevance to any given set of search criteria has increased exponentially. It's never been easier to gain access to knowledge on pretty much whatever topic one cares to name. Often, for the biggest of ideas, creating value and wealth from this easily acquirable knowledge means not only collaboration within an organisation, but also across organisations and sectors. Thus, there is a role to play in this wealth-generating endeavour for government, academia and the private sector.

The state, the ivory tower and new ideas

A chapter on innovation would not be complete without some commentary on the role of the state and the academy.

Governments should not try to pick winners and put taxpayers' money behind their choices. Government is far less capable than the marketplace of determining which ideas will succeed and which won't. Politicians and civil servants never spend their own money and therefore have a higher tolerance and lower consequence for failure than the entrepreneurs. Those who invest their limited time and money in taking a concept from idea to value have their antennae more acutely tuned to where opportunity and peril reside. If they get it wrong, they go broke, but for the politicians poor choices, we continue adding to and feeding the herd of white elephants.

That's not to say that the private sector is free of villains among its free-enterprise innovating heroes. The world of the entrepreneur most certainly has its rogues, who for example, feverishly decry paying taxes, deluded in the thought that the sole source of all wealth is their lone genius. They studiously ignore the fact that the likes of education, health, justice, defense and infrastructure are not optional extras if you are going to have a productive and competitive workforce capable of contributing to building businesses, buying products and services and growing a thriving economy.

4. INNOVATION: *Those Who Innovate Fastest Win*

It is a plague on our ideal of democracy that those with wealth are often able to buy our politicians and have them develop policies which serve their narrow interests. It has the effect of increasing the concentrations of wealth and power and stultifying the processes of developing innovative solutions to some of society's biggest issues.

It is thus the government's job, as servants of the people who elected them into office, to spend our hard-earned taxes wisely and, insofar as innovation is concerned, to fairly set the rules of engagement for ongoing success. This can be achieved through the development of a cogent policy and regulatory framework, which at a minimum creates a level playing field by legislating strong, effective competition laws. The new and valuable must be given a fair go against defensive, entrenched rent-seeking incumbents. In addition, any government framework for innovation should foster collaboration between all parties, through the development of multi-sectoral innovation hubs, playing into areas of national competitive advantage.

Governments can facilitate the coordinated development of new markets for innovative products and services through the likes of free-trade agreements, favourable domestic and foreign investment regimes and trade and cultural exchanges. While they're about it, they might want to put more effort into bringing innovation to the delivery of their own services!

As for academia, in this day and age, it cannot be the case that our universities are ivory towers, disconnected from the world we live in. Which is not to say that fundamental research should be sacrificed for only those activities passing some form of commercial test. Most of the advances in life we enjoy today have arisen from pure research. All electronics, for example, depend on the exploitation of the principles of quantum mechanics, a phenomenon that would hardly have been in the mind of Niels Bohr as he wrestled with its implications, stating famously, 'If you can fathom quantum mechanics without getting dizzy, you don't get it.'

The point is that at their best, academics are trained with a high degree of skill in rational argument and scientific method while subjecting their research to rigorous peer review. Their level of competence in bringing intellectual inquiry to identifying and solving a massively diverse range of problems provides a ready-made capability from which other sectors can benefit.

So how do we get into a virtuous cycle of value creation? It's an open question of collaboration on all sides of a triangle comprising the private and public sectors and academia. How do we best get all of what we need to make collaborative innovation happen rather than myopically focusing on our own sectoral silo?

If you think education's expensive, try ignorance.

Questions for INNOVATION

1. Why are you doing what you are currently doing? What deep-seated need does it address in your sense of your own transcendent purpose?

2. Who are the cynics and tyrants in your workplace? How can

4. INNOVATION: Those Who Innovate Fastest Win

you encourage them to seek a broader collaboration?

3. What is your role in leading your team to develop more collaborative practices within the team and across your organisation?

4. To what extent are you able to live the mantra 'fail often to succeed sooner'? What is it that you fear about failure?

5. What role do you think private enterprise, government and academia should play in your innovation agenda? What could you do to better collaborate across and beyond your organisational boundaries, including with other organisations, academia and government?

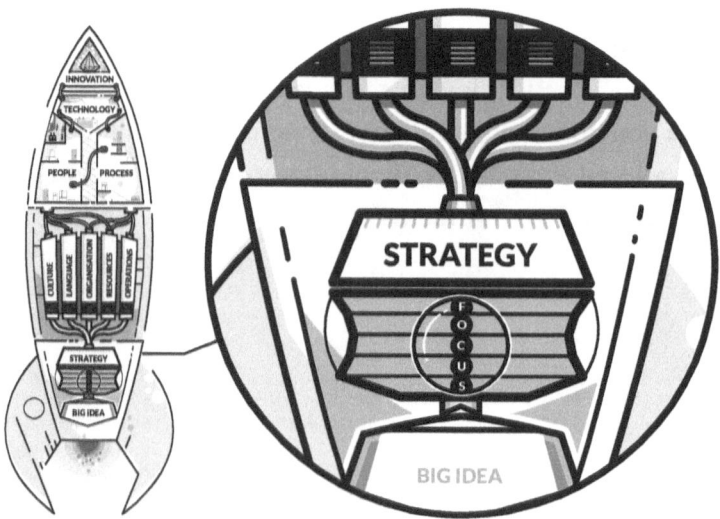

Figure 8: Strategy

Chapter 5
STRATEGY: *Thinking Tools to Reach Your Goal*

However beautiful the strategy, you should occasionally look at the results.

Winston Churchill

IT TAKES COURAGE to think and act strategically. The deeper the horizon and the broader the vision, the more the uncertainty and the greater the likelihood you are proven wrong. Safer to address only the immediate pain and let someone else deal with the long-term consequence of poor sense- and decision-making. A penny saved today is a penny saved today, whereas innovating for the revenue of tomorrow demands a long chain of risky cause and effect before it becomes cash in the bank. How much easier and less risky to save today's penny. How much poorer would we be if the heroes among us didn't take the strategic route of the road less travelled?

Having said that, it seems there are as many concepts of strategy as people thinking about it. And while my intent here isn't to compare or evaluate interpretations or approaches, I do consider a strategic mindset to be one of the most important elements needed to consistently deliver innovations in productivity. I would go so far as to say that without intentionally setting aside the time to do the work of applying mindful effort to the development and execution of strategy, an organisation leaves itself at the mercy of dumb luck. Invariably, dumb luck produces dumb outcomes.

The word 'strategy' has roots in ancient Greek and is the art of generalship, or the art and science of planning and winning a war. In business, strategising usually means doing the long-term planning to enhance the organisation's ability to achieve its goal. Strategy, therefore, must relate to the whole system and its long-term goals.

For any and all organisations, having a clear strategy helps everyone who commits their activities to the long-term sustainable success of the organisation see where they fit in with the overall plan. It is from the strategy that each of us, to a greater or lesser extent, understand the reason we are doing what we're doing, in the sequence we're doing it.

Talking about strategy inevitably also raises the related topics of tactics and operations. In the military, 'tactics' is defined as the art or science of deploying military forces and manoeuvring them in battle. 'Operations' is the state of being in action, or operative. Outside of the military, these definitions become increasingly blurred and, in business, are often used somewhat arbitrarily, depending whom you talk to and their level of work. No business has all the resources necessary to operate optimally. This means that decisions will have to be made on what gets priority at any given time. This is where tactics come into

5. STRATEGY: *Thinking Tools to Reach Your Goal*

play. They define how the business is going to prioritise different milestones in carrying out a specific strategy. They are actionable, have a purpose and a measurable result.

Leaders ought to know their organisations need strategy. But often what they call 'strategy' is merely a tactical response to some market fluctuation. After all, it's only natural that company vice-presidents want their own strategy within their fiefdom: the IT strategy, finance strategy, brand strategy, marketing strategy, product strategy and so on. To continue the military analogy, for the business as a whole to win results, these vice presidents are the equivalent of the generals who, operating within a specific theatre of conflict, must take a strategic approach to each battle with the aim of inching the whole army (and the country it represents) closer to the ultimate political victory—winning the war.

The stated strategy in service of the overall purpose of the business should cascade through the organisation, affecting the goals of each unit and, in turn, the tactics employed to fulfil the larger strategic goals. Think, for example, about a company like BHP. It's the world's largest mining company. So when it declares its strategy is 'to own and operate large, long-life, low-cost, expandable, upstream assets diversified by commodity, geography and market', it's sending a clear message to each and all of its businesses. In fact, any business within that conglomerate that does not fit the criteria should expect to be sold off as soon as is prudent for management to do so. On the other hand, the president for iron ore—a business unit that clearly integrates with the larger strategy—must determine how their own strategy contributes to the overall goal of the business.

Now, much to my surprise, this idea of 'contributing to the overall goal' holds a trap that ensnares many leaders. They don't stop to identify, or at least clearly articulate, the ultimate goal of the organisation, despite it being a fundamental aspect of running a sound business. Sadly, more often than not, the organisational goal is unclear. As you can imagine, it's hard—impossible?—to achieve innovations in productivity if you don't know what your productivity is aimed at, and therefore what it should be enhancing.

Setting goals to fulfil a purpose

Goals and purpose are often thought to be interchangeable. But there is a difference between your organisational goal and its purpose. In a for-profit organisation, the goal is usually to make more money now and in the future. In this formulation of a goal, it becomes apparent that making more money now and in the future provides the reason for shareholders to continue investing, and not take their money elsewhere. Having a goal of making a profit, though, is in itself neither good nor bad. Commerce has over the ages been the engine of progress. However, having people solely dedicated to the purpose of making money surrenders to a lazy, crass materialism that suffocates the possibility of progress associated with the heroic ideals reflected in what's best in our free-enterprise heritage.

Governments (organisations after all) can have similar ideas about productivity and purpose. They may have a goal to de-

5. STRATEGY: *Thinking Tools to Reach Your Goal*

liver the highest levels of service for every tax dollar spent. A charitable organisation might strive to achieve the lowest administrative burden for every dollar donated to the intended cause. In simple terms, each would like greater levels of output for less effort on the inputs.

From a fundamentals point of view, it is the shareholders, who have the right to set the goal. The goal, too, should have certain key attributes. You should always be able to get more of it, and it should not be stated as a target. Thus, 'We will make $x million of profit by 30th June 20xx' should be restated as, 'We will make no less than $x million of profit by no later than 30th June 20xx'.

Furthermore, the goal should be simple and easy to understand, and serve the purpose of having everyone in the organisation, from the board room to the shop floor, able to identify with it. Crucially, the goal must be understood in the context that shows how it serves the higher-order mission, vision and purpose of the organisation. Importantly, a well-crafted goal allows the actions taken when executing the strategy to be measured. Thus, it's possible to assess whether or not those actions are effective and able to deliver more units of goal achievement.

Any strategy worthy of the considerable effort required to mobilise and align the resources of the organisation must point to the achievement of its goal. And it must be able to relate individual effort at all levels of work to the system as a whole. For it is ultimately the system as a whole that delivers the best possible returns to shareholders, opportunity to employees and potential for delight to customers. No single business unit, division or part of a joint venture offers a better final tally individually than when the organisation functions as a cohesive, integrated whole.

Thus, at the systems level, if the goal is to continuously improve the owners' returns, whether in public or private sector, for profit or for cause, all organisations have a common set of critical success factors that form the building blocks of success: satisfied customers, employees, suppliers and regulators. Perhaps we should say 'delighted' rather than 'satisfied', as satisfaction palls in the face of customer's relentless demand for more. Get these right, and you at least have the necessary conditions to reliably and repeatedly deliver superior returns.

How this delight is achieved, though, depends on the dynamics of competition within the marketplace. In Michael Porter's seminal book *Competitive Advantage*, these dynamics were spelled out and include the bargaining power of suppliers, the threat of new entrants, the bargaining power of buyers, the threat of substitute products or services, and the ferocity of the rivalry among existing competitors. Porter makes the essential point that you gain competitive advantage in two fundamental ways: either you go cheaper or you differentiate your product or service. His advice for strategists is to build competitive advantage through differentiation rather than lowered prices, giving the buyer more value for the same or higher price. 'It is the worst error in strategy to compete with rivals on the same dimensions,' he says. 'Instead of competing to be the best, one should compete to be unique.' A case in point is Apple, which has only a 12–15% share of the mobile phone market but, some claim, at its peak, had a 90% share of that market's profits.

The business of business management systems

As this is a book about 'innovations in productivity', I would like to relate how strategic competitive advantage does not necessarily arise out of defining new products, services or markets, but may find its roots in the seemingly prosaic world of operations. Or, as the saying goes, 'strategy is for amateurs, logistics for professionals'.

Some years ago, I was privileged to lead my team on a global project implementing the SAP software system into a Tier-1 mining business with 13 strategic business units and over 100 operations present on every continent. The implementation was far more than an IT fix to the problem of managing the complexity of such an organisation. Their multi-billion-dollar effort aimed to standardise and simplify the core activities of the business such that all the managers and staff—whether in a copper mine in Chile, a coal mine in South Africa or an alumina mine in Australia—did their buying, warehousing, production, maintenance, finance, HR, sales and distribution in the same manner.

I understood this strategic initiative of using a new information technology platform as a means to profoundly transform the way work was planned and performed across the enterprise. This was happening during an unprecedented mining boom, with a very real risk that the existing system of management would not be able to cope with the complexity of expanding existing assets and acquiring and developing new ones. I understood the core principle behind the strategy: as a rule, adding complexity to any system increases the difficulty of managing the system not in an arithmetic 'sum of the parts' progression but exponentially, with each discretionary element multiplying the difficulty.

Successfully simplifying the running of a business from pit to port that already has millions of moving parts and tens of thousands of moving people would invariably reduce the risk of catastrophic failure. It would have the additional merit of providing a necessary condition for very reliable due-date performance, while also reducing the time between the placement of an order and delivery to the customer.

Switching on to operating discipline as a strategic lever

Many executives who have their heads in the world of strategy would argue that lead times and due-date performance are a matter for Operations to sort out. That they themselves would be better left to deal with the heady topics of competitor and market analysis and segmentation, strategic supply options, evolving technology evaluation, and organisational design and development.

And to them, I'd say it's worth remembering the famous

5. STRATEGY: *Thinking Tools to Reach Your Goal*

dictum of Taiichi Ohno, the giant of the Toyota Production System, whose ideas created one of the most admired businesses of the twentieth century. 'All we are doing is looking at the timeline,' he said, 'from the moment the customer gives us an order to the point when we collect the cash. And we are reducing the timeline by reducing the non-value-adding wastes.'

But back to our story. Some time into the project, I was working with the marketing function on their implementation of a significant part of the system. One of the executives told me about the incentive system for their salespeople, based on the positive variance they can negotiate from the traded spot price of the commodity for which they are responsible. This was a puzzle for me.

I couldn't understand how a commodity traded on the open market could be sold for more than the customer could buy it for from anyone else in that openly traded market. The proposition they offered their customers, he explained, was strategic in its nature; it didn't look at their supply chain as ending at the port, where the customer took title of the goods, but extended until they, the supplier, had solved their customer's significant problems.

By providing their product to customers in ever-shorter lead times and ever more reliably, the supplier helped the customer avoid having to invest their capital in 'just-in-case' inventory to deal with any potential failure to deliver to the promised date. Shorter lead times also meant overall holdings could be reduced, as they could be replenished in shorter and shorter cycles. Moreover, the customer's plant could be fine-tuned for the specific grade of ore that was characteristic of where it was mined, and these settings could be maintained and continuously improved without having to make adjustments every time a new source of supply entered the facility.

At that point, a big switch flipped in my mind as I realised the truly strategic nature of the project. Every part of the value chain—production, maintenance, supply, finance, distribution and people management—had to work as simply and effectively as possible to reliably deliver the product to the customer on time and in full, at ever-shorter lead times.

With so many things that could go wrong in achieving this goal, it was clear that the simpler, and more standardised, the processes—and the degree to which everyone operating them aligned to those principles—the better the performance of the system as a whole. It also had the great merit of increasing the flow of material through their supply chain, and reducing the unit cost by a far larger amount than might otherwise be achieved by looking for parsimonious reductions in labour costs and operating expenses.

Here was the best of both worlds of Porter's fundamental strategic choices: cost and differentiation. For such a product—a commodity almost completely, remember, undifferentiated from its rivals—the chosen dimension of competition was time. Specifically, lead time. And reliable delivery performance. Every other decision in the business subordinated to that simple idea—time is money.

One day, the project director joined a workshop I was facilitating. He'd just come out of a meeting with a vendor of business management system software and, wanting to benchmark his own efforts, got a surprising answer from them. Armed with this, he asked the project team if we could name a company that had done a better job of simplifying, standardising and aligning their core work processes than we were endeavouring. After much guesswork, it turned out the answer was Steve Jobs at Apple. How noteworthy that whether in the prosaic world of lumps of rock to the super-cool world of the hi-tech iPhone, operating discipline was seen as a high-value lever for sustainable competitive advantage.

A couple of years later, in a media interview after presenting his first set of results, the new CEO of this mining behemoth attributed at least $2 billion of the bottom line to the productivity improvement generated by our 'IT project'. He also quoted economist Paul Krugman: 'Productivity isn't everything, but in the long run it's almost everything.' He added the obvious but so often overlooked fact that if productivity is the ratio of outputs to inputs, whilst ever there is a need to focus on the denominator (input), there is far more leverage to be gained by addressing the numerator (output).

What, to what, and how to change—within reason

It seems fair to say that while the implementation of any strategy implies change, not all change is strategic. Naturally, then, when looking at the whole of the system, having established the system boundary and goal, one needs to ask three questions: What to change? What to change to? and How to change? In other words, what elements of the existing system need to change, what would the future look like once that change has been achieved, and how does one go about bringing that future state into being?

While reason may have its limits, we could surely do a consistently better job with our strategic initiatives if we could clearly articulate the logic of our thinking. How then can we best articulate the assumptions of cause and effects that would open the logic of our strategic reasoning to scrutiny by our peers? What benefit could be gained if we were able to use the product of such diverse scrutiny to communicate to our community of stakeholders the 'what', the 'to what' and the 'how' of the change program?

As Einstein so eloquently put it, 'Intelligence might have its limits, but stupidity knows no such bounds.' So why not improve our collective intelligence by providing ourselves with a Thinking Process toolkit to help leverage whatever natural wit, intuition and reason is, in any given moment, our individual and collective intellectual capital?

Just such a thinking process was developed by the late Dr Eli Goldratt, who discovered the Theory of Constraints (TOC). He used his background in physics to explore the relationship between manifest complexity and inherent simplicity. In a famous example he was fond of using, he talked of the immense complexity of the cosmos and how Newton was able to discover through his three laws of motion that, to a good enough approximation, all physical relations between the heavenly bodies could

5. STRATEGY: *Thinking Tools to Reach Your Goal*

be reduced to the inherent simplicity contained in his formulae.

The inherent simplicity arises from the idea that when one thinks in terms of systems, rather than in the myriad fragments of a reductionist worldview, there are very few degrees of freedom for connected entities. The reductionist manages complexity by breaking big systems into smaller and smaller parts, often thinking the best result one can hope for is to manage the parts from the bottom up and assume the whole can only ever amount to the sum of the parts. The system-thinker gives primacy to the whole, and starts their enquiry with a view as to how best to integrate from the top down.

In other words, systems thinking takes account of the fact that in an integrated system such as an organisation, what you do to one thing has an effect on another, and if you can chase down the chain of cause and effect you will, in due course, find a root cause. These root causes provide the highest leverage for systemic change.

Getting to that root cause, however, demands a certain education in the process of logical thinking. Had we been among the educated classes in the age of Socrates, we would have studied logic. Then we could construct our arguments—and challenge assumptions about that construction—without resorting to pure intuition or ad hominem attacks on people with whom we disagree.

From Chapter 2, about people, we learned some of what the Nobel Laureate for Economics in 2002, psychologist Daniel Kahneman, elucidated about important new thinking in the field of behavioural economics. He wrote the bestseller *Think-*

ing, Fast and Slow, in which he popularised the idea that we have two basic modes of thinking. Fast thinking lets us rapidly arrive at conclusions intuitively; slow thinking uses structured reasoning to explore the assumptions underpinning our hasty judgements and rigorously challenges the chains of cause and effect.

Since slow thinking takes a significant mental effort, evolution wired our brains to take the fast, intuitive route whenever possible. This works in many cases. Unfortunately, when faced with complex problems, we naturally leap to conclusions based on our inherent biases. Recognising that there are two distinctly different modes of thinking and knowing when to use each is a key to winning the results we're after. If we become intentional about taking the slow route, we afford ourselves a heightened possibility of harvesting the more abundant and attractive fruits of the well considered approach.

Goldratt's Logical Thinking Process provides a framework for navigating complexity, helping us uncover those few, inherently simple root causes that manifest all the undesirable effects of the system at large. When we use logic as a basis for decision-making, the Logical Thinking Process is a powerful ally which helps us, in the first place, understand the difference between 'necessary condition' and 'sufficient cause' logic. Indeed, one of the most common mistakes of almost every person I have worked with is to assume that what is necessary is, therefore, sufficient.

In our fast-thinking mode, we look for the 'silver bullet'— the single thing that will smash the problems we are trying to solve. We might be tempted to tell ourselves that our new computer system will deliver more projects on time, be faster to market and incorporate all the new features of the products and services our strategy demands. Yet, while the new system may be necessary, it's exceptionally rare for technology to be sufficient to solve the problems it was designed for.

What, for example, would one need to have in place to address the existing culture, the resistance to learn new ways of working and the potential upheavals in organisational structure? How does one understand what we are capable of doing now (existing capabilities) and be able to develop new capabilities? And how best to make it all operational?

The Thinking Process is a streamlined and sequential series of 'logic trees' that helps provide, for anyone willing to invest the time studying and practising it, a robust means of constructing, testing and communicating the reasoning that underlies a given approach to solving a problem.

Over the years, I've developed my own practice in the use of the Thinking Process, influenced greatly by the extensive teaching and learning improvements Bill Dettmer has made to the original pioneering work of Goldratt. These logic trees go by different names, depending on your reference source, and different practitioners use them in different sequences, sometimes as a strategic set, and other times individually to solve tactical problems. It's beyond the scope of this book to detail a complete strategic review using the Thinking Process, but for a feeling of what's involved, below is a broad outline. At the appendix is and example of a set of these logic trees.

A reason to be logical

When I conduct a full strategic analysis of an organisation's system, the general order to tackle the assignment is sown below. You can find a worked example at the appendix on p409.

Be clear about boundaries. Consider the boundaries of the system being examined. Is it the whole organisation, a strategic business unit or only a function within a bigger whole? Be clear, too, about the distinction between the 'span of control' over which your remit of authority is given and the (usually significantly larger) 'sphere of influence' within which you are expected to achieve a result.

Articulate the goal. Spend the time to properly articulate The Goal of the system you're being tasked with improving, including how it will be measured, and when you expect what results to be evident.

Build a Goal Tree. Sometimes called a Strategic Intermediate Objectives Map, the Goal Tree begins at the top with the stated goal and seeks to explore the intermediate objectives for achieving it. The top layer below the goal statement shows the three or four 'critical success factors' and, below that, the 'necessary conditions' without which success cannot be achieved. The Goal Tree is not intended to be a comprehensive plan for executing the strategy but, when done well, has the great merit of making the goal clear to all stakeholders and showing those reading it where to find their role in bringing it to fruition. Everyone can then align behind it in the way that riders in a peloton slipstream in the wake of the lead bike.

Develop a Current Reality Tree. This helps you properly understand how the existing reality is different from what's articulated in the Goal Tree. It's important to be rigorous in this phase, using logic checks to make sure the Current Reality Tree has all the logic—both necessary and sufficient—to adequately explain any diversion that might have been taken from the prescribed elements of the Goal Tree. Such logic checks include:

- **Clarity.** Are the logical statements about reality (entities) in the boxes clear in what they are saying? Can anyone involved in the system understand what is being said, and share the meaning of it in the context in which the strategy is being developed?

- **Entity existence.** Is what's being said in an entity actually true, and what data support the truth of the existence of the entity?

- **Causality existence.** When connecting one entity to another in a chain of cause and effect, what are the assumptions that underpin the linkage, and can these be changed without the logic breaking down?

- **Additional cause.** Is there another entity, which on its own would have the same effect and which, when combined with other causes, may have an amplifying effect? Alternatively, if the original cause is removed may the additional cause still play a part in keeping the undesirable effect in place?

- **Concurrent cause**. Is there an entity that needs to combine with another before it's sufficient to create the effect that's being observed?

- **Missing intermediate effect**. The proverbial 'long arrow' statement in which the distance between cause and effect is so great that one can intuit a connection, but to provide clarity, must be articulated as a full chain of causation.

- **Predicted effect**. This is the tool of the diagnostician who says if the cause is deemed to be something in particular, then it could have multiple effects, and the absence of any of those predicted effects would eliminate the possibility of the cause being what has been hypothesised.

- **Root cause analysis**. Keep looking for entities that have no other entities pointing into them, and ask if there's something in the system that's the cause of that entity being observed. At some point, you'll find you have gone down in the chain of cause and effect as far as is practicable within the span of control, and that will be the root cause of the diversion between the Current Reality and the entities contained in the Goal Tree. These root causes—and there should only be very few of them; sometimes only one—act as points of maximum leverage.

5. STRATEGY: Thinking Tools to Reach Your Goal

Test with the Evaporating Cloud. Once the root cause of system underperformance has been established, the Evaporating Cloud, also called the conflict-resolution tree, is used to examine why the root cause perpetuates within the system. It would seem reasonable to say that if the offending root cause were easy to remove, management would have done so. Assuming that everyone within the system is aligned to The Goal, then the dilemma as to which strategic direction to choose as a way out of systemic underperformance must be either one or more false assumptions about what holds the Current Reality in place. Alternatively, not all options for change have been considered and there is scope to inject new reality that will have the effect of 'evaporating' the cloud or resolving the conflict in a win-win way.

Predict with the Future Reality Tree. The evaporating of the cloud provides the direction for a systemic solution to attaining the stated organisational goal. However, before going full throttle in the proposed breakthrough direction, the Future Reality Tree provides the means of articulating the sufficiency of the cause and effects of the breakthrough's argument. We can test the assumptions contained in the argument and the results of the analysis can be used to predict consequences and communicate options. Wherever we find negative effects, this paving of good intentions on the road to ruin can be rigorously examined, corrected and re-injected into the Future Reality. We thus test and evaluate any or all plausible and relevant future scenarios.

Plan with the transition tree. This is, in essence, a variant on traditional ways of project planning. With this, the step-by-step actions at the tactical level can be taken to deliver on The Goal articulated in the broader strokes of the Future Reality Tree.

Turning common sense into common practice

Some years ago, I was involved in a very large transformation at a bank that required our sponsor, the executive in charge of the strategic business unit (SBU), to lead the integration of her business unit's products and services into a new whole-of-bank technology platform. For many years, prior to my team getting there, the relationship between our sponsor (the SBU) and IT could best be described as rancorous, with very low levels of trust, particularly in the delivery of important strategic technology projects.

Our system goal, as expressed in the Goal Tree, was rather simple: 'Deliver strategic investment in technology at an acceptable and reliable business cost, quality and due date, given the human and material resources at the bank's disposal.'

Despite best endeavours from all concerned—thinking and acting as they were within the narrow confines of the needs of their particular business function—the ultimate truth was expressed in our strategic review, using the Current Reality Tree: 'Business benefits are fewer, and bank investment in strategic programs of work is more, than is either reasonable or possible,

5. STRATEGY: *Thinking Tools to Reach Your Goal*

given the human and material resources at its disposal.' Tracing down chains of up to ten layers of cause and effect, we eventually got down to two root causes driving the dysfunction between these two important parts of the bank.

The highest echelons of the bank had determined that IT was a big-ticket item on the bank's expenditure and investment budgets, and that the best bang-to-buck ratio could be gained by compelling all demand for products and services to be channelled through the in-house capability - a fine sounding idea, but the root of a swathe of new problems.

Through the aggregation of all of the bank's internal demand for similar services, regardless of which division of the bank was using them, it was assumed that its own resources could achieve levels of utilisation and hence efficiency not possible if compared to external benchmarks. And, by having the supply internal to the bank, an additional assumed benefit was that the unit cost of labour would be significantly lower than if it was bought from contactors or consultants.

The root cause analysis led us to the discovery of a deep and fundamental structural impediment which militated against improved project outcomes for the SBU, and hence the bank. IT organised and structured itself according to the demand from all stakeholders by technology type, which limited its ability to optimise the way it used resources across the different streams of demand. It was a form of job demarcation for no good reason other than them not knowing how to better match supply and demand across the system as a whole.

The reductionist approach of looking at the parts of the technology 'factory' to be optimised wasted the chance to optimise the whole. The structural flaw and its effects were compounded by the group executive creating a single critical Key Performance Indicator (KPI) for all of IT to meet an overall utilisation rate of 90% on a rolling basis, six months out from the current date.

The debilitating effect of having such a KPI was that IT management was primarily concerned about recovering costs and not addressing the needs of the SBU in a timely and reliable fashion. This undesirable effect occurring despite the fact that the business benefits of the strategic portfolio of work often dwarfed their costs.

Furthermore, analysis using the Thinking Process also revealed (and powerfully articulated the fact) that although IT was a monopoly supplier to the SBU, it was the SBU that carried all of the accountability for the successful delivery of the technology programs, without having the requisite authority over how the work of IT—the most material part of its investment—was planned, authorised, executed and measured.

The quick way out usually leads back in

Those favouring their 'thinking-fast' conclusions argued that the easy way out was to allow for external parties to compete against IT, thus lowering the SBU's costs and raising performance. But such simple remedies fail to properly investigate the assumptions that underpin the use of a thinking-fast approach to resolving the core conflict.

5. STRATEGY: *Thinking Tools to Reach Your Goal*

In the exercise with the Current Reality Tree, a second root cause was found. The program and project management capability of SBU senior executives responsible for these significant investments was often far lower than the minimum level required to be effective in delivering the scope on time and on budget. Good bankers do not necessarily make good program and project managers.

By doing an Evaporating Cloud exercise on 'outsource vs. insource' it became abundantly clear that the simple expedient of outsourcing development would do nothing to address the low level of project management maturity and capability within the SBU. It would simply expose the bank to more risk as a consequence of not being able to properly manage the variety of types of arrangements one can have with external service providers.

When we helped define the Future Reality under the outsourcing scenario many additional issues emerged. One of these was the serious negative effect that would be felt if the SBU contracted a third party to do their strategic programs. They would be faced with navigating an even more hostile interface between the SBU, IT and the third party when it came to integrating the components into the overall solution architecture of the bank.

The Thinking Process began an initiative in which the interface between the business unit and IT was redefined. The group executive in charge reframed the nature of the relationship between the technology folk and the business owners as a 'value partnership'. and began the long-haul task of redefining processes, measures and accountabilities to ensure every decision made delivered real long-term value for the bank. People were rewarded when they had problems and asked for help, as well as when they gave help to those who had put their hand up asking for it. This represented a marked difference to the historical patterns of burying problems and casting blame. The outcome was higher speed to market of new products and services, more predictable on-time delivery and a marked reduction in cost blowouts.

Thus, if you can lead a horse to water, it's best to make it think. Or, as the American behaviourist B.F. Skinner put it: 'The real question is not whether machines think but whether people do.'

What I'll leave you with here is the thought that while the use of reason is necessary, if you're to win results, it most often isn't sufficient. What else needs to be present? Well, it's an organisation's appetite for change and how its people respond to it that plays a vital role. We'll explore this domain of culture in the next chapter.

5. STRATEGY: Thinking Tools to Reach Your Goal

Questions for STRATEGY

1. How do you define the boundary of your organisation, its goal and measures of success?
2. In what dimensions is your value chain different from your competitors', valued by your customers and hard to replicate or substitute?
3. How do you develop your organisational goal? How do you construct, test and communicate the strategic logic of the what, to what and how to change questions that your organisation must answer if it is to achieve the stated goal?

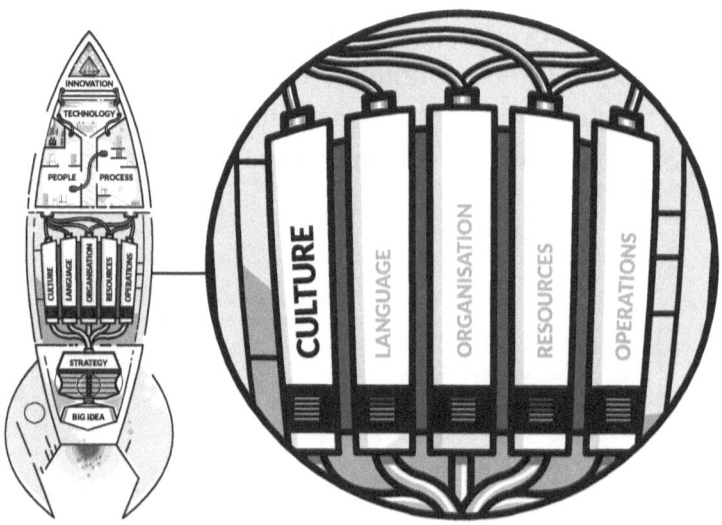

Figure 9: Culture

Chapter 6
CULTURE: *Building a Shared Vision*

> *It is not part of a true culture to tame tigers, any more than it is to make sheep ferocious.*
>
> Henry David Thoreau

CULTURE IS pretty much a force behind everything we do as human beings—it is, to we humans, both the light we project and the lens through which we see it.

Sir Edward B. Tylor, considered by many as the founder of cultural anthropology, said culture is 'that complex whole which includes knowledge, belief, art, morals, law, custom and any other capabilities and habits acquired by man as a member of society'. These attributes define us as human beings, taking us beyond mere material existence—common to all in the animal kingdom—and offering us a means of interpreting the world around us, interacting with it and creating change.

My purpose here, though, is not to look at culture from such a broad perspective. I want to narrow down the inquiry to explore what it is about the cultural domain that we need to take account of in any exploration of people at work.

Constructing culture

Several years ago, I led an intervention on a troubled construction site that was run as a joint venture between a Tier-1 Australian contractor and a European multinational. The head of the new venture needed to know when first production was going to happen. It would have a direct bearing on the total cost of the project, the timing of revenue generation and any damages they would have to pay to the owner if expectations weren't met. My firm was asked to help define the project's critical path.

A particularly difficult part of the construction phase involved choreographing the various trades—civil, mechanical and electrical—to minimise downtime and rework. Computer modelling had already provided a three-dimensional representation of the material components of the area. We added the time dimension to the model so everyone involved could visualise what was being planned, identify any clashes and make suggestions for improvements.

Furthermore, it was possible to integrate the computer-modelling program with the project's procurement system. Then, through some clever colour coding, we could identify what was already on site, what was on the way and what needed expediting. For the younger generation, who grew up doing their engineering on computers, it was the realisation of a vision, where the project could be built twice—once on a computer, the second time for real.

For the project director, however, who had worked on many

6. CULTURE: *Building a Shared Vision*

of Australia's iconic engineering projects, it was a nightmare. The man was coming to the end of his 40-year career and couldn't get his head around the idea that his command and control came from opening his laptop, clicking the mouse and striking a few keys.

This man's whole working life had involved unfurling printed drawings in construction huts, getting dirt on his boots and directing traffic around the site. To him, work meant a load of rebar steel arriving and him being on site to instruct a foreman to get one of his people to unload the bundles, group them by construction zone, and start the process of tying them into cages. The new system meant the cages would arrive pre-assembled and barcoded for scanning and positioning to the relevant part of the site.

The project director wasn't the only person having difficulty with the new system—a genuine generational divide saw splits among the professional engineers all the way through to the foreman and tradies. Some were perfectly comfortable with computers and loved the idea of the virtualisation of work; others hated it for taking away their physical control of the world around them.

Part of my process was to work with a colleague from the venture introducing the new technology in as seamless and effective a way as possible. She was a smart engineer with a doctorate in the adoption of innovation in the construction industry. One of her tasks was to turn an existing publication about the company history into an e-book so it might reach a much wider audience, especially for staff to appreciate the deep roots of their culture. Fortunately, she'd found some remarkable stories in the book about the company's early days.

Sharing stories

One story told of the owners of the business—at that time a private company in family hands—deciding to buy an aeroplane. The plane wasn't bought because they felt they'd 'made it' and could now afford the high life. Rather, it would expedite their processes and help bring their projects in on time and on budget. These men (and they were all men—another sign of those times) had to be on the ground at geographically dispersed sites to identify and resolve the most pressing problems. Since time was key, the means to travel quickly from site to site was crucial. Here, technology was solving a problem of time and space.

Another story involved the teams scheduling their work phone calls for the unusual time of 5am—not because they had a particular desire to extend their working days. In the 1960s, many places in Australia were still only served with party lines; if you didn't get in early, you took the risk of not getting your call. In a world of telegrams, a dawn phone call was a technological competitive advantage.

Similarly, whenever their supplier, Caterpillar, came up with a new bulldozer capable of moving more dirt more quickly, this company was first in the queue to buy it. Everyone, from management to workers, could see the productivity gains, even if there was an upfront investment.

Finally, my colleague found a heart-warming story of the

6. CULTURE: *Building a Shared Vision*

pregnant wife of one of the senior managers who had crossed a flooding river to carry dynamite in her 'ute' to the site where it was needed. She did this with little regard for her own health and safety. This bold woman was imbued with the spirit of doing whatever it took to build the Australia of the future. On time, and on budget!

We felt each of these anecdotes could help us in our quest to shift the perspective of the digiphobes and bring them into this brave new world. Each, we figured, could act as anchors into the past, allowing us to show that the adoption of the latest technology—in this case the computer technology we were advocating—fitted well with the organisation's 'can do' culture.

We were sure it mattered to our naysayers, that their winning culture had helped the company grow from a small family business to a listed corporation doing work in Australia and across Asia and the Middle East.

Romantic stories of derring-do, however, didn't cut it. And it seemed to matter little that their stated company values—emblazoned on their masthead—were trust, innovation, passion and excellence. It simply wasn't enough to tell them about clear productivity improvements, nor how these made them more competitive. This led me into a deeper investigation of the anxiety behind people's resistance to change.

Overcoming our learning anxiety

If ever there is to be an increase in momentum towards a concept of better ways of working, people within organisations need to increase their capacity to learn. It turns out that building a culture of learning within organisations is one of the best ways of reducing the anxiety associated with change. But achieving such a culture is no easy task.

Edgar Schein, professor emeritus at the Sloan School of Management at MIT, talks of the natural anxiety associated with any learning. To lessen that anxiety, we have to accept our own limitations and deal with the consequence that we might fail to achieve a requisite level of competence, or simply make a fool of ourselves. We know, logically, it's not possible to learn anything without making mistakes; if we could do the thing already, we'd have nothing to learn.

Schein maintains that playing against this 'anxiety of learning' is an 'anxiety of survival'. Learning only really occurs, he suggests, when the anxiety of survival is higher than the anxiety of learning. So, for example, if your boss tells you you'll be fired unless you figure out how to properly use the new performance management system, you'll probably learn how to use it; anxiety around surviving in the job trumps the anxiety about learning how to use the new performance management system. Put a little more humorously, when I asked one participant of a workshop I was running why he was attending the session, he replied, 'What interests my boss, fascinates me!'

In the case of our previously mentioned project director,

6. CULTURE: Building a Shared Vision

clearly there was anxiety that the youngsters, brought up in a digital world, would mock him for being so ineffective—or even incompetent—with the new technology. They had already laughed at the fact that he got his secretary to print out his emails, and that he crafted his grammatically perfect responses with a fountain pen in well-polished cursive writing.

But his resistance to the new technology was no laughing matter. He could not avoid the change. The company simply had to exploit the innovation in productivity the computer modelling enabled. To use an analogy he would have readily accepted, rejecting the innovation would be like insisting on retaining the pick and shovel even after the bulldozer had been invented.

The commercial imperative of survival sat on the other side of the learning anxiety scale. If he was not open to a profound transformation through the adoption of the new technology, either he or the firm would go the way of the dinosaur. Ultimately, this momentous shift wasn't his struggle. And although it took a couple of years, he escaped into retirement as the company was swallowed in a giant merger, stripped of its ability to master its own destiny.

A more humane (and therefore more effective) alternative to ratcheting up the anxiety of survival to force learning within an organisation is to decrease the anxiety associated with that learning. That is, to create the conditions in which learning could be fun, attractive and a rewarding source of personal, team and business growth.

Many approaches can foster such an environment, but perhaps the most important is to build a culture that understands the maxim 'fail often to succeed sooner' and encourages people to confess their ignorance without shame.

Successfully entering future after future

Every culture is deeply imprinted with its leader's character. In the first instance, that imprint comes from the organisation's founders and, in subsequent generations, from its CEO, executives and managers. For me, I must confess, leadership does not have the sometimes mystical elements espoused by writers who privilege the idea above mere 'management'.

To describe leadership and management as two separate things is as foolish as talking about the quality of your cabin as being independent of the engines that power you to your destination. Sitting in your lap of luxury, unable to move from the tarmac for want of an engine may satisfy your vanity, but sooner or later, you'll want to get a move on. Conversely, getting to your destination with engines firing, but sitting on bare aluminium floorboards, without seat strap, service or steward may get you moving, but you're unlikely to choose this option if alternatives are available.

'Managerial leadership', as described by Elliott Jaques, is in fact the correct term given to that activity that takes an enterprise and navigates the complex path by which it enters future after future.

A leader always operates within a managerial context. As Stalin so brutally reminded Churchill: 'How many divisions does the Pope of Rome have?' A political leader operates in a

6. CULTURE: Building a Shared Vision

different managerial context to a military one, and both of them differ to one whose prime concern is that of his congregation or flock. One can hardly imagine Pope Pius XII leading Stalin's Red Army, nor Stalin managing the Holy Roman church, yet both were leaders.

For me, the most useful definition of leadership comes from the Karpin Report, commissioned when Paul Keating was Australia's Prime Minister. 'Leadership,' it states simply, 'is that quality that has people do what you would have them do without having to resort to the authority of management.' This is a very high bar to achieve, for it demands that people of the organisation feel so connected to its purpose, goal and values that they would willingly subordinate their personal agenda in favour of the collective good.

Being a leader means travelling the road less travelled, and demands a great deal of courage. You are never sure if others will willingly follow where you lead; and if they don't, you're thought a fool. Further, leadership calls for the ability to create a shared vision of the future in which the range and diversity of personal visions can be given expression. This demands the fusing of the personal with the collective and requires high levels of competence in conducting conversations that matter; the art of dialogic exchange. (We'll explore this more in Chapter 7).

The likelihood of resorting to managerial authority can only be reduced if management is increasingly grounded in 'systems thinking' which, in turn, finds its fulfilment in a culture that favours learning. Here's the rub. In my experience, it is near impossible to change culture per se. Edgar Schein talks about culture manifesting itself at three different levels: 'artefacts', 'espoused beliefs and values' and 'basic underlying assumptions'.

The artefacts include the visible structures and processes, as well as the observed behaviour, which in themselves are difficult to decipher. For culture to change, it is necessary to change deep-seated underlying assumptions about the situation in question and what will work to improve it. The values of the construction company we referred to earlier might seem to be grounded in trust, innovation, passion and excellence. But as we saw, it wasn't like that at all. Indeed, all too often, what is espoused is not what's lived. One has to dig deep into the basic underlying assumptions, where, in the words of Schein, 'the unconscious, taken-for-granted beliefs and values determine behaviour, thought and feeling'.

Internal cohesion and external adaptation

It's worth at this point noting Schein's definition of culture in full:

> The culture of a group can be defined as a pattern of shared basic assumptions learned by a group as it solved its problems of external adaptation and internal integration, which has worked well enough to be considered valid and, therefore, to be taught to new members as the correct way to perceive, think, and feel in relation to those problems.

6. CULTURE: *Building a Shared Vision*

Understanding culture therefore rests on two principles: how the organisation perceives, thinks and feels in relation to the problem of coming together as a whole; and how it adapts to the forces that prevail in the marketplace in which its products and services are exchanged.

Schein goes on to explain the problems of an organisation coming together as a whole. The challenges are:

- creating a common language and conceptual categories
- defining group boundaries and criteria for inclusion and exclusion
- distributing power, authority and status
- developing norms of trust, intimacy, friendship and love
- defining and allocating rewards and punishment
- explaining the unexplainable

So how might these items fit the industrial project outlined earlier? Our team provided a useful one-time solution to the direct problem of bringing order, speed and reliability to the performance of the work on the major project. But as with the ailing patient who goes for a blood test to determine the cause of their malady, whether the sample is taken from the left or right arm, the pathology belongs to the body and is found wherever the blood flows.

Having solved the lesser problem of getting the project on track, subsequently, we were asked by the senior executive of the construction organisation to conduct a deeper study. This study looked at the root cause of a problem that had reared its head in our project, but was clearly systemic across all projects within the group.

From an extensive series of in-depth interviews across a comprehensive diagonal slice of the company, we identified the problem in the executive summary of the final report thus:

- The construction planning practices have devolved to a state where the work output from the planning discipline has little-to-no influence on the execution of physical work, particularly at major projects.

- There is a breakdown in the flow of information and communication across the distinct process phases, from the bid through to commissioning and handover.

- There has been a significant increase over time in the specialisation and number of disciplines and roles within typical large projects, making more complex the flow of timely relevant information crucial to bringing large projects in at a profit.

- Different business units and customer types have different, and sometimes distinct and prescriptive, requirements as to how they want their projects managed.

- There is a generational gap in attitudes to the use, and value, of IT tools insofar as they support effective sense- and decision-making.

The senior executive who had commissioned our assignment was as concerned as we were with the depth of the challenge. How does one begin to approach a problem as big as this, involving projects worth tens of billions of dollars and affecting tens of thousands of employees, consultants, contractors and customer representatives?

Hiring Hercules to lift your vision

Cultural transformation takes nothing less than a Herculean effort. When we consider the problems of coming together as a cohesive whole to the practices of the business, we can understand that success demands an unshakeable leadership from the top. Only such an open will has the power to create a resolute constancy of purpose and a vision to inspire everyone—from the shop floor to the boardroom.

In *Built to Last*, Jerry Porras and Jim Collins characterise 'truly great companies' as those that 'understand the difference between what should never change and what should be open for change; between what is genuinely sacred and what is not'. This gets to the heart of what a genuine culture is all about. The balancing act of managing this change while maintaining continuity takes, they say, a rare ability 'requiring a consciously practiced discipline—closely linked to the ability to develop a vision'.

So much for internal cohesion. To shift an entire organisation to meet the second component of culture as defined by Schein—that is, adapting to the changing demands of a free and highly competitive marketplace—you must first unfreeze the current situation; which means the organisation's leaders recognising progress is blocked. Like someone entering rehab, the first step is acknowledging there's a problem. After all, as

Deming put it, 'survival is optional'.

When change is on the cards, our primal emotions come into play. We fear loss of power or position; there is shame attendant on being discovered as being temporarily incompetent; we fear being punished for such incompetence, and we worry about losing our personal identity and group membership. These fears usually trigger quite predictable responses, often summarised in the literature as denial and 'resistance to change'. Or—in terms everyone who's ever worked in an organisation can recognise—dodging and manoeuvring, scapegoating and passing the buck.

So, if you are a leader and you'd like your transformation to succeed, you're well advised to back up your compelling vision with psychological safety. Isn't it true we all seek safety in the crowd when unsure of the situation? Buried deep in the herd, we feel secure in the idea we won't get noticed.

But there are paths to safety besides hiding in the crowd. These include formal training in the new way of working, involvement of the learner in the learning and how it is delivered, and informal training of relevant groups and teams so that learners don't feel like deviants when they decide to engage with the new learning.

Once the anxiety of survival has been recognised, you can amplify the effectiveness of any intervention by consciously decreasing the anxiety of learning. Providing practice fields, coaches and feedback all help create positive reinforcing loops.

Of course, systems drive behaviour, and thus systems and structures must be designed in a way that encourages and fosters new ways of working.

6. CULTURE: Building a Shared Vision

In summary, Schein gives us five principles for cultural change.

1. Make survival anxiety or guilt greater than learning anxiety.
2. Reduce learning anxiety rather than increase survival anxiety.
3. Define your 'change goal' concretely in terms of the specific problem you're trying to fix, not simply as 'culture change'.
4. Realise that old cultural elements can be destroyed by eliminating the people who 'carry' those elements, but new cultural elements can only be learned if the new behaviour leads to success and satisfaction.
5. Remember that cultural change is always transformative change and requires a period of unlearning that is psychologically painful.

To understand the obstacles to change and the fears and anxieties within organisations, I have found Schein's insights invaluable. But it's one thing to have an idea of what's going on. It's quite another to be asked to intervene and help align a company around a new vision and goal. As important as diagnostics are, the patient wants a cure.

At a practical level, I have found Peter Senge a torchbearer lighting the path for new ways of thinking about work. Schein was, in fact, one of Senge's mentors at the MIT Sloan School of Management. So it makes perfect sense that the younger man sought to build on these ideas about culture. The remainder of this chapter, then, introduces Senge's systems approach and how as a framework rooted in culture, it is capable of extending to affect the whole organisation.

Innovating fast means learning fast

There's a whole field of academic and corporate study devoted to organisational learning. Perhaps you already work in that field and are looking for ways to connect the 'thinking' with the 'doing' and 'being'. My thesis is that whatever you try to achieve within an organisation will come to naught unless you take a holistic 'systems' approach, and also consider that people are not automata (the famous 'human resources'). We have free will and so we need a way of talking about this aspect. It's a key component of what I call the 'value-creation engine'.

Through his seminal book, *The Fifth Discipline*, Peter Senge sets out a clear and memorable framework that gives a coherent approach to what Schein describes. The book received a lot of attention when it was published in 1990. In my experience, though, too few executives have grasped the profound and beneficial implications of Senge's ideas. Fewer still have taken advantage of the power gained by aligning the five disciplines in support of sense- and decision-making when undergoing transformative change.

Senge's thinking is a powerful ally to the more mathematically based focus of Eli Goldratt (which we'll investigate in Chapter 10). His organisational learning approach has become ingrained with my own 'ensemble' view of organisations and projects.

With this brief synopsis of each of the five disciplines, I've brought in my own and others' additional thoughts to demonstrate the value of viewing culture through these lenses—for the sake of productivity, engagement and the joy of learning.

6. CULTURE: Building a Shared Vision

Personal mastery: Achieving mastery over one's own responses to the multitude of stimuli that living in the world brings provides one with a far greater range of thinking, feeling and acting than would otherwise be the case, when we might descend into what George Bernard Shaw describes as 'a feverish selfish little clod of ailments and grievances complaining that the world will not devote itself to making you happy'.

When a high degree of personal mastery has been achieved, there is a deep sense of participating, actively and consciously, in the growth of your highest future self. You have the courage to create a lofty and even heroic vision of possibility, but can ground this creative tension between the future and the present with an unvarnished view of current reality.

You have a deep sense of connection to a narrative of your past, present and future and are, at all times, tuned into your own and others' thoughts and feelings. Personal mastery is that perpetual dance of being and becoming, which philosopher Martin Buber expressed as 'quitting defined for destined being'.

Shared vision: More than a lofty statement about an unachievable end state, shared vision is an articulation of the future the organisation would like to bring into being. It can only come after listening to others and sharing personal visions. In its fullness, a shared vision should have a sound understanding of current reality and, through the envisioning process, create commitment and will on the part of each person in the organisation to bring the desired future state into being.

With a powerful shared vision, a sense of partnership arises among the people who have created it along with a strong commonality of purpose. The vision is rendered from the point of view of the desired future. But it should be able to be thought of as if it were already in existence, in the present tense.

The richer the rendering of the holographic elements of the vision, the more powerfully does such a vision breathe life into a future that hitherto could only be imagined. I use the metaphor advisedly, as a vision requires nurturing to flourish. Placing attention on the intention contained within the vision animates its 'presencing' into the world.

Team learning: Despite the fact that we may speak the same language, or share a common culture, whenever we are in a group that extends beyond ourselves (and sometimes even in conversation with ourselves!) one of the most difficult things to accomplish is understanding one another: deciphering meaning. The word for conversations that look to explore meaning is dialogue, which when split into its Greek components gives us *dia* (through) and *logos* (word, speech, thought, reason, principle and logic).

The essence of team learning resides in the practice of dialogue, when we are able to suspend our assumptions, surface our defensiveness and listen with head and heart to another. To be in the shoes of the other. We lean in and listen empathically to discern what is truly meant. With this foundational skill of dialogue mastered, teams have the means of becoming increasingly effective in collectively harnessing the creative impulse and imagining new ways of being and aspiring to futures that redefine possibility.

'We have grown accustomed to changing,' says Senge, 'only in reaction to outside forces, yet the wellspring of real learning is aspiration, imagination, and experimentation.'

Without the alignment that comes from the collective intelligence generated by team learning, the net result of our endeavours falls short of its mark. Instead, we spend energy exercising our defensive routines through the percussion of our discussions. The way out of being stuck is through the quality of our listening and the conversation that follows.

Mental models: It seems rather strange that, though we live some 500 years after Galileo proved Copernicus right, we still refer to that wonderful time of day when the sun retreats below the horizon as a 'sunset'. The sun is doing no such thing, but the mental model we have from our lived experience in the world has the sun setting. In fact, at the equator, we are retreating from the sun at some 1,600km/hr.

A credible argument could be made that everything we think we know is nothing more than a construction of our minds, educated and acculturated to see things in a particular way. The great minds who have lived among us have sought a deeper truth and opened their minds to different ways of seeing. They have gifted us ever-better mental models to accommodate the evidence of observed phenomena. They have been masters of the ability to balance inquiry into how things are, and advocates of the truths they have discovered.

If we are to reap the benefits of working within a learning organisation, we must be able to cultivate our love of truth and openness. We must test assumptions, distinguish data from our mental models' abstractions based on that data, and learn how to balance inquiry with advocacy. In short, the future is not what it used to be—we are forever required to challenge our assumptions and find new ways of thinking, being and acting in the world if we are to live the good and beautiful life.

Systems thinking: Where do I end and where does the rest of the universe begin? At the edge of my skin? The furthest reach of my breath? As far as my eye can see? The same length an email travels as it transmits my thoughts? A Skype call from the other side of the world?

What is the nature of the system within which you operate? Where do you draw its boundary and what is its goal? Is it you, your family, your colleagues, the company you work in, the country you pay taxes to or the planet we live on? And why stop there? What of other systems? Computer systems, nervous systems, production systems, cardiovascular systems, air-conditioning systems, flight control systems, traffic systems, management systems; the list is endless. Systems thinking is seeing the parts only insofar as they relate to the whole and giving the whole primacy. According to Senge,

6. CULTURE: Building a Shared Vision

systems thinking is 'the fifth discipline' binding all the others together.

Seeing system archetypes

The essence of all systems thinking is that everything is connected, whole and of value. The work done by Senge and others in their systems work has enabled them to identify numerous archetypes, such as 'the tragedy of the commons' (of which global warming is a prime example) and 'success to the successful'. Understanding these archetypes allows us to discern deep patterns that reveal themselves time and again in any number of different contexts.

Living systems are in a constant cycle of being born, growing and returning. Non-living systems break. Non-living systems always exist within living systems; we are not separate from the biosphere, but a product of it. We forget this at our peril; most obviously, for example, the threat to a thriving physical environment on our planet. As US Senator Gaylord Nelson put it, 'The economy is a wholly owned subsidiary of the environment, not the other way around.'

A piece of code in a computer program has a bug and a developer must fix it. A car gets a puncture and it needs repair. If we apply the rules of non-living systems to living systems, we are making one of the most common and serious errors of our age, with often tragic consequence. The archetypes help us understand how structure and policy influence behaviour and what levers are available to amplify systemic change through powerful, focused interventions. Change your organisational hierarchy and introduce a policy that rewards experimentation and a change in outcomes is inevitable. Using systems thinking, we can test our hypotheses about cause and effect by simulating larger system dynamics.

In the workplace, the demand of systems thinking, if it is not to be a purely mechanical construct, leads inexorably to an orientation of servant leadership—that is, leading from the place that serves the highest possible good of the system's future.

A notable paradox in this idea is that the most significant changes anyone can bring to bear in the vast systems of which we are all a part comes from our individual ability to recognise ourselves as agents in these systems. The quality of our agency has a profound effect on systemic outcomes and, in turn, our ability to boldly develop innovative solutions to real-world problems.

If it is true that those who innovate fastest win—where innovation is the rate at which knowledge is converted into additional value and wealth—then it must also be true that those who innovate fastest learn fastest. The rate at which innovation flows through an organisation is the rate at which the people within the organisation learn. The central question then must be, 'What limits are there to the growth of my learning?' whether as an individual or as part of a collective?'

To be sure, when envisioning bold visions, it is never easy to overcome the anxiety of survival. The uncertainty of what comes next is directly proportional to the power of your vision. And luck, both good and bad, will have its often-unfair say.

6. CULTURE: Building a Shared Vision

Having said that, if you fail to summon the courage to break out of the fear and into a fair dinkum, fully expressed life, then I recommend you close this book and retreat quietly. Put its ideas into the too-hard box. If you dare to succeed, read on.

Questions for CULTURE

1. Identify three to five top factors that best describe your organisation's culture, its internal cohesion and its ability to adapt to external forces?

2. What three things can you do to decrease the anxiety of learning in your organisation?

3. Why do you think cleaving to the principles of a learning organisation could help you and your organisation win results?

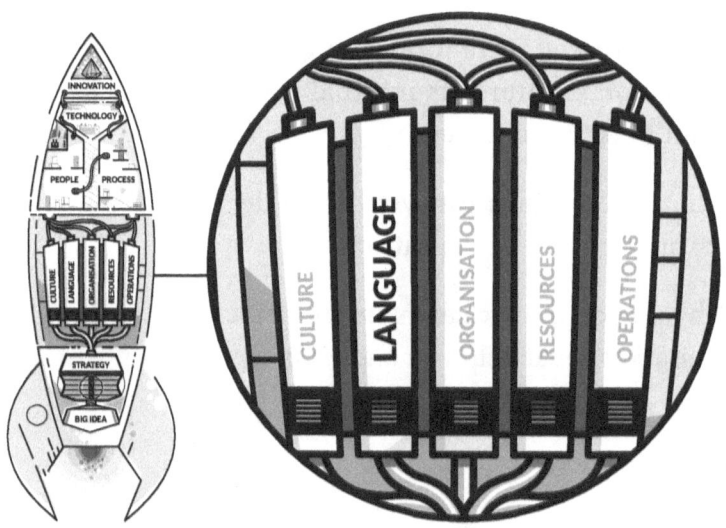

Figure 10: Language

Chapter 7
LANGUAGE: *Step into their Shoes*

The language of friendship is not words but meanings.

Henry David Thoreau

A FOREIGNER NEEDS A TRANSLATOR in court to defend herself against the accusation that she has killed her neighbour's dog. The judge asks through the translator, 'Did you kill the dog?' The translator interprets it as a question: 'You killed the dog?' The accused, reading the question as a statement, responds with another question and a gesture of her hands opened up towards the ceiling of the courtroom and a look of incredulity on her face, 'I killed the dog?' At this point the interpreter tells the judge that he now has a confession.

We are meaning-making machines, inferring meaning from language. By that, I don't mean only the world's different spoken and written language, although those do provide plenty of tripwires for us. In business, we have the language of the balance sheet and profit and loss; the language of the graph showing revenue versus costs; the language of the Gantt chart timeline; the language of the architecture and décor of the office; the language of the clothes we wear; the language of the music playing in the background; and the body language of folded arms or a 'power pose'. Everything we do carries subtle—and not so subtle—signals that convey meaning for both the transmitter and the receiver.

Experience has taught me that we are woefully inadequate in attending to the creation of shared meaning through this multitude of language types. We are often able to misinterpret each other's meaning as easily as my apocryphal dog story. Why is this? Why do we so often talk at cross-purposes? Could it be that at the base of all our communications and interactions—at the root of how we listen, talk and organise—we need a grammar that can help us better understand not only what is being said, but where the centre of the communication is coming from and where the centre of the listening resides? Often, the intention of the messenger has as much to do with the message as its content.

A grammar of the social field

With gratitude to the work of David Bohm, Bill Isaacs and Otto Scharmer, I have come to understand that one can construct a 'grammar of the social field' that deepens and enriches the pool of shared meaning between two or more individuals in a given situation. By social field, I mean any charge or energy that is created when one listens, converses or organises with others.

By its nature, this field is invisible—in much the same way as a magnetic field is invisible. Just as you need to sprinkle iron filings around to see the effects of magnetism, we need a way of making manifest the underlying structures and effects of our communication. This grammar of the social field, as defined by Scharmer in his book *Theory U*, offers a means by which we can describe what arises in our interactions with each other. So let's take a short sojourn to get a taste of what this might look and feel like.

If we work through an example or two, we can see how social fields take shape and understand how knowing their patterns are useful to meaning-making. It's analogous to the invisible force of magnetism and how that can lead to the development of electric motors, which do real work in the world of things.

Imagine yourself in a closed loop at the centre of your own attention, downloading whatever touches your senses through deeply ingrained habits of thought. There is no possibility of learning anything new, because any stimulus you get is fed through the projector of your mind onto the screen of your ego. Anything that it doesn't like, simply doesn't show up.

For example, if you have a deep faith in the idea that the earth is at the centre of the universe and are not willing to peer into Galileo's telescope, then you are stuck with habits of thought from the past and will have no access to the profound mystery of our little blue earth suspended in its orbit around our pretty average star, itself part of a galaxy in a cluster of tens of billions of other galaxies, and a universe so vast it is beyond any personal conception we might have of time and space.

Let's bring things back to earth with a more prosaic example. At an assignment in a bank, I put it to one of the senior executives that it would be a major boost to productivity if the people skilled in the areas of risk and product were shared as a pool across all the industry sectors into which the relationship bankers did deals. She told me categorically this would never happen because the patterns of thinking, feeling and acting were so ingrained that no one would even be able to contemplate such an eventuality, let alone know what to do to make it happen.

But out on the horizon, on the periphery of the executive's vision, was the daily news about major changes happening in the banking sector—crypto-currencies, new payment mechanisms, non-traditional lending, foreign competitors better able to service multinational clients, and the euro crisis and its implications for the global credit system.

Here was disconfirming data shining a light on the inadequacy of the mental models of the players. From thinking the shadow on the wall was the bear, they too stepped out of Plato's Cave to see for themselves what a real bear looks and feels like. She confessed to me she would need to explore a whole new way of listening and speaking, as dealing with shadows was far less consequential than wrestling with bears.

It is not so simple, however, to move from the autistic projection of the download to the rational arguments of fact-based reasoning. According to Scharmer, there is a voice in the head, the 'voice of judgement', which stands in the way, as sentinel. It is the inner voice telling you that you have no talent, your analysis isn't good enough and you cannot believe in the evidence your own intelligence tells you is the truth.

The voice of judgement keeps you in that sanctuary where you tell yourself that whatever needs doing is someone else's

7. LANGUAGE: *Step into their Shoes*

work. You convince yourself this is simply the way the world works and there is little you can do to change it—your small contribution cannot possibly make a difference to the situation. So you proceed to continuously repeat patterns of the past, sleepwalking your life away.

When the voice of judgement is powerful enough, even the ability to learn becomes atrophied. In its most extreme form, this inability manifests as the egotism of the tyrant. Such people characteristically fail to accommodate new information that would disconfirm their world view, increasingly attempting the ultimately futile job of bending the world to their will. The consequence of persistently inhabiting this domain is almost always some form of mental disorder, and a diminished ability to participate in the richness of what it is to be human. As if this weren't bad enough, it is often accompanied by inflicting misery on others—especially those over whom they have power.

Overcoming the voice of judgement, one learns to see afresh—but now from the periphery of vision. Disconfirming data streams in as the windows of the mind are opened. One must take account of the evidence of the objective facts. Galileo was able to demonstrate, by virtue of his study of the moons of Jupiter, that the earth cannot possibly be at the centre of the universe; rather, as Copernicus theorised, we are in orbit around the sun. Paying attention in this mode is not dependent on emotive content; it is fact-based and how all good science is done.

To return to my bank executive, who is very smart and able to admit the times they are a-changing, she develops a new model of her competitor environment and what needs to be done to adapt. She enters countless arguments with her colleagues, especially those who fear losing power through changes to the existing arrangements.

She spends days gathering evidence to prove her case, marshalling facts and figures the way a general musters troops for parade. She beats down naysayers with the compelling logic of her reasoned argument. It is all highly adversarial, draining, and, regrettably, she says, the 'normal way of getting things done around here'. In fact, it's much like our parliament—the power of two competing arguments fighting until one dies or is beaten into submission. She feels deeply the stress of the gladiatorial contest, but gains some small comfort from the important discoveries made in the heat of battle. But at what cost? And what are the alternatives?

Feeling what we're seeing

We humans are emotional as well as rational beings. As you move to the next level in an exploration of the social field, you notice the boundary of the system is made permeable. You are no longer in your closed loop, and the focus of your attention is not wedded to your point of view. You develop a sense of what it feels like to stand in the shoes of those you are talking to. You abandon the dry fact-based mode of paying attention, where the other, until now, has been little more than an interchangeable thing—a human widget. But there is a guardian standing at this gate of knowing from the heart—the 'voice of cynicism'.

7. LANGUAGE: *Step into their Shoes*

This voice shields us from disappointment, rejection and disconnection from others. The price we pay for this shield, though, is a cauterising of our emotions. And while this may save us pain, we become increasingly less able to feel the joy of being connected to our deepest, authentic selves, to experience the mystery of our profoundly gregarious species. In the words of Brené Brown, who has made a life's study of the topic, 'Vulnerability is the birthplace of connection and the path to the feeling of worthiness. If it doesn't feel vulnerable, the sharing is probably not constructive.'

Back with Galileo again, imagine the shock even his closest friend would have experienced at discovering that everything he had known and held dear was no longer true? We may mock the church now, but how would you respond if you lived in the 17th century and were told you should not believe what your own eyes were telling you about the sun 'setting'? Or try to comprehend the terrifying thought of things falling off a world not fixed in space, as the wisdom of the previous 6,000 years of civilisation had it?

What deep anxiety and fear would come over you as you consider the implications of this new and alien world? Would you want someone to listen to your fears with an open heart? This new level of the social field treats the other as sacred and whole, a child of the universe entitled to compassion—not simply a brain on legs, with an instruction to get on with it.

But it doesn't have to be as grand and epic as all that. My bank executive took some time out to think about what was being demanded of her counterpart in the technology services division. She was surprised to discover the key performance measures used in that part of the business demanded utilisation of resources at greater than 90%, on a rolling six-month forecast—despite the fact the business case was rarely developed that far out. Senior managers lived in terror of not meeting these targets, as it had implications for their own and their team's jobs. For her part, by listening from a place of compassion, my executive could give expression to her counterparts concerns and vulnerabilities.

Success in her business-critical project was a prerequisite of her long march to the boardroom. The fear of failure woke her up at night in cold sweats. Having the courage to expose these vulnerabilities to each other set the relationship off in a whole new direction. There was at least the willingness to explore options, a greater desire to expose assumptions keeping them from reaching a winning solution. They both acknowledged seeing more of the whole human being in each other, each striving in their own way to do the best they could for themselves, their team and the company.

There is a yet deeper level of the social field, where you have already opened yourself up and are mindfully stepping into the shoes of the other. You sense a new generative energy arising from living fully into your truest self and doing the work that is both your bliss and your destiny. There is a guardian of this gate, too: the 'voice of fear'. The deepest source of this fear is our fear of death—the fact we won't be around forever and, despite this, the world will continue to turn.

It is a fundamental quality of nature that the old must die in order to make way for the new. At a level not quite as dramatic as drawing our last breath, we must be fearless in the face of the death of our ego construct if we are to live a life in which we come to know our own lived experience in its most deep and meaningful way. We must learn afresh what it means to be fully alive in this moment—and the next, and the next. It is only when we surrender completely to the inevitability of the constancy of being and becoming that we slip the shackles of the voice of fear. We come to understand the aphorism 'mourn the fear of death, rejoice the death of fear'.

From this place of listening, Galileo's friend might have felt that what he witnessed through the telescope was not limiting at all, but revealed a far deeper mystery of a universe beyond comprehension, beyond rendering in words by even the finest poet. He might have been filled with a sense of beauty and awe known and recounted in the blissful raptures of the mystics. This level of the social field is highly creative in its nature and profoundly generative of new ways of being.

The stop at the top of the trajectory

You may recall the introduction to Part 1, where I left us hanging before the biggest workshop of my life. I arrived at the workshop to find a lot of tension between the players. Many mistakes had been made in the huge and important technology transformation project affecting the future of the enterprise. If we were going to achieve any kind of breakthrough, I knew on the plane that something different had to be done. And a breakthrough was absolutely what we needed.

The whole day had been full of tough arguments, fierce debate about what had happened and the best way forward. In my role as facilitator, I had spent most of the day trying to get the participants to see the value of opening their hearts to the others in the room. It was clear to me that so long as the conversation remained stuck in the mind, we would not be able to unlock the endless debate about who was right and who was wrong.

At afternoon tea, I decided to take a chance by building a five-minute meditation into the start of the final session. I was very nervous about doing this, as most people there would never have meditated before, and in the room were people whose careers were mostly in engineering and technology disciplines, and whose more usual concerns were with facts, figures, processes and beer.

An image came to mind of a pebble thrown into the air, which at the top of its ascent froze for a moment before changing direction and commencing its descent. This became my metaphor. Before we could change direction, we had to have a moment where everything stopped. The effect the meditation produced was stunning. The energy of the room was completely transformed. No sooner would one of the participants begin to talk of an idea, someone else would finish the sentence—idea building upon idea in a chain reaction, each person visibly excited as a witness and co-creator of the unfolding conversation.

The meditation alone was not the cause of the breakthrough. I have introduced meditation to workshops on many other occasions, mostly with positive effect, but never before had some-

7. LANGUAGE: *Step into their Shoes*

thing so powerful been unleashed. What I believe the meditation did on that occasion was to open a space in each participant, allowing for the possibility of something new to be created. They became willing to let go of their old positions, suspend their more habitual rules of engagement and disidentify themselves from the nature of the problem being tackled.

When these old patterns 'died', it made way for the collective flow of intelligence, deeper insight into underlying causes and a desire to collectively create new possibility. Grace had entered the room. I have come to call this 'the decisionless space'. It doesn't mean no decisions get taken, but the generative nature of the field created opens up the possibility of new framings of the problem.

The eminent physicist David Bohm did significant work in the realm of dialogue and the processes which underpin it, particularly in *On Dialogue*. Following in his footsteps, Bill Isaacs explored the issue further in his book *Dialogue and the Art of Thinking Together* which summarises a way of thinking how conversations, once started, can follow different pathways. Both inform my approach to learning how to better hold conversations in which the kind of generative space mentioned above can be created. Figure 11 is a diagram from Isaacs' book.

As we turn to each other, we will often make near instantaneous decisions as to our mode of entering the conversation. We face a fundamental choice of defence or suspense. In defensive mode, which is by far and away the more common, our defensiveness can either be productive or unproductive. When productive, we use analysis, hard data and explicit reasoning to

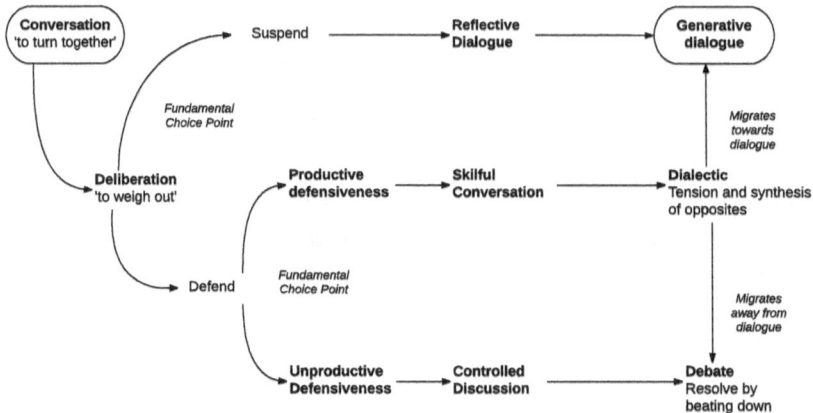

Figure 11: A dialogue process map
From *Dialogue and the Art of Thinking* by Bill Isaacs

win the argument. We are not so stuck with our view to defend it at all costs; a good counter argument will see the conversation migrate towards dialogue.

When the defensiveness is unproductive, the conversation turns to discussion—a word with the same root as concussion and percussion, and often with the same net effect. In this mode, there is a migration from dialogue and the conversation is all about advocacy for a given point of view, working on beating down the opponent in often fierce debate, until there is surrender on one side or the other. Relationships are the collateral damage of such encounters.

However, at the critical point of deliberation, a richer alternative is available to us. In choosing suspension, we intentionally listen without resistance—we disidentify from an egocentric attachment to what is being heard. Skilled practitioners of reflect-

7. LANGUAGE: *Step into their Shoes*

ive dialogue explore underlying causes, rules and assumptions to get to deeper questions and better framing of problems. This practice of suspension and reflective dialogue moves the conversation towards generative dialogue, where fresh insights allow for the invention of unprecedented possibilities. It is a field of collective flow.

If we aspire to bring a new world into being which is more just, kind and wise, then we need to become skilled in the 'art of thinking together' and learn how to move to the top-right-hand corner of Isaacs's diagram.

Beyond the definitions of the dualities of ideas—such as order and chaos, life and death, good and evil—lies the realm of bliss. This is the arena occupied by the saints, sages and mystics. When we mere mortals are touched by grace, we get short tantalising insights into the eternity that is this present moment. It is the realm of an ineffable God, if we use the word to mean a signpost to ultimate truth, meaning and mystery. Or alternatively, as the first words of the Tao Te Ching put it: 'Tao called Tao is not Tao.'

In a similar way, language can only ever be a signpost to what is really happening and the depth of your experience of it. Do not mistake the name of the thing for the thing itself. There are ways of knowing that go beyond our capacity to render them in language—whatever its form.

In the world of more than just work, we are well served by studying these different aspects of language as a means of enriching our experience of life itself. But we must also not lose touch with our ability to understand our world of work when it transcends our ability to express it in words, pictures or symbols.

Questions for LANGUAGE

1. If you stop for a moment and contemplate everyone and everything around you, what meaning do you give to the first dozen things that grab hold of your senses?

2. How does language express itself in the structure of your organisation? What is the geometry of power?

3. If you accept that all levels of the social field are all available to you at all times, what three things do you do that might be stopping you from accessing the deepest levels?

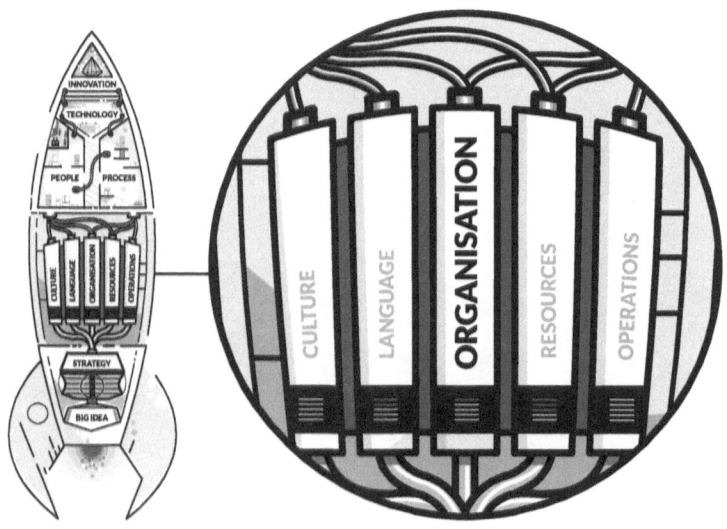

Figure 12: Organisation

Chapter 8

ORGANISATION: *The Strange Freedom of Hierarchies*

> *Those rampaging against hierarchies today rarely stop to consider that hierarchy as a form of social organisation occurs throughout nature. Instead of throwing rocks at hierarchies, it behoves us to try to understand why hierarchy might actually be important, and the principles that might guide leaders to distinguish functional from dysfunctional hierarchy.*
>
> Peter Senge

IN 1883, the Catalan architect Antoni Gaudí took over the design of a new cathedral in Barcelona following the original architect's resignation. Gaudí had a vision for a magnificent construction unlike any seen before. At his death 43 years later, his extravagant ideas were only a quarter completed. But he had put in place the organisation to see to it that work would continue. His energy, intellect, aesthetic and organising ability ensured that since his death in 1926, the cathedral has continued to be built, the completion of which is planned to occur more than a hundred years after he drew his last breath.

What level of thinking was required by this great man to bring such a vision into existence? How many of us can cast out our intention to 100 years after we die and know that what we imagined would only then be coming to final fruition. What kind of hierarchy did he imagine was necessary to organise all the aspects of bringing his vision into the cityscape of modern Barcelona? How did he go about organising the architects, the engineers, the stone masons and the carpenters; the town planners, the politicians, the financiers and the priests; the recruiters the accountants, the managers and the supervisors?

Taking over after the original architect resigned, Gaudí transformed the plans with his remarkable vision for this one-of-a-kind cathedral. He had to have the mental ability to span the time-horizon of his historic achievement, as well as all the component parts of the organisation that would turn his intention into reality. What, he would surely have thought, is every member of the team going to do today, this month, this year and this decade? In his mind's eye, beyond the immense vision itself, I imagine he had a plan that would bring together all the disciplines from each domain to make his intention manifest in the world. Bringing something as complex as the *Sagrada Família* into being was a major feat of taming complexity through a hierarchy of accountability. He couldn't possibly have done it all on his own. Incidentally, when pressed to explain the long construction timeline, Gaudí is said to have commented: 'My client is not in a hurry.' We should all be so lucky.

8. ORGANISATION: The Strange Freedom of Hierarchies

The paradox of a hierarchy of freedom

For many of us, hierarchies seem to go against the ideal of freedom. How can someone, by virtue of their organisational position, have the authority to tell me what to do and hold me accountable for my work? Surely, we think, there are better ways to organise and collaborate than establishing formal accountability hierarchies. It seems so old fashioned, so bureaucratic and so antithetical to the modern idea of the flat, egalitarian structure. We instinctively feel we should be masters of our own destiny and rebel against the idea of being told what to do—especially if we sense that the person doing the telling is not up to the task of effectively managing the work of the deeper horizons.

When I first came across Stratified Systems Theory in Elliott Jaques's seminal book *Requisite Organization*, I found rather offensive the idea that my mental processing ability could be measured and that the trajectory of my lifelong capability could be plotted after submitting myself to a single battery of tests. Surely, I thought, we are all capable of great things, given enough time, effort and education.

Yet here was a theory that seemed to limit my potential and tell me I would never rise to rule the world! On more sober reflection, I reasoned that whatever my deep desire, I could accept I just didn't have it in me to be, say, the world's best rugby player, singer-songwriter or physicist. Despite whatever hard work I might do, I realised that I didn't have those gifts, whether physical or mental. Why should the ability to manage and lead within an enterprise be looked at any differently to those whose natural endowments enable them to rise to their future of highest potential in rugby, songwriting or physics?

Overcoming my natural aversion to the inegalitarian spirit of the Stratified Systems Theory were two things: the overwhelming mass of data Jaques found to substantiate his ideas and the thought that what really mattered most to me was having interesting, challenging work to do, suited to my level of capability.

It would also help if I had a good boss who was clear about what I was being held accountable for and who gave me the requisite authority over the resources I needed to deliver on those accountabilities. To make the whole puzzle complete, I would need a clear means of assigning work between myself and my reports as well as an effective way of initiating work with colleagues who were not in the same functional part of the organisation as me. That is, those reporting into a different part of the hierarchy—with a different boss.

What Jaques discovered is that there is a natural layering or stratification of complexity in human organisation and a natural recognition of authority and subordination among the people working within these layers. This 'stratified system' is, he argues, not only natural but 'requisite'—the system will fail if it doesn't acknowledge this need for hierarchy. Many a startup has failed not because of a poor product, but because of internal strife once the organisation grows beyond the original small band of founders.

8. ORGANISATION: The Strange Freedom of Hierarchies

As required by nature

Requisite organisation (the process as well as the book title) takes the concepts of stratified systems theory and applies them in the structuring of the organisation—based on the time-span necessary for work at each stratum to be completed, and in the description of each employee's current level of cognitive maturation or time-horizon.

When the time-span of the work and time-horizon of the individual assigned to that work match, there is deep job satisfaction for the employee and rich, creative outputs for the organisation. The organisation whose lines of authority align with the requisite step change between the strata can foster and marshal—and benefit from—the creativity and problem-solving capability of the right people placed at the right level of organisational complexity.

Nearly all organisational dysfunction can be traced to poor structure and systems, not deficient employees. Organisation development interventions should focus on fixing the organisation rather than fixing employees. Fixing the organisation (structure, role relationships, policies, systems of work, managerial practices) frees employees to work at their full potential, creating increased efficiency, effectiveness and employee satisfaction.

Examples of fixing the organisation include science-based methodologies for:

- Matching employee capability to job complexity
- Appropriately spacing employees' capability with that of their managers to improve leadership and communication

- Ensuring the right number of organisational layers
- Explicitly defining managerial authority and accountability
- Explicitly defining managerial leadership processes
- Explicitly defining cross-functional working relationships
- Matching compensation to job complexity ('felt fair' compensation)

Coming to understand and appreciate Stratified Systems Theory proved to be the equivalent of turning a big conceptual key to unlock understanding as to why it is so difficult to bring systems thinking into organisations. The puzzle applied to the general principles of systems thinking, but I was particularly interested in its relevance to the Theory of Constraints—an operations management suite of methods and tools that made so much sense but has struggled to find a sustainable place in the world of management.

A standard response to the adoption of systems thinking is that it needs to be led from the top. While this is almost always necessary, it is by no means sufficient. What is of fundamental importance is the cognitive capacity or mental processing ability of the people leading the design and implementation of this better way of managing work.

It is one thing to operate and continuously improve an existing system designed to manage work. It is quite another to bring into being an entirely new way of thinking, upend 500 years of enculturation which, by its nature, calls for an end to its supporting worldview, steeped in mechanistic reductionism.

In short, many people are in positions of power and authority which exceed their innate ability to deliver the changes demanded by systems thinking. In such situations, it is inevitable that they will drag their organisations down to their level of thinking. They are simply incapable of lifting it to the requisite level for profound change. It's the equivalent of asking the captain of the high-school rugby team to lead the national squad and expect victory.

Start with end-to-end thinking

Some years ago, I made my first foray into the financial services sector, having previously spent most of my time and energy working in manufacturing, engineering and construction. After some considerable sales effort on my part to convince the company that my approach could work in their sector, I was pointed to the area of one of Australia's very large banks which operated as an in-house consultancy for continuous improvement. This particular unit had the strong support of the CEO, who had done much to beef it up when he was group executive in charge of strategy.

The big theme was productivity, as measured in the way banks usually do—the ratio of cost to income. A significant amount of work had been done to incorporate the principles of Lean and Six Sigma into the solution-set of any problem the business units brought to their door. They had even developed councils for common functions across business units—for example, a lending council to agree on as standard an approach to lending as possible, whether for personal loans, asset finance, mortgages, corporate or institutional loans.

A big topic of conversation, current at the time when I first met my sponsor, was the desire to create end-to-end processes. If I were a customer requesting a mortgage, somehow the response to that request would be designed to receive end-to-end treatment to overcome the functional barriers within the bank's organisational structure: product, distribution, risk, operations and technology.

Significant work had been done to develop courseware to build capability in the fundamentals of the Lean Six Sigma toolkit and they had the usual array of Green, Black and Master Black Belt practitioners. These people were deployed to improvement projects of varying sizes, and had early success in many areas of the bank. For example, something as simple but effective as instituting the holding of daily stand-up meetings to go through the classic Shewhart–Deming cycle of Plan–Do–Check–Act.

I have subsequently become a good mate with my sponsor, as we enjoyed a period of deep learning together. Early on we concluded that despite the significant investment made in continuous improvement, some of the underlying assumptions about their applicability was deeply flawed. It was a classic trap of thinking that what was necessary was also sufficient.

At its root, the biggest flaw lay in the deeply embedded mindsets of the systems versus reductionist mental model. Once exposed, it was illuminating to recognise how often the mindset of managing complexity through its division into smaller and more manageable parts led organisational leaders to structure their endeavours less effectively. The underlying delusion was that by some magic, these disconnected parts could be reas-

8. ORGANISATION: *The Strange Freedom of Hierarchies*

sembled into the whole. While integration may challenge at its limits, reductionism knows no such bounds. Indeed, it produces a Frankenstein's monster—primacy must reside in the whole if truth and beauty are to be fully realised.

The fundamental issue at hand, then, is how best to manage complexity. When one looks at extended processes such as managing the life-cycle of a home loan, it is effected by all the departments of the bank. From those functions directly involved in the process such as risk, product and distribution, but also the threading functions of HR, Finance, Security, Compliance and the like.

The ability to give effect to the intention of an end-to-end process depends profoundly on the extent to which the HR function can provide critical thinking on the appropriate design of the organisation. It must consider the requisite layers of management, from the shopfloor, to supervision, to management and long-range executive planning and control.

Many an HR team approaches their own work in a fragmented manner, reducing the complexity of different aspects of the job to the sub-functional heads of recruitment, industrial relations, organisational development, organisational design, remuneration and other roles. This case was no different. The thing is, I noted to my friend, that in the same way a customer walks into a bank for a home loan and doesn't really care how the innards of the bank works, a member of staff arrives for the day's work as a whole human being. He or she isn't really concerned with how the HR function organises itself. Unless, of course, it is more dysfunctional than their experience has hitherto become accustomed to; or, indeed, if you are one of those arriving to work in the HR function!

I made the case to my friend that it would be a welcome change to find people who had made their careers in the science and art of Human Resource management willing to put their knowledge and experience of the behavioural aspects of the HR function at the disposal of managers and staff. Such knowledge must as a minimum, I suggested, include an understanding of the fundamentals of Stratified Systems Theory and the Requisite Organisation. The ideas contained within them, I continued, are grounded in decades of empirical research. Just as one wouldn't do accounting without knowing the fundamentals of double-entry bookkeeping, I felt it hard to think anyone could do a proper job of organisational development and design without knowing the work of Jaques.

When properly understood, stratified systems theory and requisite organisation provide a powerful means of getting people to bring the best of who they are to the workplace. It creates wins for their personal development as well as results for their organisations. My friend laughed as he reflected that most of the people who run their race within the organisation under the HR banner wouldn't have heard of either the theory or of its associated book on organisational design, and would thus be ill equipped to provide any advice.

8. ORGANISATION: The Strange Freedom of Hierarchies

Fully defining the work

The first principle must be to understand the minimum requirements for defining a piece of work. To this end, it is useful to understand the acronym CPORT, which stands for context, purpose, outcome (both quality and quantity), resource and time. It is remarkable that billions of work instructions are given every day and most of them end up missing one or more of these vital components.

Let's take two examples to illustrate what I mean. I am the branch manager and I want one of my supervisors to reconcile the cash received during the day.

The **context** is that I am accountable for a true reflection of the branch's cash position on a daily basis. The **purpose** is to reconcile all cash receipts and payments to the general ledger. The **outcome** is a reconciliation sheet that shows the count of the cash at the beginning and end of each day, in accordance with normal banking procedures for branch managers. The **resource** required will be a bank teller trained in cash reconciliation, access to that part of the bank's IT system that facilitates cash reconciliations, and a security officer to handle the cash movement from the ATM to the counting room. The **timing** is set for 4pm every day when the branch doors close. Now, that is a relatively simple instruction, and the time limit of discretion to whom it has been issued is a day. Nothing too complex at all.

But let's now take what might have been our mandate for end-to-end processing:

The work: Build an end-to-end capability for mortgage lending.

Context: Bank customers, in survey after survey have shown that they deeply resent being pushed around from department to department whenever they have a problem with a product they are trying to buy or a service they are trying to use. Often, resolution of their issues takes a long time and as a consequence we lose their business. It also costs us a lot of money in rework.

We believe that if we can find an innovative solution to providing the customer with a one-stop shop for their needs and we develop systems and processes allowing us to keep them informed of where their query is at any given time, we will speed up time to resolution and provide better customer satisfaction. This will be a source of competitive advantage against the low benchmark our industry sets. Our research shows us mortgage lending represents our biggest problem, but also our biggest opportunity.

Purpose: The purpose of the work is to shorten the lead times and provide greater transparency of the end-to-end mortgage lending process.

Outcomes: The following deliverables are required to progress this work:

- A paper detailing and quantifying the nature of the problem, its costs to the bank and the benefits an investment in fixing it might realise.

8. ORGANISATION: *The Strange Freedom of Hierarchies*

- A conceptual design of a solution.
- A preliminary budget costing, to ± 25% of the final investment.
- A preliminary target operating model for the solution.
- A project plan done to the standard set by the continuous improvement function.

Resources: the Continuous Improvement function will give $100,000 of initial seed investment to get phase one deliverables completed. A suitably skilled person from IT will be made available to the project as part of this funding. Continuous Improvement will put together a detailed resourcing plan and schedule to determine how the $100,000 will be spent.

Timing: It is the intention of the mortgage lending part of the business to include this work as part of their strategy for the forthcoming year, with an implementation of recommendations to be completed within 3 years from approval. The business case will thus need to be presented to the Senior Leadership Team no later than the end of this financial year.

This is not a definitive document, or the best example of what a CPORT instruction might look like, but it provides clear direction. We know the context, the purpose, the outcomes demanded, when they're required and what resources we have to work with. The time limit of discretion is measured by the end-date of the overall implementation, which would be June 2019.

We now have a means of defining work in the same way—a simple checklist that works for something simple that happens every day as well as for a longer-range project with strategic implications for Continuous Improvement, the business unit and the bank as a whole.

The big question, then, for a bank wishing to run end-to-end processes across functions is how does it address the need for a person from one function to accept work requests from someone who is in another function, with a completely different reporting line? How do we get them to do what needs to be done and subordinate their impulse to optimise their own function to the stated requirement of giving superior customer service?

Crossing the silos

To return to my friend's situation, he had by virtue of the bank's org chart a **T**ask-**A**ssigning **R**ole **R**elationship with all his subordinates or a 'TARR'. It follows that he cannot be effective in acquitting that for which he is held accountable if he doesn't have the requisite or matching authority over the bank's resources to get the work done of turning intention into reality—in this case, an end-to-end process for a home loan.

Whether he calls it a 'TARR' or not, my friend fully understands that his role within Continuous Improvement enables him to instruct his team to develop training courses, hold workshops, facilitate process analysis in different business units and help design and implement solutions for their most pressing needs. However, he has no authority over the resources of the target business unit.

8. ORGANISATION: The Strange Freedom of Hierarchies

These people often have a desperate conflict between getting through the work of the day and doing that which will provide benefits over a longer time-horizon. Furthermore, there is often a direct conflict between the measures used to manage and control the business unit for its performance over the short term and the need to deliver a result over that deeper horizon.

The relationship that exists for example between Continuous Improvement and Mortgage Lending we call a Task Initiating Role Relationship, or a 'TIRR'. This relationship is established as part of the overall organisational design, and can vary in its type from being merely advisory (A can have access to B to try to persuade B to take some advice) to being prescriptive, in which A can often have as much authority as B's direct boss.

These kinds of relationships are common in places like the military, where a military policeman can arrest a superior officer, or in dangerous industrial environments, where a health and safety officer can stop the whole plant without reference to anyone else if he or she feels the risk warrants such a move. Indeed, such arrangements already exist in a bank, where a person in the risk function can determine not to proceed with a loan even when someone of higher rank from a different function within the bank has determined the transaction should go ahead.

It was clear these ideas had hooked my friend, but he had some questions. Particularly, he felt that his continuous improvement division, generally worked on a different time horizon to the core business which was obsessed with trying to hit their numbers for the day, week or month, as well as expediting work relating to customer complaints, attending to the demands of risk and compliance, internal audit, finance and everything else. 'When it comes down to it,' he said, 'they don't have very much time to address the underlying causes of why life is such a turbulent rush of random, incoherent events.'

Time to think of chronos, kairos and modes of work

His own role required him to consider improvements to business units, within the context of the productivity agenda of the bank, three or even five years out. He explained how, as a mechanical engineer undergraduate, he had studied fluid mechanics and the concept of the boundary layer of fluid passing over the surface of an object—for example, the wing of an aeroplane. Under certain conditions, the flow within the boundary layer would be very turbulent, lots of tightly wound vortices, and a whole lot more drag than lift. Under different circumstances, though, the flow at the boundary layer would be far more laminar and smooth, with layer upon layer of air taken on in an orderly way over the geometry of the wing, thus providing the maximum lift with minimum drag.

'I feel the business is often operating in the turbulent layer,' he said, 'while we're trying to design something that goes beyond that layer of turbulence. Through our design, we make the whole process deliver the equivalent of more lift for less drag. What do these ideas about requisite organisation have to say about that?'

8. ORGANISATION: *The Strange Freedom of Hierarchies*

In fact, this is a fundamental concept of stratified systems theory. What Jaques discovered in his research over decades, and with tens of thousands of data points, is that there is a correlation between the time horizon of the work, its complexity and the mental processing ability required to manage it. Jaques makes the point that if ever we are to make progress in evolving our organisations from the constraints imposed by an industrial-age view of how best to manage, we need to take into account the idea that there are actually five dimensions of time and space.

There are the three dimensions of space with which we are all familiar: breadth, depth and height. Jaques adds two axes of time: chronos and kairos. Chronos is the one with which we are most familiar—measured by a clock and proceeding from the past through the present and into the future. Kairos, at right angles to the familiar left-to-right timeline, deals with the dimension of memory of the past and intention for the future in any given moment. Jaques is particularly interested in the future time horizon of an individual.

If the simplest way of defining work is that action which turns intention into reality, an obvious question arises when examining anyone in their situated workplace as to what their intention is. How far out does it go? What degree of complexity does it have?

It's worth noting that this intention is not in the realm of fantasy, but is measurable through psychological testing that assesses the ability to think in one of four basic patterns: declarative, serial, cumulative and parallel. Each of these modes is as different from the other as water is from ice or steam. Jaques also proved that not only can these tests determine someone's current level of cognitive capacity, but can reliably indicate that individual's trajectory of thinking power from when they start work, at say 20, through to retirement.

My friend felt as uncomfortable about all this as I had initially. We all like to think we can do anything if we apply ourselves to it with sufficient rigour, but Jaques says this cognitive capacity or mental processing ability is a function of our genes. It's one reason why Jaques's ideas have not been more widely adopted. People misrepresent his work as a form of eugenics when in fact he was deeply empathic and wanted everyone to reach their full potential.

As I alluded to earlier, most of us accept our physical genetic limitations. I'm six-foot-two and weigh 105kg, so I could never have been a champion jockey. Why do we shudder at the thought of our limitations in the realm of mental processing? Wouldn't I be able to make a much better contribution to my own development and to society if I were doing work that was sized correctly for me at the point in my career when I was doing it? Surely it would help me to recognise that as I get older, not only from experience, but because of the inherent nature of my brain, that I will move into different modes of work? If I have a job that's too big for me, then I end up getting ulcers; if the job is too small, I get bored. So isn't it important that I have one that is the right size for my ability?

Jaques groups these different cognitive levels into four bands, each of which relates to the different types of thinking listed above: declarative, cumulative, serial and parallel. Once

8. ORGANISATION: *The Strange Freedom of Hierarchies*

the fourth mode has been reached, the modes keep repeating as a series of fours, much like the idea in music of pitches repeating at higher frequencies in subsequent octaves.

It helps my understanding to ground all this in a little practicality. Mode I has a horizon of one day to three months, Mode II three months to one year, Mode III one year to two years, Mode IV two years to five years. Mode V is five to ten years, the mode occupied by the CEO, and it is at this level of work where we return to declarative processing, with the difference being that the fundamental unit is not a discreet packet of work, but a discreet unit of an overall business. A group executive of a strategic business unit of the bank might thus be doing Mode V work, with the overall CEO doing Mode VI work at a ten- to twenty-year horizon.

Thus, if I am a teller at the bank, the horizon of my work is at most last month, this month and next month. My work entails for the most part conforming to the detailed policies and procedures of the bank. Mode II would be the work of a supervisor or team lead, who would have to deal with their subordinate's queries. They would have work to do that looks both backward and forward, recording important measures and for example, managing a staff roster over an extended period.

Mode III work is that of the manager who has accountability for whole systems—perhaps a branch manager. They might be responsible for the P&L of the branch and for preparing the budgets. To a large extent they would be using the systems of management developed by others, but would have a key role in soliciting and developing continuous improvement ideas.

It is only really at Mode IV that the problems being solved step out of the realm of the existing paradigm and genuine innovation is required. It becomes a design problem that proceeds from a hypothesis, and cannot reasonably be expected to be an extant system of management for a suite of products or services within anything less than a three- to five-year horizon.

A group executive operating at Mode V would be best occupying themselves about the overall strategic direction of their business unit. How is technology changing to provide new threats and opportunities? And how does their business unit of the bank protect against the disruptions and profit from the possibilities? Which markets and geographies should they be paying more attention to and which should they be exiting? What is the nature of the talent pool they need to develop so that all levels of work are properly populated to deliver the capabilities the business unit requires over the next five to ten years?

At this point you may be wondering how all this works in companies where pressure from investors and shareholders to deliver quarterly gains are chased at the expense of long-term growth. The answer is it usually doesn't. Either you end up with CEOs who are not up to the short-term task—and get fired—or you see them do a quick patch-up job before moving on to new pastures where their talents can be appreciated.

Much of the hero-worship around Steve Jobs was due to his ability to look beyond the short term. Because it's only when the CEO can take a long-term view—while enabling short-term operational excellence—that great step change happens. Today, Jeff Bezos of Amazon personifies the visionary leader who has

8. ORGANISATION: The Strange Freedom of Hierarchies

said from day one (and it's always 'Day One' with Bezos!) that he's only interested in the long game and that profits will be ploughed back into the business. It's one thing to say you 'think long-term'; few have the ability to imagine their organisation stepping into that future—seizing every opportunity along the way—as Bezos does.

So, how did all this knowledge of modes of work apply to him in his current role? My banking executive friend was excited by this new way of thinking and told me the penny had dropped as to why he felt so unsatisfied in his existing role. His boss, he told me, was at best running at Mode III, and yet as the head of the continuous improvement function of the bank nothing less than Mode IV would be required if they were to achieve the kind of goals they had set themselves. The existing systems of management had to be comprehensively reimagined if ever the intention of turning the vision of end-to-end processes were to become a reality.

He now understood the profound consequence of these insights from stratified systems theory and the requisite organisation for the structure of the management accountability hierarchy of the bank of the future. There was not enough distance in cognitive ability between himself and his boss, and thus the whole agenda of the continuous improvement function had descended to the level of its leader.

There was a mismatch between what he was being held accountable for and the authority he had over the resources at the bank's disposal. There were no real mechanisms in place to work out cross-functional collaboration and assignment of accountability, other than a general intention to get the work done, the goodwill of the business units and the persuasive powers he and his team could bring to bear in any given situation. He had nothing more he could learn from his boss, nor the situation, so he quit.

Team of Teams

Before leaving the topic of Organisation and returning to our spaceship, I'd like to make mention of the fact that I find the whole idea of a team of teams the most exciting innovation in organisational design since Elliott Jaques published *Requisite Organization*. There have been many new fads proposed by the supposed gurus of corporate design, but they don't pass muster against the rigour developed by Dr Elliott Jaques with his Stratified Systems Theory. Besides his theory about the three-way correlation between cognitive ability, time-horizon of work and complexity, he also developed a means by which you can exercise effective management accountability both functionally and cross-functionally.

General Stanley McChrystal and his team prove the exception to the rule of fads. He was the head of the Joint Operations Command of all special forces in Iraq – numbering some 7,000 people. Along with his team, he reinvented how to get the best of bureaucratic command and control to work with the speed and adaptability of a networked organisation. They had made a virtue of the necessity of moving faster than their Al Qaeda in Iraq enemy while bringing to bear the fearsome organised

8. ORGANISATION: *The Strange Freedom of Hierarchies*

power available to the coalition forces.

Two observations stayed with me once I understood the concept from McChrystal's book *Team of Teams*: the degree to which the US military had perfected Taylorism and its bureaucratic tropes, and how radical transparency and subsidiarity (devolving decision making powers to the lowest level competent to make those decisions) were used to re-energise it.

The courage required to embrace the radical departure from our existing 'need to know' and 'command and control' norms would make most CEOs I know run a mile. But I am confident that what McChrystal led in the heat of battle—and what his aide-de-camp Chris Fussell has written about in One Mission—represents the start of something completely new in the field of organisational design and effectiveness.

Questions for ORGANISATION

1. How do you issue work instructions for all levels of work within your management accountability hierarchy?

2. Why do you hold yourself, your subordinates and your collateral relationships accountable for work in the way that you do?

3. How many layers of management do you have in your overall accountability hierarchy, and why are they there?

4. Do you have the authority over the resources you need to complete the work for which you are held accountable?

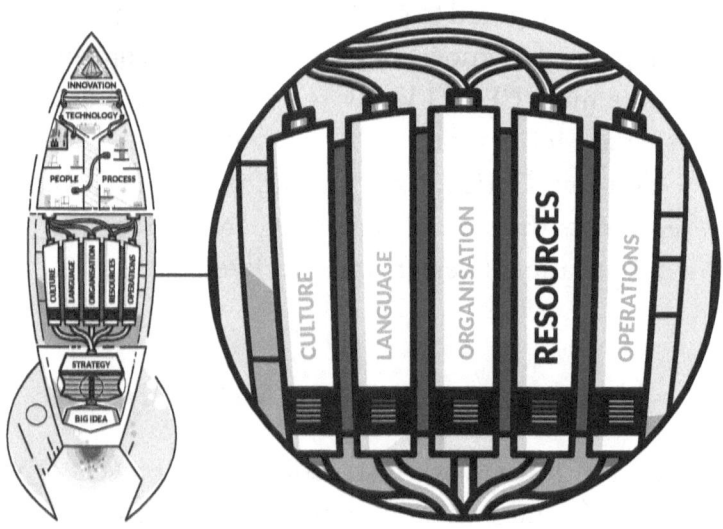

Figure 13: Resources

Chapter 9
RESOURCES: *What's Reasonable and Possible*

Innovation is the specific instrument of entrepreneurship. The act that endows resources with a new capacity to create wealth.

Peter Drucker

MANY YEARS AGO, when reading *Servant Leadership* by Robert Greenleaf, I was struck by an expression he kept using: 'What is reasonable and possible, given the human and material resources you have at your disposal?' I have never stopped asking that question, as it so well frames the conversation about innovations in productivity. What might we mean by reasonable and what by possible? Is 'reasonable' a set of objective criteria by which we can determine what we should expect from a given set of resources? And 'possible' the extent to which you meet or exceed that expectation?

Greenleaf was a senior executive in the telco giant AT&T in its early days, before automated switches were the norm. I could imagine him wondering how many calls were likely to be made, how many an operator could connect, and therefore the reasonable number of operator resources required to fulfil the service obligations of AT&T. As for the possible part? Well, perhaps he was talking about the behavioural and motivational component. Just because it's reasonable to expect someone to connect a certain number of calls an hour doesn't make it possible, be it because of operator incompetence, the human need for breaks, unsteady demand or any other reason.

Whatever the case, the question has been a constant muse of mine. I have expanded the resources from 'human' and 'material' to include 'finance' and 'information'. I could just roll those two categories up into materials, but I have found it useful to call them out because they play such a big part in the success of any initiative to improve productivity.

Digging a little deeper into his question, what happens when innovation is introduced to the mix? For example, instead of phone-switching being done manually by operators, today's exchanges automatically and instantly make those connections. What becomes the rate-determining step for what's reasonable and possible? Is it the number of skilled engineers to design and build these new switches? The capital required to invest in their design, production, commissioning and operation? The information needed to determine where these new services will yield the highest return on investment? And what of the people—the human resources? Do they have the right skills? Are they well managed and led? Are they motivated to meet or exceed what is reasonably expected by making the 'impossible' possible?

9. RESOURCES: *What's Reasonable and Possible*

Human resources

Like many people, I feel a little uncomfortable with the word pair 'human resources'. It seems to objectify the experience of actually working with people—real human beings, whose hearts beat and whose minds think (often not about work) while they go about earning their daily bread. Many HR departments unwittingly reinforce this negative idea, too often seeing employees as 'things' they need to manage through recruitment, induction, performance review, remuneration, personal development, grievances and exit—voluntarily or otherwise. It is easy to only go through the motions of applying all the 'people management' systems and overlook the actual individuals who turn up at work each day. What work is reasonable and possible for each of them, on any given day?

I shouldn't just single out the HR professionals; we are all guilty of it to some degree. Just because we are humans, in daily negotiations with all sorts of other humans who cross our paths, we assume we know what motivates people and therefore how to define what is both reasonable and possible.

Some years ago, I was involved in an extremely large business management system redesign. This complex global project was into its second release, the first release being more about defining scope and firing up the engines. Release 2 was the real deal when it came to the heavy lifting on the functional design, and the deployment scope covered four out of 12 strategic business units, scattered across Asia, the United States, South Africa and Australia. As the project progressed, it became clear that business demands well outside the control of the project were pressuring the release for completion in a seemingly unreasonable and impossible timeframe. Indeed, an expert independent review of the plans for the release put the odds of completing on time at 3% or less—in other words, a 97% likelihood of failure.

In a series of extraordinary workshops, which on occasion had a hundred senior project people in the room from all over the world, we explored why we felt so connected to what we were doing—what it meant for us as individuals, the meaning for our teams, the project and the different organisations we all represented. The leadership team took an enlightened view about investing in the best possible methods and systems of work management. They gave weight to the idea that if the project was to make the impossible possible, then representation from the whole system had to be in the room—stream leads, solution architects, engineers, developers, subject-matter experts and project managers.

At several points during the two-day workshop we referenced Roger Bannister's four-minute mile as a metaphor for conquering what had, until then, seemed impossible. We invited people to recall a time when they had exceeded their own expectations. Many remembered similar feelings to Bannister's description of his state during the run: 'No longer conscious of my movement, I discovered a new unity with nature. I had found a new source of power and beauty, a source I never dreamt existed.'

People are human and we should never treat them the way we would a super- efficient machine. However, given the right motivation and connected to a mighty purpose, we are individually and collectively capable of being highly effective and of making the impossible possible. So what does reasonable and possible really mean when you look at your people?

Material resources

To me, 'material resources' refers to anything we apply to our work that's not human, financial or information. That means the equipment we use, from a crane to a hammer; the materials we consume, from paper and plastic to wood and metal; and all the physical parts of our production, distribution and exchange systems, such as machinery, trucks and shops. Under this definition of material, what could it mean when we talk about doing what is reasonable and possible?

I was once working with a global food company that had two manufacturing units in Australia and one in New Zealand. Head office in London had asked the local team to analyse the potential effect of consolidating their manufacturing in one location. With the regional operations director, I designed a thought experiment for all the managers and line supervisors across the three units. To remove the influence of which location might be most cost-effective or geographically suitable, I invited them to imagine the new site as a floating island in the middle of the Tasman on which all the materials and equipment from both sides of the divide would be set up.

The manufacturing process was simple enough. Raw materials came in and were blended under heat and pressure, then passed through a moulding line which fed the output into unit packs and box packs for shrink-wrapping onto pallets, ready to ship to their own distribution centres and onward to those of their big retail clients. Far and away the most expensive pieces of equipment were the moulding lines—one in New Zealand and four in Australia.

Everyone at the meeting was very proud of the fourth of these, only recently commissioned at a capital cost of some £23 million. As we worked through the calculations, I asked them all to assume that each piece of equipment could run at the manufacturer's 'nameplate' recommended capacity, and that it ran 24/7, as was the existing case at the two factories.

These folks were intimate with their facts and figures, so it took less than an hour to arrive at some staggering and embarrassing conclusions. They could produce everything they were then producing on a 24/7 shift pattern in a remodelled 24/5 shift with enormous savings from overtime and weekend loadings. But the real kicker came when the GM of the bigger plant let those assembled know of a trial he had been running for the last few weeks.

To get more output from one of the products, he'd been turning up the feed speed of the moulding line. Each time he did so, he was surprised to find no negative effect on the quality of the product. All this spare capacity on the critically constrained resource was possible, he explained, because the heat exchanger was over-specified and could thus comfortably cope with the additional load.

These two discoveries—later validated in a very detailed piece of analytical work—meant that the whole £23m invest-

9. RESOURCES: What's Reasonable and Possible

ment had been a waste of scarce capital. Moreover, the reduction in overtime materially improved the labour productivity per unit of production. At this point, it might be worth laying aside the book for a few moments to consider the implication for you on your journey to improve labour and capital productivity. What if you approached the use of the materials of your enterprise in such a way—unconstrained 24/7capacity versus actual load?

Financial resources

The game of business is played by rules largely written by finance. Indeed, the very language of business is the language of accounting. So it's surprising how willingly management accountants step off the field of play, proclaiming their role as merely scorekeeper.

No less an authority than Charles Horngren, professor emeritus of accounting at Stanford University, declared: 'Relevant information is the predicted future costs and revenues that will differ among alternative actions. The existence of a limiting factor changes the basic assumptions underlying the cost and revenue opportunity of a particular action.' This is also sometimes expressed as, 'An enterprise will profit maximise when it makes and sells the product or service with the highest contribution margin per unit of its scarce resource.'

And yet, even though most accountants will be familiar with this concept, when one asks what that scarce resource is, they will usually demur and say that's an issue for Operations to sort out. On the other hand, when one asks someone from Operations the same question, they will usually have a good idea of what this limiting factor is, but will complain that the way the measurement system is set up makes it very difficult to act on this knowledge.

Whether using absorption costing methods in manufacturing or earned value in project management, both forms of accounting depend on measuring activity and assigning value according to that activity. This affects behaviours—and hence results—that favour optimising the parts at the expense of the whole.

Under this system of accounting, if I am running a factory and I over-produce in my section, my expenses are credited to the profit and loss while that cost is capitalised into inventory. Likewise, on a project I can 'earn' a significant amount of value by completing a big piece of work, even if it's not on the critical path. This makes people far more likely to seek that credit than spend time on a fiddly bit on the critical path that earns a minute amount of value by comparison. In the case of the factory, we burn through cash and have piles of inventory no one wants to buy; in the project world, we unduly delay project completion and erode the business case that supported doing it in the first place.

So why do we continue to scupper our chances of better results? What is the source of these counter-productive measures? To find out, we need to dive deep into the fundamentals of our worldview of systems and their parts, as well as what Deming called the psychology of people, society and change.

The accounting principle called 'matching' attempts to identify the costs incurred for a product or service in one ac-

9. RESOURCES: *What's Reasonable and Possible*

counting period with the revenue for that same product or service delivered in another period. If revenue and costs are not matched, one could be losing money without ever knowing it. However, this matching principle takes no heed of the existence of the limiting factor to which Horngren refers, and treats all activity as the same, whether at a production bottleneck in a factory or on the critical path of a project.

The matching principle drives the delusion that every unit of normalised activity—whenever it occurs and whatever the circumstance—delivers the same value to the enterprise. It is a delusion because we know that all systems have constraints and that constraints determine the rate at which value is created (more on this truth in the next chapter).

Hence, measuring activity at each node in the value chain and concluding that the product of this activity and a normalised unit cost will maximise profit is misguided. But it's a hard belief to shake. Or maybe it's not a belief, but self-interest. Machiavelli's warning comes to mind:

> It must be remembered that there is nothing more difficult to plan, more doubtful of success, nor more dangerous to manage, than the creation of a new system, for the initiator has the enmity of all who would profit by the preservation of the old institutions and merely lukewarm defenders in those who would gain by the new ones.

Eli Goldratt, the brain behind Theory of Constraints, called his system Constraint Accounting. It provides a powerful means of managing system performance by adopting a unified set of measures to encourage people with a stake in the system's outcome to apply a focus at their local level in such a way that their efforts deliver the best possible result for the system. In other words, it defines what's reasonable and possible given the finance one has available. There will be more on this in the section on Reporting and Analytics in Chapter 14.

Information resources

Goldratt said that the difference between information and data is that information is the answer to the question you ask of your data. Value resides in the flow of information to the extent it can provide timely answers to relevant questions, supporting effective sense- and decision-making. However, getting those who have custody over the information assets of the business to ask the right questions has been a source of enduring bemusement and pain.

Not that long ago, I was involved in a significant piece of work to expand a mine's operations at its port facilities. To get this work done, we counted up all the information systems, excluding standard productivity products such as email, Excel, PowerPoint, Word and a few Access databases (Table 1).

Trying to keep such a multitude of systems up to date results in several related issues. It's cumbersome and requires significant disciplined effort to keep current. People end up planning on spreadsheets on their local computers. The different systems, even collectively, do not accurately represent all work 'not started', 'in progress' and 'complete'. Individuals are neither clear on the work they are accountable for, nor on the context and

9. RESOURCES: *What's Reasonable and Possible*

Product	Vendor	Primary purpose
SAP	SAP	Procurement and accounting
Primavera	Oracle	Project controls
MS Project	Microsoft	Scheduling
Concerto	Realization	Finite scheduling
EZ Trac	Fluor	Milestone and time tracking
Aconex	Aconex	Workflow traceability
Autodesk	Navisworks	Building Information Management (BIM) operations
Smartplant 3D	Intergraph	Engineering design Facilities life cycle
Tekla	Tekla	Specialised shop detailing and fabrication features

Table 1: A selection of a mine's information systems

purpose of their work in relation to the organisation's goals. Managers are not able to easily gauge who is available to do what work.

These issues cascade up the organisational hierarchy resulting in executives not being able to see a true, real-time picture of their value chain. Is their organisation doing the right things in the right order? How can such disparate tools be effective in giving executives, managers and staff the means to continuously improve their business performance?

Then there's the human side of poor data and information. Poorly implemented management tools can reinforce a poor working culture, characterised by individuals and teams disproportionately loaded with work. Not knowing which way to turn, people respond in an ad hoc way to the wheel with the most squeak. This thrashing around, or multitasking, leads to lower productivity and quality, longer working hours, higher levels of stress, suboptimal performance and general dissatisfaction.

And yet, stitching all this together is not as difficult as it may seem, given an understanding of its importance, and the will to get it done. For example, a data object in the engineering model refers to an item in the schedule, which refers to the same item in the procurement packages, shop detailing, fabrication and construction work. With a little bit of thought and coding, all these disparate parts can start to come together.

The problem is the shortage of brave souls to take on the mission of fighting the 'owners' of these disparate systems to answer the simple but reasonable question: 'What can I achieve when given the human and material resources at my disposal?'

9. RESOURCES: What's Reasonable and Possible

Questions for RESOURCES

1. What are the human, material, financial and information resources you have at your disposal? How do you keep track of what they are?

2. How do you go about establishing what outcomes are reasonable and possible given those resources?

3. Why is it important for you to integrate the disparate systems you use to instrument and control your value-creation engine? How might you go about doing it better?

Figure 14: Operations

Chapter 10
OPERATIONS: *Playing on Cue Every Time*

The theory that can absorb the greatest number of facts, and persist in doing so, generation after generation, through all changes of opinion and detail, is the one that must rule all observation.

Adam Smith

TOC: *Theory of Constraints*

THE THEORY OF CONSTRAINTS (TOC) is a profoundly paradoxical approach to the identification and resolution of problems, in that the basic idea is extraordinarily simple, but the ability to make it work in a sustainable way is extremely difficult.

I first used TOC as Managing Director of South Africa's largest commercial refrigeration contractor. Our number one customer had all but ignored their fleet of fridges for several years and, after some market shocks to their business, they decided to take the brakes off and accelerate their transformation program. This called for an unprecedented amount of work to deliver a whole new concept in the way fresh and frozen food was displayed and sold.

When I asked my boss at the time for the money to get some consulting advice on the TOC approach, he replied, 'I don't believe in theory and especially not a Theory of Constraints.' One way and another I got the prototype going using the principles and took 26 days off a 71-day program of work. The result was enough to convince me to start my own consulting practice. I went back to my boss to hand in my notice. In our amicable parting, I believe I said, 'I may not believe in the theory of gravity, but that doesn't mean my arse doesn't point to the ground!'

The idea that systems have constraints relative to their goal seems self-evident when one considers that no enterprise can achieve an infinite amount of goal units, whatever those might be. In the for-profit sector, no company has yet been able to provide an immediate, infinite return on investment. If it did, there would be no need to invest anywhere else. No project has ever been done with zero lead-time. No product has been made, shipped and replaced in the instant another of its type has been sold. If any of this ever becomes possible, the Theory of Constraints will be exactly like science in the way science itself moves forward, step by proven or falsified step.

Being good scientists, though, we must tread carefully when making grand assertions about any given theory's universal relevance or application. We must look for the evidence. We must seek out the disconfirming data. We need to remind ourselves of the limits of our understanding of natural laws, bound as they are by our container of time and space. Over the thousands of years we humans have puzzled together theories on how our natural universe works, again and again, those ideas are overturned by new ones which more closely represent the observed data. Why should we think we have reached the end of the mystery?

The 5-Step FOCUS

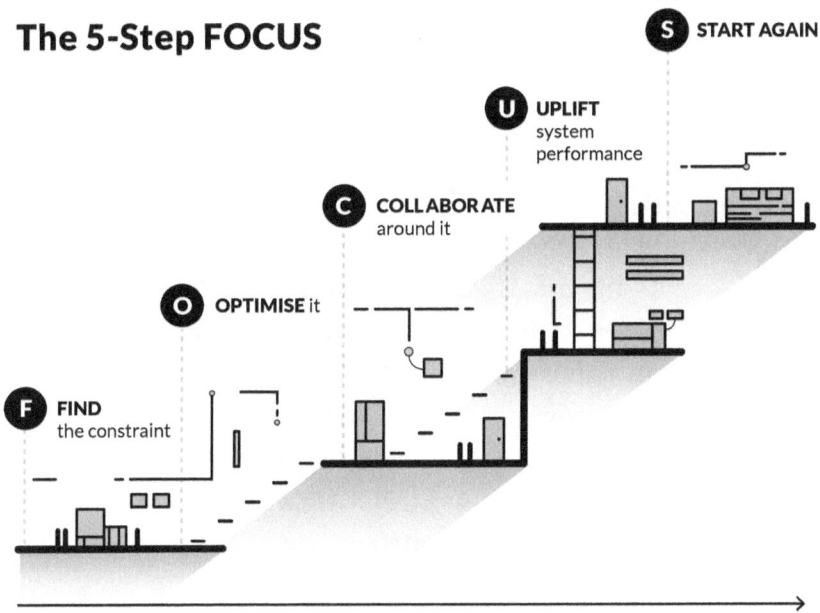

Process of continuous improvement

The 5-Step FOCUS

When we deal with more prosaic matters, an approximation to reality might not be 'ultimate truth', but 'good enough' to turn out a useful result. By analogy, one need not know the details of quantum physics to understand how a car will behave while driving—Newton's laws of motion will suffice.

Theory of Constraints offers an approach to managing the operations of a business which allows for the application of sound reasoning to the theory's prime insight: even in the most complex endeavours, very few things (and sometimes only one) govern the rate at which value is created. Any system can produce only as much as its critically constrained resource; were it not the case, the output of the system would be infinite or would collapse to zero.

If this basic statement of the theory itself is true—and remember, one would need the equivalent of a perpetual motion machine to disprove it—the first order of business is to identify that constraint, the bottleneck blocking the path to goal achievement.

Goldratt provides a very useful process for examining and continuously improving systems, known as the Five Focusing Steps. In my organisation, we have adapted his original language a little and used the word FOCUS as an acronym to help in remembering its key elements.

Find

If all systems are governed by their constraint, then the first order of business to improving system performance is to identify where that constraint is. But, how are we to use the word 'find'? Is it a case of 'where the hell is it?' or rather 'given that a constraint exists, where would you choose to have it if you were to design it into your system?' If your intention is to have control over how your system performs, clearly it is better the constraint is selected as a matter of design. Your system will have a constraint either way. So either you manage the constraint, or it manages you.

Constraints in production systems can be found in one of two ways—by doing the analytics of load versus capacity, or often more simply, by looking for build-ups of work in process. If you're in projects, the constraint of a project is its resource levelled critical path.

Optimise

Optimisation within the 5-Step FOCUS involves the science of scheduling. That is, getting down to the nitty-gritty of ensuring none of the capacity available of the constraint is wasted. It should always be busy, and working on the right tasks. If someone takes a break while doing the work of the constraint, wherever possible, someone else must take their place. If a work centre breaks down, or a process is stuck, attention is prioritised to that area.

Collaborate

The third focusing step is to 'collaborate'. It's worthwhile to think through what it takes to have people truly collaborate in the horizontal flow of value across the functional silos of the organisation, rather than vertically to its power structure. This collaboration step goes to the heart of effective teamwork and calls for high levels of understanding between functional teams and their leaders.

Teams must acknowledge that the basic organisational fabric of the management hierarchy could be changing daily. In the words of W. Edwards Deming, the grandfather of all continuous improvement: 'The object of any component is to contribute its best to the system, not to maximise its own production [...] Some components may operate at a loss themselves in order to optimise the whole system.'

So, collaborating means everyone helps the constraint: if there are tasks that can be offloaded to non-constraints, they should be. Non-constraints must ensure the constraint isn't starved of work because of upstream delays. Work is removed from the constraint to ensure there is no downstream blockage. Work is released in the correct sequence, and at a rate which matches the rate at which the constraint is performing. Flooding the constraint with excess work in process costs money, creates clutter and slows the flow of value.

Uplift

The uplift step is undertaken once everything possible has been done to optimise the constraint—now it's time to invest in additional capacity. As one of the doyens of TOC put it, 'When you've squeezed all the blood from a stone, get more stones.' It is quite common to get 25% or more system output from the first three steps alone: find, optimise and collaborate. One of the most common errors made in managing systems is to invest in new capacity before the find-optimise-collaborate steps have been carried out. When making the investment decision, though, you must be careful where you want the constraint to be, and ensure your new capacity delivers that outcome.

10. OPERATIONS: Playing on Cue Every Time

A constraint can exist in one of three fundamental places: in supply, make or the marketplace. Depending on where you are in the supply chain, one person's supply-side constraint is another's production bottleneck. During the time of the investment boom in Australia, iron-ore prices were increasing at a crazy 70% per year. From the perspective of the iron-ore producers, they had a production bottleneck, but for the steel mills, they had a supply-side constraint. By contrast, once the investment cycle was over and all the new capacity was brought on stream, prices tumbled and the iron-ore producers then faced a market constraint. Deciding where you make your investment, or in the language of the 5-Step FOCUS, what you choose to uplift, will have fateful consequence.

Start again
With more capacity now available at the constraint, you'll find that the constraint will have moved. So now we start the 5-Step FOCUS again and, hopefully, find the constraint where we planned and designed it to be.

In summary, if the existence of a constraint is axiomatic, then following are some valuable mantras which can be used to bolster business performance:

- Constraints govern the rate at which value is created.
- Any system has one constraint that has most impact.
- A gain for the constraint is a gain for the system as a whole.
- The constraint must do only that which only the constraint can do.
- Non-constraints have capacity relative to the constraint.

Part of the challenge of managing the transformation to an operations management philosophy grounded in systems thinking is met through applying Theory of Constraints to the different types of flow encountered in any group activity. Below the level of theory, then, are the methods and tools that bring those theories to life.

Having said that, I am heartily sick of the wars over which method is the best. Is it Agile or Waterfall? Lean or Six Sigma? Or Lean Six Sigma, even? ABC, Balanced Scorecard, Earned Value? Critical Path or Critical Chain? My starting point is always that work is work—regardless of the way it is planned, done or improved.

If I could take *The Matrix*'s 'blue pill' instead of investing all the time and energy in figuring out better ways to do better work, I most assuredly would. For the issue is not which method is best, but how good is it at solving the problem you have defined. Too often I have seen people disappear down the rabbit-hole of getting better and better at doing their work in a particular way while completely losing sight of why they are doing it at all. It's like taking the 'red pill' and knowing Kung Fu but without any idea of what you could do with it.

What method is used, if any is to be used at all, should be determined by whether or not it is fit for the purpose to which it is being applied, and what the likely results will be. If all you have is a hammer, everything looks like a nail, so rather understand as many tools from the toolkits as you can, and choose the ones capable of solving the problem at hand.

If you are looking for a breakthrough in productivity, there

10. OPERATIONS: *Playing on Cue Every Time*

is an irrefutably strong case for starting with TOC. Its virtue lies in its grounding in the science of system dynamics and the order of the questions it asks when looking to improve system performance. The correct identification of a constraint, after all, provides a powerful focus on the places of high leverage, which in their improvement lift overall system performance.

Just as Bernoulli's principle accounted for how the geometry of a well-designed wing provides sufficient lift for a heavier-than-air object to fly, TOC provides the means to achieve profoundly improved productivity outcomes. The kind of aircraft one makes as a result of understanding Bernoulli's principle is a matter for the aircraft designers and their markets. Likewise, what one does with the principles of TOC is a matter for those who are charged with determining how resources work across time and space to achieve the organisational goal.

But ignoring the principles turns business leaders into the equivalent of those poor souls who tried to fly by tying bird-feathers to their arms, hoping their furious flapping would take them anywhere but where gravity invariably and unceremoniously dumped them. Substituting eagle feathers for chicken is no alternative to science.

Below, I briefly outline what the constraints-based management world calls the 'proven solutions'. Proven means they have produced sufficient empirical evidence over countless cases, small and large, to materially improve revenue, reduce costs, minimise investment of capital, shorten speed to market and improve due-date performance. I should add that these thumbnails do not represent the depth of the body of knowledge that TOC has become. Moreover, the state of the art in project, production and distribution management are constantly on the move, and being improved. However, if you can get your head around the basics to see the merit in what the proven solutions say about the world of managing work, there are many places to go for further help.

Project management

Critical Chain Project Management (CCPM) is the TOC-based method that defines what is reasonable and possible to achieve in environments with finite resources and high levels of uncertainty. It can be used for the planning and execution of work as well as for reporting on work that may be happening at a more granular level than is typically manageable with standard project management approaches.

For example, a project task might appear on a Gantt chart as a single bar taking ten days. But within that task, on any given day, a team of ten people might be working on two or three tasks, with this more granular work managed by another work-management system.

The singular innovation of CCPM that is sui generis is how it treats the uncertainty inherent in any given project task. Consistent with the systems thinking that underpins TOC, at one level it looks to optimise the project, rather than the tasks within a project, and at another level a portfolio of work rather than any given project within that portfolio. Thus, tasks are estimated according to their touch time, with management attention

10. OPERATIONS: *Playing on Cue Every Time*

and resource allocation prioritised according to how the longest chain in a given network is progressing against its consumption of the aggregate protection available to the whole chain.

Without knowing anything about CCPM, one can readily create finite schedule plans, whether in a spreadsheet or in very sophisticated project management tools. However, without the benefit of the CCPM method to manage uncertainty and focus the application of resource effort during execution, such schedules become brittle. People working on projects fairly quickly end up working to their own drumbeat, to the detriment of the value delivered through the systematic application of CCPM principles.

I once led an assignment on a large industrial plant being built from the ground up. When I first met the project director and asked him where the critical path of the project was, he told me he had 12! 'Wrong answer,' I replied, a little less Socratically than I might do today. 'By definition, there can only be one. If you can't identify it, or if all the feeding paths are so close that as soon as one workstream jumps off it another randomly jumps on, then your system is out of control. The constraint is managing you.'

I asked him where he would choose it to be, and why. He started at the top with the need to get first product out by a certain date from the first part of the plant. 'If we don't,' he said, 'we'll be paying liquidated damages and will be in breach of our banking covenants. As a consequence, we'll attract penalty interest rates and our reputation will be shredded courtesy of a hostile media.'

I agreed. They clearly needed to get some temporary water

rigged up to that part of the plant so they could proceed at a pace. Doing so required pouring a concrete plinth of a couple of cubic metres onto which the temporary arrangement could perch. The project director protested that the concreters were doing a fine job pouring hundreds of cubic metres over on the other side of the site to build the new water storage and filtration systems. 'We get paid for every cubic metre of concrete poured,' he said, 'and they can get really efficient if they set up for big pours. Putting that poxy plinth in place has major nuisance value.'

Some nuisance. He had 100 days before hitting the date for the liquidated damages when all hell would break loose. By my estimation he had 100 days of work left to do to get to that point, assuming nothing went wrong in the meantime. That meant no buffer. Against that, he may have had a temporary cash-flow advantage from pouring hundreds of cubic metres without interruption from the 'poxy plinth'. What, I asked, was the opportunity cost of focusing on that big pour versus collaborating on the needs of the real critical path? He moved the concrete team and poured the plinth.

Production management

When I talk about production, I don't necessarily mean a factory filled with machines that churn out widgets. Any context in which there is a high degree of repeatability in a process lends itself to the application of Drum Buffer Rope (DBR).

The method of DBR is contained in its name—the 'drum' being the critically constrained resource whose 'drumbeat' sched-

10. OPERATIONS: *Playing on Cue Every Time*

ule provides the signal for the synchronisation of all other parts of the system. A minute lost at the drum is a minute lost for the system as a whole, so the 'buffer' is a store of work immediately before the drum to ensures the drum never starves (runs out of work). The 'rope' is a pull signal on the release of new work into the system from its most upstream gating activity, designed to match the actual rate of work completion at the drum. In the same way the drums keep the beat of the music, so DBR keeps the organisation playing on cue, every time.

Another story to illustrate. My client made cables used in microelectronics, fibre optics, high-voltage transmission lines and everything in between. Their large factory handled the whole process from drawing out the copper wire and plaiting it to the desired thickness, to applying insulation to the strands and across the whole bundled arrangement, before reeling it onto spools for storage and shipment.

We identified a particular machine in the production process that was more loaded than any other against the week's production schedule. The bottleneck. A rough calculation put the gross margin generated by this machine when running at production speed at $1,200 per minute. Because it was the bottleneck of the whole production line, when it stopped, the whole factory began losing $1,200 per minute.

An industrial agreement at this firm stated that the hourly pay of someone working as both an operator and a maintainer must rise from $36 to $40 to recognise their greater skill level. In their wisdom, senior management had decided to employ only operators to run the machine, thus saving the additional $4 per hour due to people who could function as maintainers as well.

While touring the facility, I saw the machine go down in front of my eyes. The operator told me he could have sorted the fault in a matter of minutes. Thanks to the agreement, though, he wasn't allowed to repair the machine, but had to call his supervisor to request a maintainer. Unfortunately, the maintainer was in the middle of planned maintenance elsewhere in the plant and had a machine in pieces. He was deep in the rhythm of his assigned work for the day and loath to transfer.

Two hours later, he arrived to fix the machine: cost of difference in labour between maintainer and operator $8; lost margin to the business $144,000, with banked-up inventory and blocked production everywhere upstream of this critically constrained resource.

You might say it's fairer here to give an annual labour cost difference of $7,680—based on a 240-day year of 8-hour days—rather than only count the two hours when the machine broke. But even considering an annual increase of $4 per hour to the operator/maintainer, the machine would have to go 18.75 years without breaking before it would pay to heed the difference. How likely is that?

DBR is, of course, well suited to say a car-manufacturing facility with highly sophisticated software tools to look at the scheduling of the factory floor, taking into account complex bills of material and production routes. But it's equally valuable in running a process to assign the work of fixing defects in software, technical queries in engineering or salesmen to a call roster. In all cases, it delivers results that would otherwise be considered neither reasonable nor possible.

10. OPERATIONS: Playing on Cue Every Time

Distribution and replenishment management

The replenishment solution defines the minimum amount of inventory that must be held to provide an agreed level of service. Most usually this is applied in areas such as retail distribution chains, manufacturing facilities, maintenance depots and shared service work. In these situations, the absence of a stocking item might mean the loss of a sale, a halt in production or the delay of return to service of an item being maintained. This solution is called Dynamic Buffer Management (DBM).

The DBM solution can equally be used to manage the 'bench' of large consulting firms, where the skill types are treated as virtual inventory and demand is aggregated across large numbers of projects. The essence of the solution depends on understanding average rates of consumption for a given item, the variability in that consumption and the different types of lead-time involved in moving the item from its point of production through to its point of consumption.

Besides dramatically improving service levels, DBM manages to do so with a lesser investment of working capital. The key lies in understanding how much easier it is to provide agreed service levels to all nodes of consumption, if inventory is held and aggregated close to the point of production. If this sounds a little counterintuitive in today's world of fractured supply chains, let's look at an example.

A large national furniture retailer asked my team to look into how their imports supply chain was doing and what we could do to improve it. They felt they had too much money tied up in inventory. Although some items achieved a stock-turn of three to four times per year, a significant amount of stock turned much slower. In the words of the manager in charge, 'We have slow stock, comatose stock, dead stock and archaeological stock.'

I asked him how often they placed orders on their suppliers.

'Once a month we have sales and operations planning meetings,' he said. 'That's when we collect together the orders.'

Since they owned the retail outlets, I wondered why they didn't place an order for one item at the factory in China as soon as it was scanned through the point of sale.

'Ah,' he said, 'because they have minimum batch quantities for production.'

'How do you know that?' I asked.

'Because that's what our computer system tells us,' he replied, a bit perplexed.

I asked if anyone had actually been to the factory and talked with their production planner. Might the Chinese supplier consolidate their orders with other global buyers? What do they do to deal with the peaks and troughs of demand on their facilities? Maybe my client could make an arrangement to place a replenishment order as soon as anything is sold, which the supplier would then make when ready, or once they hit a minimum trigger amount.

'Sounds reasonable,' he said. But after thinking for a moment, he found another reason for the status quo. 'If we did that, we'd have all these small batches to ship, and we couldn't possibly afford the additional freight.'

10. OPERATIONS: *Playing on Cue Every Time*

'By that logic,' I said, 'Why not wait until you can fill a super-tanker to ship your goods and get the absolute lowest cost of shipping possible?'

That absurd suggestion illustrates this kind of reductionist thinking focused on cost-cutting without seeing the other available options.

The best outcome would involve consolidating shipments from a number of suppliers at a place close to the production points. The cost advantage gained on any given product by having it made outside the geographic cluster is very likely massively outweighed by the operating expense of managing it—and the investment in additional inventory needed—by not taking advantage of a logistics chain capable of providing quick and inexpensive replenishment. In my client's case, the only inventory they needed to carry locally was equal to one shipping lead-time from the consolidation point close to their production centres.

It took all my skills in change management to overcome my client's fear of doing something that seemed so counterintuitive, even though it stacked up logically. We decided to start it as a prototype across a small range and, building on early successes, eventually, by dramatically reducing lead-times, got to halving the amount of money stuck in excess inventory while simultaneously improving due-date performance to unprecedented levels in the high 90s.

The principles behind each solution (CCPM, DBR, DBM) all derive from the logical thinking at the heart of Theory of Constraints. As I said at the beginning of this chapter, though, the principles are simple. It's the consistent and sustainable application of the principles that is hard. That, and getting whole teams to change the way they have been trained to identify problems and solve them.

The issue is often one of methodology fatigue. Many methodologies promise radical improvement, but their foundations are usually in social science. TOC fits the criterion of a falsifiable hypothesis and can therefore be considered scientific in a way that a social science cannot. When people understand this new kind of thinking for themselves, profound change can occur. Whether people accept it or not. as we've noted earlier, there really are only two choices: either we manage the constraint, or it manages us.

Questions for OPERATIONS

1. How do you define the boundary of inclusion for your system?

2. What is the goal of the system? A properly defined goal has the following characteristics: you can always get more of it; it is straightforward and easy to understand, from the shopfloor to the boardroom; it aligns everyone to a common purpose; it makes decision-making easy by acting as a reference point (i.e. is the decision going to help us get closer to our goal or will it subtract from it?).

3. What is the one thing that prevents you from getting more of your goal? What is the system constraint?

10. OPERATIONS: *Playing on Cue Every Time*

4. Are you, or your team, ever the system constraint yourself, either permanently or during a phase of a project? How do your colleagues rally around you to make sure you're being effective at doing only that which only you can do?

5. If you, or your team, are not the constraint, how do you go about offering spare capacity to your constrained colleagues so the organisation as a whole can achieve more?

Part 3
What to Change to?

Playing in Time

When we have a good balance between thinking and feeling ... our actions and lives are always the richer for it.

Yo-Yo Ma

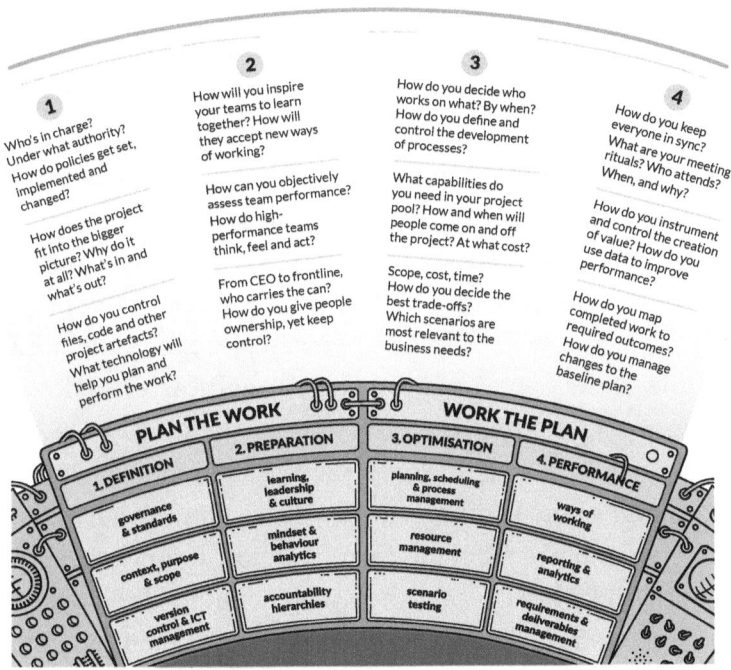

Figure 15: The value-management office

WE COME TO KNOW THE WORLD through pairs of opposites—order and chaos, good and evil, love and hate. It's the Yin and the Yang, male and female, birth and death. So in what way can we think about *More Than Just Work* in terms of pairs of opposites? What useful thinking frame will allow us to dive deeper into the realm of the problem we're trying to solve—how to lead a more productive and beneficial work life. Or, put another way, how to create better ways to do better work. Could the basic pair be the constant navigation of the interplay between the 'why' and the 'what'? The story we tell ourselves about the 'why' and how we go about doing the 'what'? The mythos and the logos?

As we saw in Chapter 7 on Organisation, the ancient Greeks defined two different concepts of time: chronos and kairos. We're most familiar with the former—the progression of the seconds into minutes, hours, days, months and years. It's what a clock and a calendar measure. All our business measures use this concept. A company's balance sheet states the assets and liabilities at a point in time, just as the profit and loss statement shows how much money has been made over time, and the cash flow, as its name suggests, how much cash has flowed in and out of the business over time.

So, at one level, the real constraint to the achievement of any organisation's goal is time—the supply of it and the demands on it. Taken to its absurd, but logical conclusion, if time were infinite, then everything we ever desired to do could be done, with time to spare. Constrain it to the 25,550 days of our biblical allotment on this good earth, though, and we must make choices.

The other dimension of time is Kairos, which exists in every present moment and calls to mind the past and its memories, as well as the future and its intentions. Thus, if we are to be fulfilled in our work, it will not happen without examining the intention behind what we do in the Kairos dimension. If our life is limited to a finite number of tours around the sun, and we aspire to live the good and beautiful life, we ought always to consider not just the 'to what' and 'by when' of our work but, importantly, to first explore the 'why'.

Invitation to a meditation

I invite you to pause for a moment, really relax and get a sense of what you want to do with what you have left of this lifetime. I mean really relax. All too often, we're so caught up in our daily busy-ness that we forget to deeply relax. Even for a few seconds. And for many, even a few seconds of this kind of attention makes us feel guilty that we're not 'doing'. The common equation is: activity equals value.

So take a deep breath and 'feel' (don't 'think') into your deepest sense of what life calls on you to do with your days, your talents, your resources. In the words of Lao Tzu, the ancient Chinese sage:

> Attain complete emptiness,
> Hold fast to stillness.
>
> The ten thousand things stir about;
> I only watch for their going back.

> Things grow and grow,
> But each goes back to its root.
> Going back to the root is stillness.
> This means returning to what is.

From such a still place, ask yourself, what do you really want to have happen? Picture yourself three to five years from now. Cast your intention out as far as your imagination will allow. Dream big. Let go of your fear that your dream is too crazy, too unrealistic—out of your reach. What does the courageous hero in you want to do? What do you see out there on the horizon that you want to get done? What is your intention?

Before we start, let's hear from Bill O'Brien, the ex-CEO of Hannover Insurance and a leader in the world of developing organisations capable of learning:

> The fundamental problem with most businesses is that they're governed by mediocre ideas. Maximising the return on invested capital is an example of a mediocre idea. Mediocre ideas don't uplift people. They don't give them something they can tell their children about. They don't create much meaning.

Where are you? Who's with you? What are you doing? How are you feeling? Can you see it? Who are you? What material things would you like to own? What is your ideal living environment? What is your idea for health, fitness, sports and anything to do with your body? What type of relationships would you like to have with family, friends and others? What is your ideal professional or vocational situation? What impact would you like your efforts to have? What would you like to create in the arena of individual learning, travel, reading, or other activities? What is your vision for the community or society you live in? Now is the time to redefine what's possible.

When you're good and ready, take some crayons and as large a sheet of paper as you can find. And, for about ten minutes, start freely drawing the vision you see in your mind's eye.

(It's okay, the rest of life can wait a few minutes.)

Don't worry if you think you can't draw. This isn't about how artistic you are; it's about letting your imagination access a different place in your head and heart, and tapping into your dreams. Avoid putting words down. Let your hand guide where your soul wants to go. Make a stab at picturing that future place and time and bring it into this moment.

Then, when you think you've drawn for about ten minutes, stop and come back to the book.

So how did it feel? What did you draw? What future did you see? Can you give it a name? Are there words and a story you can now associate with it?

Are you excited? Energised by your new vision? Surprised by your boldness? Were you able to silence—for a few moments—that inner voice of judgement?

If perhaps you haven't been bold enough and need more practice, don't fret. We'll return to this idea of a 'retreat to reflect' in Part 4.

What's what?

Let's say you now have a strong picture—your vision splendid—a noble purpose, a possibility to live into, a meaningful contribution. You've narrated the story about the 'why', but how are you going to bring your intention into reality? What is the connective tissue between the vision and what you accomplish on the ground? What's the 'what' of what you're going to do?

Picture in your mind's eye, if you will, a balance beam, like a pair of scales you might find in an antique shop, with its plates pointing up to the ceiling, and the middle anchored in a base that looks something like a see-saw. On the right of your scales, place three bundles of work—those from past, present and future: the story you tell of what got you here; who you're now being; and the final legacy you imagine you'll leave behind.

On the left, are equal and opposite bundles of capability—what you and everyone who ever worked with you brought to the party to get you to where you are now; what they now bring to getting your current life projects done; and what you will have at that place in the future as you fulfil your life's purpose.

If you are to be a good steward of your resources in leading your team over the long haul, then creating a healthy balance between work to be done and the capabilities demanded to make it so is non-negotiable. In other words, if you don't pay attention to supply and demand, which are the fundamental pair of opposites of business, and indeed whole economies, then your best-laid plans will unravel. To arrive at a balance between supply and demand, though, takes more than dumb luck.

Playing in Time

Four pillars hold up the goal

Your goal rests on many critical factors for success. But when it comes to work, these can all be aligned under four fundamental pillars that describe ways of:

Defining demand for your capabilities in and across time and place

Preparing your resources to supply the capability to meet that defined demand

Optimising the proposed resources in good time, for the duration of the work

Performing work, addressing both its planning and execution in a coherent and synchronous fashion

These four elements are the critical components you need to 'plan the work' then 'work the plan'. Everyone, from the corner store to the largest organisation in the world has to a greater or lesser degree, engaged in those elements of work. The more complex the work, the more sophisticated these four fundamental pillars become and the greater the need for standards, with defined processes for managing the 'planning' and 'performance'.

Let's start simple and see how 'planning the work' and 'working the plan' play out in a small business, say our favourite corner store.

Somewhere, whether on a scrap of paper or in a diary or electronic calendar, the owner has written a roster of what needs to be done for which shifts, from the cashing-up routines to the defrosting of the fridges, from the cycle of orders from suppliers, to paying the rent to the landlord. Perhaps on the wall will be a sheet of paper that has the numbers that list the capabilities required to keep the store running: casual staff, grocery suppliers, fridge mechanics, emergency services and so on.

When it comes to managing the range of people needed to keep the business ticking over, you can be sure it will be someone's duty to make the phone calls, write the emails, deposit the cash or place online orders and receive them. Whether in a structured and routine way, a completely ad hoc way, or anything in between, there will be appointments in diaries, meetings between people who keep the store going, and a range of reports to establish profitability, supplier performance and customer preferences. Perhaps some of the staff meet every time there's a shift changeover, others on a weekly basis to decide what's going to be put on special and how it will be displayed.

Thus, if you're looking for it, even the corner store plans the work and works the plan.

Looking through different lenses

I have had the good fortune to study a wide range of workplaces during my career. When I step into a business, I imagine in my mind's eye, a binocular-like contraption used by optometrists to measure the lenses you need to correct imperfect vision. When I look at an organisation—the corner store or the multinational—through my optometrist machine, it is as if I'm changing lenses over, turning the dials and trying different combinations until finally the test pattern on the wall comes into sharp focus. Too much supply means money is wasted on costs, with people falling over each other. Too little and the demands build up, along with the stress of being under-resourced.

Stretching the metaphor, if my optical device had poorly ground lenses it would be impossible to accurately measure the balance between capabilities and work—between supply and demand. The test lenses are ground to a standard so they can reliably and accurately measure the best fit, then they are sent off to the supplier who grinds the actual glasses calibrated to the same standard as the testing machine.

For similar reason, then, if ever we are to establish a rational means of determining a good balance between capability and work, we need standards to govern the quality of how we define them. A great quality system develops standards that are fit for purpose and easy to use. It empowers the 'amazing' such that average people going about their work can achieve remarkable results.

Innovating across all types of work

Whether you run the corner store, work in the largest of multinationals, or are beginning your start-up, there are many different types of work to do to turn the best of your ideas into tangible value. There is the work of generating the big bold ideas in the first place! Then, because 'just' an idea is not enough, one must do the work of creating a strategy to turn the idea into value. Will that idea flow through the enterprise in a seamless manner? Perhaps there is again work to do—in the field of culture—to pave the way for it to flow.

And, the work doesn't end there; more activity is needed in the field of language such that everyone at all levels can come to share the meaning attached to developing the idea into additional value and wealth. Then, it's vital to know if your organisation, in its current form, is suited to bringing this boon into the world. If not, there is the work of organisational design to be done. Do you have the resources needed to allow the idea to deliver its promise of value, or is there work to be done in that domain as well?

If you have figured out all the above, you must still make the shift from the one-off project, which develops your idea, into the repeatable 'business as usual' that makes, distributes and sells the products and services that are its fruit. This is your innovation made real—travelling the whole cycle from idea to realised value.

But all the work behind it demands capability, in the right place, at the right time, to bring your intention into reality. This is the perspiration turning your inspiration into value—wealth for toil.

Intention and reality, supply and demand—critical pairs of opposites in bringing to the world better ways of doing better work.

But to fulfil the promise, we need to explore another pair of opposites: planning the work and working the plan—how we plan to get it done and then doing it.

So, let's get on with it.

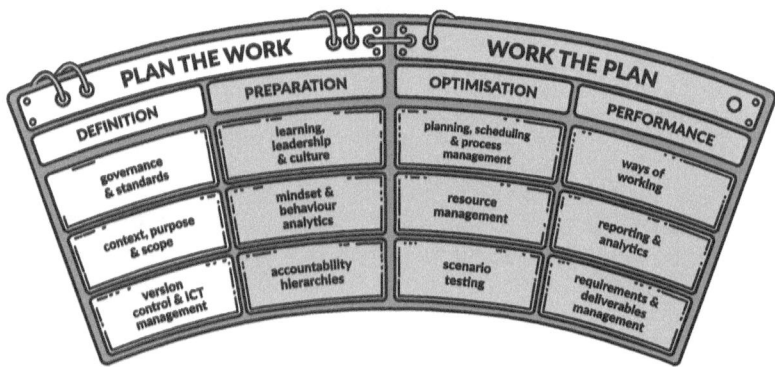

Figure 16: Plan the work: Definition

Chapter 11
DEFINITION: *The How, What and Why*

Music is a moral law. It gives soul to the universe, wings to the mind, flight to the imagination, and charm and gaiety to life and to everything.

Plato

THE ORCHESTRA FALLS SILENT as the oboe sounds a pitch, lightly piercing the audience chatter. Gradually, section by section, the musicians take their cue and tune their instruments to this lone vibration. The conductor walks on stage. The concertmaster rises, the orchestra follows. A hush descends on the auditorium. The conductor smiles, raises an eyebrow, lifts the baton. And the music begins.

With a wave of the hand, the room reverberates with the technical virtuosity of the players, each having easily fulfilled the requisite 10,000 hours to mastery. Yet we do not measure the efficiency of their playing by the quantity of notes per player, or the volume they are collectively capable of producing. Rather, we marvel at the way each musician, engaging head, heart and hand, joins with another to animate a rich musical story.

This is the ensemble effect, giving an audience of strangers the possibility of knowing the parts—composer, conductor, musicians, instruments, concert hall—as an emergent, living orchestration of the whole. And yes, the concertgoers themselves are also actively contributing to the performance.

Imagine for a moment that your business could be as gifted as such an ensemble, with exceptional levels of personal mastery, precision in synchronisation and a shared passion for delighting your customers. What would it do for your bottom line? How much value could you and your organisation create if all of the parts were connected in a way that thinks, feels and acts as a unified whole?

Let's face it, organising work is really difficult, whether of the orchestral variety or the more prosaic daily grind. Even when we discount the human factor and just look at the processes and technologies supporting them, there is no end of opportunity for confusion, poor synchronisation, overloading, nugatory work, rework and other missteps. Think about the number of different ways you get and give work instructions: by phone, in meetings, via Post-it notes, email, calendar appointments, to-do lists, electronic notes, spreadsheets, flight plans, Gantt charts, workflow tools, business IT system screens and more.

Start with your own work

Whether you're responsible for managing people or a project, it helps to see the complex challenges of coordination you face by looking at your own approach to work. Perhaps you see your-

11. DEFINITION: *The How, What and Why*

self as highly efficient, or perhaps you feel you procrastinate. Maybe you get off to a flying start, but flag in the middle. Or maybe you're a perfectionist who spends too much time gilding the lily, when 'good enough' is really what was required.

Maybe you've read and absorbed all the personal development books and podcasts out there but have found the remedies too difficult to integrate into your personal ways of working. Most likely, though, your mental self-image is neither as good as you believe, nor as bad as you fear. We need a reality check.

Let's look at an exercise we can all do to develop insight into personal productivity. Try keeping a very strict diary of your activity for, say, a month. I recommend you record in it everything you plan to do for a particular planning cycle, be it a day, a week, a fortnight or a month. At the end of each planning cycle, reflect on what you actually did with your time. You can do it electronically but I find it more convenient to make entries as they occur in my pocket notebook, then transfer the entries into a spreadsheet for analysis later.

In this spreadsheet, use one column to classify the type of work, another for the project or function it is coming from, and yet another for who is asking for it. Be sure to include yourself when you're either setting yourself or someone else to do the work.

In short, create a simple system to enable you to forecast all the work you have to do, by when, for whom and why. The million-dollar question, of course, then becomes: what parts of all that work got completed—and why. Or, indeed, why not?

I'm pretty sure the correlation between the forecasting and the reality will surprise you. On more than one occasion, you'll most likely be asking how all that time slipped away without getting done what you'd set out to do. This happens to all of us. I'm not questioning how hard you work, nor the intention with which you step into the work. The truth is that you can reduce and reduce the packets of work—you can make them so tight, they're the quaver on a musical stave. But as life ticks away the seconds—still there would be a gap.

And even as you get better at estimating the time required to get individual tasks done, when you string a few of them together, the cumulative effect of delays in one is not made up for by the gains in those completing early. When you then add in what everyone else is doing—those on whom you depend as well as those who depend on you—you're deep into a logistical nightmare.

Going back to our orchestra, imagine what it would be like if every musician, armed with the repertoire for the evening performance, was given free rein to determine which piece they would play, and licence to play it when they wanted. And, if by some happy circumstance they happened on playing the same tune, they all did so in a different key and tempo.

That's the world of work I witness. The musicians sit in their chairs, with the covers from the pieces of work they're there to perform on the stands in front of them. But when they fold open the manuscript, the inside is blank. That's the second viola you hear, calling out to the conductor, 'Hey boss, which note now?'

Of course, there are a number of helpful tips and tricks to getting the work to work. With the late Stephen R. Covey's analogy of big rocks, stones, pebbles, sand and water, we have

11. DEFINITION: *The How, What and Why*

the picture of how planning and sequence can make a significant difference to getting more important work done. If you had to fit all those elements into a bucket, you would place the big rocks in first. The stones, pebbles, sand—and finally water—can then fit in around them. Put the sand and water in first and you'll never get the rocks to fit.

But just how big is the bucket? How large are the rocks? What is the consequence to someone else down the line of leaving out one of the elements because there's no room? And what of the effect of the drip torture of email, texts and instant messaging, relentlessly demanding attention and classification into urgent, important or both?

I remember my first boss telling me I could never use the words 'as soon as possible' when asked when a given task would be ready, as it allowed for a get-out clause. When feet were held to the fire—'Well? Where's the output of that task?'—it was too easy to say 'Sorry, boss, it wasn't possible!'

Joking aside, there can be few things more important to success than the ability to reliably deliver to promise. Doing what you say you're going to do, when you say you're going to do it, is a fundamental that underpins trust. If there's more trust, you have lower costs and greater possibility. If I trust you to deliver, I don't need to invest time and effort in detailing and checking your work.

Of equal importance to keeping your promise, there can be few levers of competitive advantage more consequential than agility. That is, the ability to respond to your market, and the customers you serve, faster than your rivals.

For the whole to be heard the way the composer intended, the conductor 'plays' the orchestra on time and in tune. But, it is not the regimented tic-toc of the metronome that enlivens the players as they interact with the conductor, each other and the audience. They feel into the pulse their music generates—they are always at the ready, and poised to respond in a heartbeat. That's how we'd like our organisations to be—in sync, at the ready, and poised to respond in a heartbeat.

GOVERNANCE AND STANDARDS

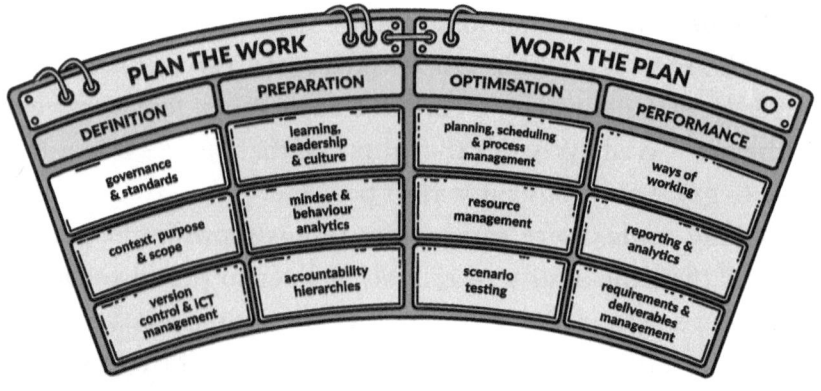

Getting to the happy state of a high-performing team takes real work, and for the rest of this chapter, I'd like to focus on defining the work—what we should be thinking of as the minimum necessary conditions for repeatedly and reliably winning great results.

I invite you to think of all the types of organisation you encounter—from the corner shop to a Fortune 500 business;

11. DEFINITION: *The How, What and Why*

from a government department to the faculty of a university; from a trade union to a non-governmental organisation. They all have, to greater or lesser extent, a need to address the questions described below.

Furthermore, you don't need to be the owner, senior executive, professor or shop steward. Indeed, you may be a valued consultant or contractor to a larger organisation, or a micro-business operating on your own from your home office. Whoever you are, I believe you will find it useful to think of how these questions affect you, your organisation, those who provide services to you and those who you serve.

In broad terms, definition allows you to clearly articulate how the work is to be run, exactly what it includes (and doesn't), why you are doing it, and the infrastructure you require to control the deliverables—be they the likes of documents, code, materials, equipment or services—to a defined standard.

As more than half of a good answer is a good question, here are some questions to help you gain deeper insight into this aspect of planning the work.

1. In the planning and performance of work, who speaks and acts on behalf of the owners—both for their rights and for their obligations about opportunity, risk and regulatory compliance?

2. Who speaks and acts for the employees and their rights and obligations? Who has what accountability, with what authority? Are they the same people?

3. How do the rules of the organisation get set and enforced—

who writes the 'thou shalts' and the 'thou shalt nots' of the planning and performance of work?

4. What are the quality standards that govern the demand for work and the supply of capabilities to perform that work?

Maturing from the start, one step at a time

A friend's favourite saying when someone calls into question his insistence on observing standards: 'Better to have double standards than none at all!' Notwithstanding the humour, if we are to create better ways of doing better work, we need to take the idea of standards seriously. Why do we require them? How do we go about continuously improving them?

A useful starting point for thinking about governance and standards comes from the work done by a variety of universities and industry bodies on capability maturity models (CMM). Capability is defined as the ability to perform or achieve certain actions or outcomes through a set of controllable and measurable faculties, features, functions, processes or services. Maturity means the ability to react, cope and reason in an appropriate way for the given situation.

An immature organisation is one whose processes are improvised during a project. Where processes exist, they are largely ignored. The organisation reacts to events rather than being proactive. Unrealistic budgets are set, schedules are sacrificed to scope or cost and there are no objective measures for quality.

By contrast, a mature organisation has high levels of inter-

11. DEFINITION: *The How, What and Why*

group communication and coordination; work is accomplished to plan; practices are consistent with processes; there exists a way to update processes in a controlled fashion when necessary; there are well-defined roles and responsibilities; and management formally commits to using the systems and processes as defined in the standards until methodically improved.

One of the most effective capability maturity models—CMMI, the 'I' standing for integration—combines many different models into one industry-standard framework. It was developed by members of industry, government and the Carnegie Mellon Software Engineering Institute (SEI). The main sponsors included the Office of the Secretary of Defence (OSD) and the National Defence Industrial Association who wanted a way to gain control of cost-plus contracts by building improved management capabilities—and thus avoid taxpayers funding million-dollar toilet seats.

While the CMMI may seem biased towards projects and services, it can just as easily be thought through in the context of a supply chain. Have a think where your organisation might rank on the defined levels of maturity:

Ad Hoc: Process measures are not in place and the jobs and organisational structures are based on the traditional functions, not horizontal processes.

Defined: Representatives from functions meet regularly to co-ordinate with each other concerning process activities, but only as representatives of their traditional functions.

Linked: Cooperation between intra-company functions, vendors and customers take the form of teams that share common process, measures and goals.

Integrated: The company, its vendors and suppliers, take cooperation to the process level. Organisational structures and jobs are based on process.

Extended: Competition is based upon multi-firm networks. A horizontal, customer-focused, collaborative culture is firmly in place.

What do you think it would take to move up the scale, and what would be the benefit?

Accountability must start from the top of the organisation and flow down the hierarchy. If the lowest level of worker is to be held accountable for performing to a standard, then so too must shareholders, the board, all executives, projects and all business as usual.

Clearly, the ability to move along the maturity levels of the capability model demands a system of governance that has the governing body develop policies and continuously monitor their implementation and improvement.

Going back to our orchestra metaphor, let's imagine a concert put on at the Sydney Opera House. You arrive at the magnificent Bennelong Point with the iconic sails on your right and the Sydney Harbour Bridge on the left. You go into the building, have a glass of wine, and at the sound of the gong make your way to the auditorium. The lights dim; the musicians, dressed in black, file in. And we're back where we were at the beginning of this chapter. The oboe has put them all in tune. The conductor

11. DEFINITION: *The How, What and Why*

has appeared, given a nod to the orchestra and acknowledged the applause of the expectant audience.

As you lean into the music, you consider this snippet from a pamphlet left on your seat, telling of the project to upgrade the whole Opera House precinct:

> The Sydney Opera House Trust operates and maintains the Sydney Opera House for the State Government and the people of NSW. Our mission stems from our founding Act, which as well as protecting, maintaining and developing the building as a performing arts centre charges us with: promoting artistic taste and achievement, and encouraging innovation.

Well, there you have it. There's the governance of an accountability hierarchy tracing back from the people who sold you your glass of wine and ushered you to your seat, through to the director of the Sydney Opera House Trust who contracted the orchestra and conductor, acting on behalf of the government of NSW who ultimately answers to the people of that state whose taxes partly fund the beloved institution.

As the final applause resonates in your memory, you think to yourself that the whole experience has really been terrific. Not only has the display of musical virtuosity been outstanding, but every step of the adventure—from buying the tickets off a well thought through promotional email, to being courteously filed out of the building—has been to an exemplary standard.

How do the governance and standards within your organisation shape up against the virtuosos?

CONTEXT, PURPOSE AND SCOPE

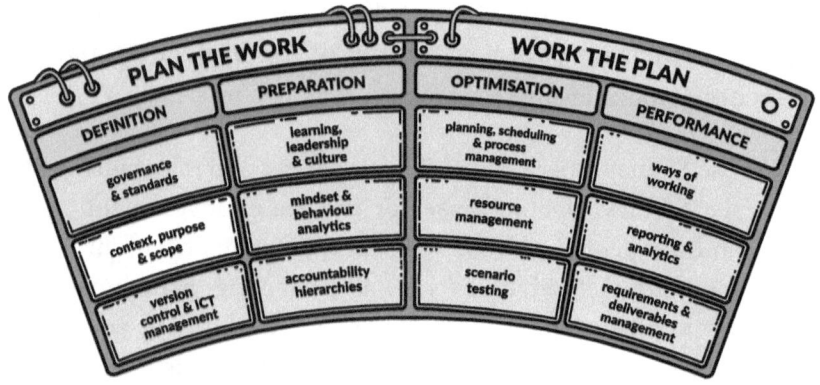

Whenever we approach the planning of our work, we need to be clear about context—the sometimes shifting banks through which the river of meaning flows. That is, how what we plan fits into the bigger picture, as well as the reason for doing it. Only then can we start to determine what scope will be included and what left out.

The Sydney Opera House's mission statement is very helpful here:

> The Sydney Opera House embodies beauty, inspiration and the liberating power of art and ideas. It is a masterpiece that belongs to all Australians. We will treasure and renew the Opera House for future generations of artists, audiences and visitors. Everything we do will engage and inspire people through its excellence, ambition and breadth. We will strengthen our central role in Australia's life and identity.

11. DEFINITION: *The How, What and Why*

That articulates a very clear context for this Australian institution, with a powerful and inspiring description of its purpose. I can well imagine that every person who works there, at any level of work, would read it and be infused with a deep sense of commitment to the cause, and that it would provide a high level of motivation for each, individually and collectively, to make a meaningful contribution.

This context becomes the governing idea for any project, large or small, as well as injecting a sense of purpose into the prosaic work of the day-to-day. It has the power to inform how people turn up to themselves and each other, what gets talked about and the quality of what gets done.

Given that example, I invite you to take a few moments to think of the following questions insofar as they relate to your organisation, or one you are trying to work with:

1. What is the organisational context for a given piece of work? What difference does it make to its planning and performance if the completion horizon is an hour, day, month, year or decade away? How is this communicated to the different levels of the organisation who have ownership of those horizons?

2. What is the purpose of the work? Why are you doing it? To 'liberate through the power of art and ideas' like the Sydney Opera House? To make a living? To make a profit? To comply with a regulator? To save costs? To satisfy a customer? To seize an opportunity in the marketplace? To learn and grow? To make a contribution? To do something significant?

3. What is the scope of the work? What has to be done, what is optional and what will expressly be excluded?

This third question, of scope, cannot properly be answered until the context and purpose of the work have been defined. We know from our example that the Sydney Opera House Trust, the governing body, 'will treasure and renew the Sydney Opera House for future generations of artists, audiences and visitors'.

Within the scope of that renewal is the building itself:

> As custodians, we will do the building justice, honouring the Utzon design principles, its standing as one of the world's pre-eminent works of architecture and performing arts venues. To do this, we will work to conserve and renew the building, preparing it for future generations of artists, audiences and visitors.

Thus, when the architects, engineers and tradies come to do their work, they will know that anything that honours the design principles of the original architect, Jørn Utzon, is in scope—and that which doesn't is out. They know conservation and renewal is in, whereas any radical change is out. Eventually this will boil down to defined streams of work such as exterior, interior, acoustics, lighting, seating, food and beverage, back of house and so on.

For each of those there will be contracts, bills of materials, requirements, procurement packages, work plans and deliverables. The scope is, in a sense, the equivalent of the musical score, bringing people, materials, information and money together, as an integrated statement that addresses the question: 'What is the work?'

11. DEFINITION: *The How, What and Why*

Perhaps almost as important as defining at the outset what is in and out of scope, is the ability to control whatever changes are made on the way through to completion. This is the dwelling place of the notorious 'scope creep'. As one colleague of mine puts it, 'Plans are for getting you into things—you've got to get yourself out.' Or, in the phrase so favoured by the military, 'No plan survives contact with the enemy.'

A significant element of planning the work is ensuring that the means exist to effectively regulate any changes that may be made to what you first thought of. To deliver high-performance outcomes, it is fundamental to have a structured process by which any changes to scope are measured against their impact on budget and schedule before they are either approved or rejected.

VERSION CONTROL AND ICT MANAGEMENT

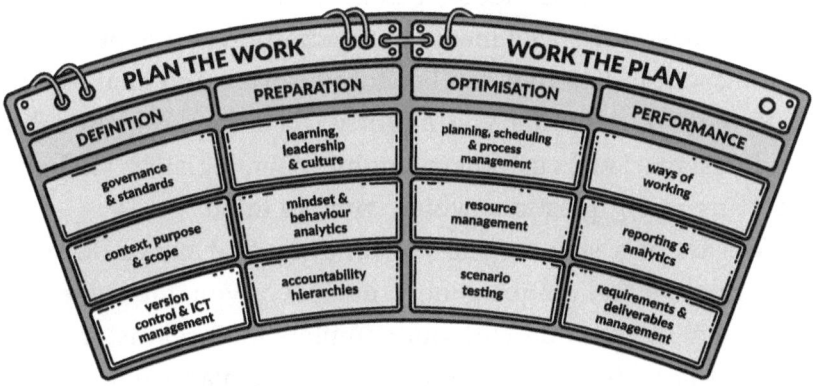

We live in the digital age. When I plug a query into Google asking, 'How much data is created every minute?' I get an answer whose figures refer to items per minute—every minute, of every day—and are, as you read this, no doubt long since out of date:

- Email users send over 200 million messages
- Facebook users share nearly 2.5 million pieces of content
- Twitter users tweet over 500,000 times
- Instagram users post over 277,000 new stories
- YouTube users watch 4,500,000 videos
- Device users download over 390,000 apps
- Google conducts almost 5,000,000 searches
- Amazon ships over 1,100 packages
- Tinder users swipe 1,400,000 times!

We are all far more connected than we have ever been, and are getting ever more so. We share documents, spreadsheets, presentations, photos, videos, technical drawings, and on and on. Our business and social media transactions generate petabytes of transaction data that can be stored, sorted and analysed to yield most of anything you might wish to know about sales, products, markets, customers, engineering, logistics, staff and most any other questions which come to mind.

We are at a stage, given the funding, that we could store the complete and unique genetic dataset of you, me and every individual alive, along with our complete medical history. The Square Kilometre Array, the radio telescope planned to answer questions about the origins of the universe will generate an

11. DEFINITION: The How, What and Why

exabyte (a billion gigabytes) of raw data for every day it points to long ago and faraway places.

It seems logical, then, that along with the multitude of benefits of this proliferation of data, we ought to think about a rational, reliable and consistent way of storing, retrieving and securing it. You would be a rare beast indeed if you could keep ahead of the torrent of emails arriving in your inbox every day, with their attachments, and links to storage systems such as Dropbox, Share Point, Google Drive, OneDrive, iCloud and the rest.

If you're like me, you'll have work spread over several of these storage solutions. And if you collaborate across organisational boundaries for a living, you will likely have to access client or supplier storage systems as well.

It's a constant battle to try and abide by the Lean principle of 'a place for everything, and everything in its place'. And then of course there are all the challenges around the administration of security, access and disaster recovery. How much more complex our interlocked lives have become since the days of paper-based filing systems. And we still have to operate and maintain those as well!

While we are living in the digital age, we are also living in the communication age. Being a baby boomer, I am not a digital native, and still get an enormous thrill every time I hook up on the likes of Skype, WebEx and Zoom.

On a recent call, it was seen as perfectly ordinary that we had two participants in Cape Town, one in Prague, two in Sydney, one in Devonport, one in Auckland and one in São Paulo. And there we were, on video with each other, reading facial expressions, talking in our turn, sharing screens and doing what only the science-fiction writers had imagined a generation ago. What was once a pure flight of fancy has increasingly become a necessary condition of doing business in a borderless world. And, it was all recorded—leaving us with the issue of determining where we would store it, and how we would index it for future retrieval.

The Nike mantra of 'Just Do It' just doesn't work if ever you want to deliver high-performance outcomes. On many occasions, it's not even a case of high performance—as when the systems fail completely.

In the definition phase of any given project, it thus behoves you to consider carefully the following questions, and invest the time and energy to develop solutions.

- What is the systematic way you are going to document the requirements and deliverables of the work and manage all the different modes of communication supporting their development?

- How will you ensure that the change control of the code base for any applications you use or develop is effectively managed?

- How will you ensure that everyone is working on the latest version of any given work artefact? How will you control valid changes and preclude those not authorised from altering it?

- What information and communications technology systems

11. DEFINITION: *The How, What and Why*

are you going to use to host your work, document and collaboration management systems? How reliable does each have to be? What is the consequence of failure and what processes are in place to mitigate such an eventuality?

Now draw a deep breath, stand up, breathe in and out ... and relax. Considering each of these points may not be the sexy stuff of the grand concepts, but it is the foundational infrastructure if you are to reliably—and repeatedly—turn great ideas into realised value. As the words of my adopted country's anthem declare, there is 'wealth for toil'.

Just as the musician devotes time to practising scales and arpeggios, so too must we resolve to properly define our work before we launch into performing it. It takes a certain courage to stare down your own misgivings about dedicating time to an activity which at first blush seems far removed from the excitement of bringing a new idea into the world. It takes even more courage—and not a little guile—to persuade others to develop and continuously improve governance and standards as a means of supporting and unleashing the amazing in people. We all fear being labelled the killjoy bureaucrat.

So, with that in mind, let's turn to the second part of planning the work—the preparation activities.

Questions for DEFINITION

1. Does everyone in your organisation understand how it is governed and the standards expected for the effective planning and performance of work?

2. How well does everyone from the board room to the shop floor understand the context within which your organisation is operating? Do they feel connected to its purpose? How do you decide what you are not going to do?

3. Insofar as the storage and retrieval of your organisation's information is concerned, how well are you doing in having a place for everything and having everything in its place?

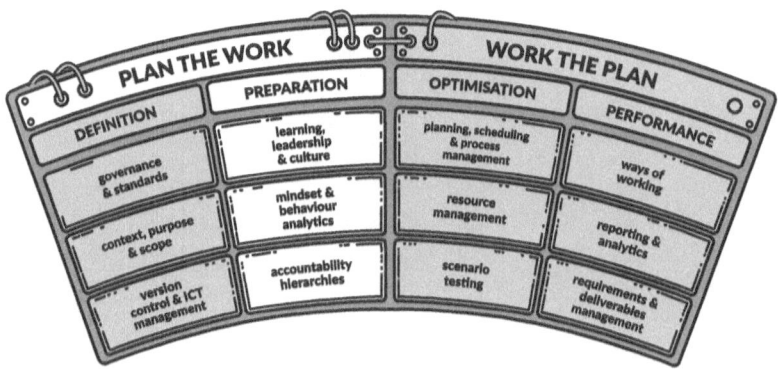

Figure 17: Plan the work: Preparation

Chapter 12
PREPARATION: *Getting Ready to Perform*

Success depends upon previous preparation, and without such preparation there is sure to be failure.

Confucius

THE PREPARATION ACTIVITIES are all about taking stock of what you have in terms of culture, mindsets and structure so they can be continuously improved. Why are these dimensions of preparation particularly important?

Innovation is the ability to turn knowledge into additional value and wealth. The rate at which knowledge is turned into additional value and wealth will depend on the rate at which people within organisations learn—either to integrate new knowledge to their work, or apply old knowledge in new ways. So, having a deep understanding of your culture, the mindsets and behaviours informing them, and whether or not your organisational structure is conducive to learning or not, will have a profound effect on your ability to innovate and prosper.

LEARNING, LEADERSHIP AND CULTURE

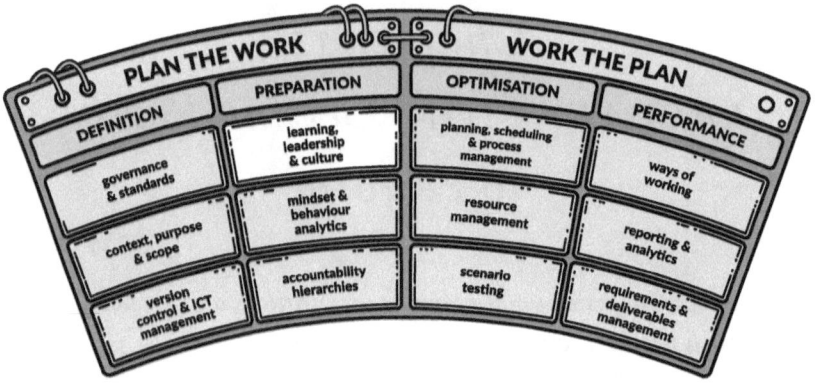

Perhaps you are familiar with the Plan–Do–Check–Act (PDCA) learning cycle first developed by the pioneers of the quality movement, Deming and Shewhart. This four-step learning cycle can be applied at all different levels of an organisation, and across any time horizon.

The 'plan' step establishes the objectives and processes necessary to deliver results with the expected output. The 'do' step is the execution of the plan. The 'check' establishes whether or not the do step has delivered the plan's objectives. The 'act' step calls on you to take the learning from the check, establish reasons why the result may be better or worse than expected, and incorporate those learnings into a new plan. The cycle continues ad infinitum in a process of continuous improvement.

Sounds simple enough. As with all simple ideas, though, their enduring value comes from the deeper truths they hold.

12. PREPARATION: *Getting Ready to Perform*

Learning, leadership and culture do not happen in a vacuum and cannot be mandated from on high. The powerful boss cannot, by diktat, produce greater learning, powerful leaders or a desired culture. What the empowering boss can do, is to create the conditions in which more productive learning fields are developed. These safe spaces empower people to lead from wherever they stand and learn from whatever they do.

Even the smallest organisations are complex. One way to look at complexity is across three different axes: dynamic, social and emergent.

Dynamic complexity describes the world of rational cause and effect—the stock and flow calculations of a supply chain, the articulation of task dependencies in a Gantt chart, or the process diagrams of an operating model.

Social complexity adds the people dimension to the equation and brings free will into play, with its attendant cultural biases, mental models and unexamined assumptions.

Emergent complexity adds the dimension of learning from a future that is as yet unknown and, to a greater or lesser degree, unknowable.

The type of learning required to address these dimensions of complexity is quite different in their nature.

Single-loop learning is the act of performing the same basic task again and again, gradually achieving mastery in being able to repeat it with zero defects. The cellist sits in the rehearsal room and stares at her newly commissioned concerto, due to be performed at a rehearsal in a few days with her orchestra and a world-famous guest conductor. She's analysed the score and is ready for a read-through. A deep breath of courage drowns out the anxiety as she adjusts her posture, grips the bow and opens to the first page of the manuscript sitting lifeless on the music stand.

Initially, it sounds awful. Strange bowing, difficult fingering—so many notes! She moves closer to the music, makes a couple of marks with her pencil, puts it down, arms herself again with her bow, and a better idea of how she's going to attack the piece. It's not quite as scary as the first time round. There has been progress. A certain familiarity emerges with each additional go round.

Before too long she can play whole phrases without reference to the score. She moves beyond the metronomic counting of each note in its time. Soon, a piece of herself is in the notes, creating the phrases and completing the tune. Again and again practice goes on—plan–do–check–act. When the time arrives for rehearsals with the great one, she's ready.

Social complexity calls for more than simply repeating a routine until it is perfected. If we are to understand and be understood, we need the scope of our learning to be broader, and its impact deeper. Double-loop learning addresses social complexity and is associated with high levels of emotional and social intelligence. You ask the deeper question, 'Why am I doing it this way, if at all?' For what is the benefit of being super-efficient at chopping down trees if you're in the wrong forest?

Emotional intelligence helps because, to be effective, you

12. PREPARATION: *Getting Ready to Perform*

must know your heart's response to what's in front of you, while social intelligence relates to our powerful human need to connect with others to feel most fully alive.

Our cellist does not practice her new piece for days only to stay locked in her practice room. If she chose to do so, she would gain none of the joy to be had from sharing her learning and accomplishment with others. And of course, had she not mastered her part of the whole, she would have had the shame of turning up to her colleagues having failed to do her duty of learning the piece.

Her instrument's held by the scruff of the fingerboard as she enters the Opera House for the first rehearsal. The casual jeans and T-shirts betray the seriousness of the task at hand. Each musician, including the conductor, has their own idea of what they think the composer was trying to say. And they each in their turn have a piece of themselves they would like to contribute to creating memories for their ensemble and audience.

Over the rehearsal period, as excitement builds towards the premiere of the new season, the conductor welds the orchestra into a cohesive, expressive whole. He has a primal influence on how the musicians will turn up. Is he the stern taskmaster who autocratically dictates his interpretation of the long-dead composer's intent? Or is his social intelligence such that he, without making a sound, can lead each and every player to bring out all they have to contribute to the performance? Can he have them play in such a way that they feel the breath of the audience being taken away by the virtuosity of all those parts coming together to form a whole, an order greater than the sum of its parts?

And what of emergent complexity? What kind of learning and leadership is associated with that? It could be referred to as triple-loop learning, descending deeper than the other two types, into the question about the intention behind the situation or events you are trying to learn about. It is learning from the future, and the quality of that future is shaped by your ability to concentrate attention on intention.

The conductor has an idea of the rapture he would have his audience experience based on what he is able to move his orchestra to do. He places his attention on the vision of what he wants to achieve. How the concert hall will reverberate to the music, hold the silence between the notes, resonate to the applause at the close.

He projects what the audience and musicians will be thinking and feeling as they experience together the musical vision he inspires in them. At the moment he lifts his baton for the concerto's first bar, none of this intention is yet manifest. But, as each phrase builds, it has an emergent property, calling on the future to unfold. Many great performers attest to the fact that the audience is an active contributor to the performance; that they can feel their attention even (or especially) through their silence—an active energy of listening. He is learning from the future he has created with his imagination. (More on 'learning from the future' in Part 4.)

These fields of learning, leadership and culture are closely related to each other. Whether preparing for a single project or developing a systemic capability to assess and improve what

12. PREPARATION: Getting Ready to Perform

exists within and across your organisation, it makes sense to systematically go about understanding these fields.

To get the best possible performance from your people, it is helpful to reflect on how you'd answer these questions:

- What is the capacity of the people within your organisation to learn more about themselves and the work they do?

- How safe is it to explore better ways of working?

- How can you build capacity, at all levels of work, for people to lead themselves and their teams without resort to the authority of management?

- To what extent can personal mastery and shared vision be developed as a means of surfacing the amazing in people?

- What is the culture of your organisation? How do you go about building internal cohesion and adaptability to the external environment? Are you bureaucratic or laissez-faire? Market competitive, or close knit as a family?

MINDSET AND BEHAVIOUR ANALYTICS

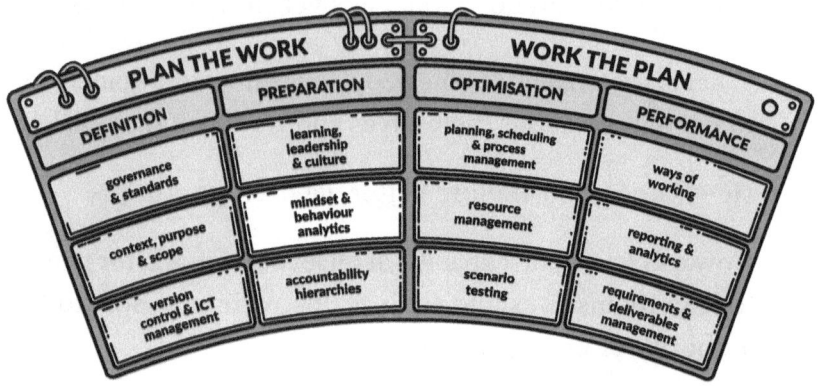

What mindset sits behind the mask you wear—whether looking at the mirror, a hall filled with people or an exchange on a webcast? Dan Siegel, inventor of the concept of 'mindsight', gave us a powerful definition of a mind as 'an embodied and emergent relational process that regulates the flow of energy and information'.

This definition is particularly useful as a way to explore mindsets and behaviours. For all of us who have a brain, there is a mind at work. What the mind does, sitting in the body, is to regulate the flow of energy and information as we go about our daily lives. That energy and information could come in many forms. For example, the sound of music and traffic are both forms of energy which the mind must regulate. The response to either could be quite different, but it is your mind doing that regulating. Your mind is at work on the information contained in the words on this page, using the symbols of the alphabet to make sense of the words, sentences and concepts you read.

In all of this, what is important is what Siegel defines as the emergent relational aspect of the definition. None of us is an island—we come to understand ourselves only insofar as we relate to what we find around us. We are constantly comparing, using the natural taxonomic engine of our minds to classify what we see and think of as good or bad, or something we like or don't like, and want or don't want.

According to the man who founded analytical psychology, Carl Jung, we are all endowed at birth with a bias towards one of two basic attitudes—expressed in the well-known idea of the introvert and extrovert. Joseph Campbell describes Jung's introvert as 'a power-oriented person who focuses on their own internal image of how things should be'. The extrovert, on the other hand, turns outward, losing themselves in another object.

Jung made the point that no one is wholly introvert or extrovert. We all occupy a point on the scale and, whether through our genes or upbringing, we'll have our preference as to how we interact with the world. Building on this model, Jung went on to describe two other pairs of opposites, forming the foundations of the human psyche: sensation against intuition, and sensibility against intellect.

Sensation refers to our capacity to use our senses to relate to the space around us—the sensory reality of the here and now. The sensates use sight, sound, touch, taste and smell to know the world.

Intuition is the orientation that relies on instinct rather than conscious reasoning, and intuitives seek out what's possible based on an instinctive understanding of their life circumstance.

Sensibility refers to the capacity to feel, emotionally, all that life has to throw at you. Knowing what you like and don't like, what you are attracted to and that which repulses you.

Intellect, as the word suggests, calls on faculties of thinking and reason. In the same way that we all occupy a position on the continuum of introversion and extraversion, we are also on a continuum with regard to sensibility and intellect or sensation and intuition.

From such individual building blocks, which form the foundation of many popular psychometric tools used in business, such as Myers–Briggs (Katharine Cook Briggs collaborated with Jung; Isabel Briggs Myers was her daughter), we can build a picture of the rich diversity in our organisations.

More recently, with the advent of massive computing power and statistical factor analysis techniques, the study of personality has become far more empirically sound. The Big Five personality traits have been developed using the 'lexical hypothesis'— that is, in the words of professor of psychology, Jordan Peterson

> Each and every human language contains a relatively complete description of the important similarities and differences between individuals. Language has encapsulated such description because human beings are ex-

12. PREPARATION: Getting Ready to Perform

ceptionally social, and need to understand each other to cooperate effectively and avoid conflict.

The five major traits and their aspects are:

1. Agreeableness: compassion and politeness
2. Conscientiousness: industriousness and orderliness
3. Extraversion: enthusiasm and assertiveness
4. Neuroticism: withdrawal and volatility
5. Openness to experience: openness and intellect

But knowing what each individual is endowed with is not enough to understand how the whole behaves. It says little about what happens when each of us become part of a team. The orchestra, like any organisation, is much more than the sum of the personalities of its musicians.

Building on these elements of the individual psyche, we can establish a broader picture of what comprises a more comprehensive mindset. My friend David Levy, an ex McKinsey Consultant who is doing pioneering work in the field of quantitative mindset and behaviour analytics had this definition: *Mindsets are a set of beliefs* (in and about self and how the world works), *attitudes* (towards others and situations) *and heuristics* (biases, shortcuts to decisions, actions) *that directly and significantly shape a person's outlook and behaviours* (with feedback loops via learning) *and interact with a person's inherent qualities, source of drive, state and contextual orientation.* Below are some examples of more common mindsets.

'Abundance' versus 'scarcity' mindset

In his *7 Habits of Highly Effective People,* the late Stephen R. Covey popularised the notion of the abundance versus scarcity mindset:

> People, teams and organisations with the scarcity mindset believe the world has a finite amount of the good stuff to go around, and the big choice is to determine who the winners and losers are. In contrast, people with an abundance mindset see the world as unlimited in its bounty, and a share in that bounty is constrained only by imagination, intellect and a willingness to collaborate with others.

'Fixed' versus 'growth' mindset

Carol Dweck, a professor of psychology at Stanford, has a theory that individuals can be placed on a continuum according to their implicit views of where ability comes from:

> In a fixed mindset students believe their basic abilities, their intelligence, their talents, are just fixed traits. They have a certain amount and that's that, and then their goal becomes to look smart all the time and never look dumb.

> In a growth mindset, students understand that their talents and abilities can be developed through effort, good teaching and persistence. They don't necessarily think everyone's the same or anyone can be Einstein, but they believe everyone can get smarter if they work at it.

'Productive' versus 'defensive' mindset

According to the late Chris Argyris, a pioneer of organisational learning and Professor Emeritus at Harvard Business School, the two dominant and competing mindsets in organisations are 'productive' and 'defensive':

> The productive mindset seeks out valid knowledge that is testable. The productive reasoning mindset creates informed choices and makes reasoning transparent. The defensive mindset, on the other hand, is self-protective and self-deceptive. When this mindset is active, people or organisations only seek out information that will protect them. Truth can be shut out when it is seen as threatening. The defensive mindset may lead to learning based on false assumptions or prevent learning altogether.

Mind the gap

It's important to develop a proper understanding of which mindsets cause the behaviours you see in your organisation, which ones matter for performance and what their current baseline is. Without that, you will never effectively detail, prioritise and close the gap of those which lead to superior results. Understanding mindsets is a key component of being able to propel leaders and the workforce into a brighter future, energised with the knowledge of how team composition and dynamics can be used to leverage individual capabilities and preferences.

Work is now being done to define the surveys and sensors capable of directly correlating particular mindsets and behaviours with organisational performance. This work is not being done in the abstract, but is grounded in the specifics of people in their workplaces, providing empirical answers as to which mindsets and behaviours are associated with, say, outstanding frontline bankers. Or likewise, how certain mindsets and behaviours can be directly correlated to performance in large, complex programs of work.

When we move away from seeing the people we work with—and the teams we form for our projects—as mere objects on an organisational chart or cost items in a spreadsheet, we have taken a bold step. We trade the two-dimensional certainty of the abstractions that the org chart and spreadsheet represent for a richer and more dynamic model of the fullness of human experience.

We surrender to our ignorance of what lies behind the mask and are ready to be vulnerable in finding out. A vital component of being prepared is having a means of doing the analytics, and committing to doing it on a regular basis. It is a sure way of providing invaluable insight into how to continuously improve performance.

- What are the mindsets and behaviours that lead to winning better results? In which areas of your business? Sales? Production? Projects?

- What means do you have of proving empirically that the mindsets and behaviours you have chosen are in fact correctly correlated with performance?

- What data do you use to provide feedback to individuals so that they know their strengths and weaknesses with

12. PREPARATION: Getting Ready to Perform

regard to proven mindsets and behaviours for success in their endeavours?

- How do you look at the whole population of your workforce to see who the benchmark performers are? Where are they working and how can you learn more from them?

- What are you doing about getting those people who, from a mindsets and behaviour point of view, are genuinely not suited to the role they are in 'off the bus'?

ACCOUNTABILITY HIERARCHIES

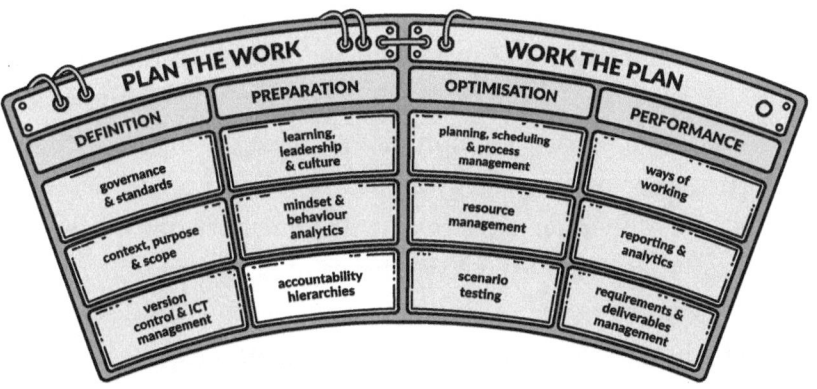

By now, we know what we're going to do, where it fits into the bigger picture and why we're doing it. We know how it's going to be governed, and what kind of questions we'll be asking of our learning, leadership and culture. We have called out the criticality of mindsets and behaviours and are ready to undertake the detail of working the plan. Or are we? What's missing?

Let's return to the board of the Sydney Opera House Trust and their document titled *Enterprise Strategy 2013*. I choose this example as the principles involved are universal. The document identified five key areas of strategic focus over the next ten years: stakeholders, the building, performing arts, visitor experiences and our people, and business agility.

Think about this organisation for a moment. It has deep associations with culture and the arts, and is a government-owned entity. But does it not, at root, face the same challenges as our retailers, airlines, hospitals, banks or mining groups? Isn't every organisation ultimately trying to deliver better performance in the face of complexity?

For the Sydney Opera House strategy to be successful, there would need to be an accountability hierarchy flowing from the board, through the CEO to the heads of each of the strategic pillars of the plan. While the CEO is accountable for the whole of the ten-year plan, it's simply not possible for her to attend to the articulation of the strategy at the lower levels of the hierarchy. It will take individual executives with time horizons of three to five years to develop their hypotheses of how they will achieve the goals stated in the overall plan and then go about the work of designing, testing and implementing their ideas.

Below these executives sits another level of management in the accountability hierarchy, tasked with looking after the one- to two-year horizon—the development of the budgets, plans and processes of specific streams of work within the silos of the strategic pillars. Theirs is the world of the general manager, accountable for the compliant use of the overall systems of man-

12. PREPARATION: *Getting Ready to Perform*

agement and contributing to their continuous improvement.

Below them sit the supervisors who look out anywhere from three months to a year. It is their accountability to muster the troops and ensure they are adequately resourced to do the work contained in the plan, delivering according to the defined processes, just in time and just on quality.

Elliott Jaques, among others, has established beyond reasonable doubt the direct and empirical correlation between the time-horizon of the work being considered, its complexity and therefore the cognitive capacity needed to manage it (see Chapter 8 for more detail). Any more than this number of layers and you risk having people feeling squashed into a job that is too small for them. Leave out any of the layers and you'll create high levels of anxiety in those who feel their jobs are too big for them.

Before closing this topic, we need to resolve one more issue. How to be effective in the cross-functional relationships required to bring the whole strategic plan into being. The stakeholders need to know what is happening with the building. The building needs to accommodate the needs of the performing arts and visitor experiences. To make it all come together without wasting public funding and goodwill, it will need to incorporate the People and Business agility team, and their ideas.

How, then, is the organisational structure of the strategic program designed? How does it accommodate the assigning of work through the hierarchy of a given functional silo, and hold accountable those doing work initiated by a collateral function?

If you were responsible for this step of organisational design, would you have the courage and foresight to avoid the trap of creating a Tower of Babel where no one is clear on the horizon, context, purpose, outcomes or timing of what they are being held accountable for? We may speak the same language, but do we share the same meanings?

The instances are legion where people have been elevated to managerial positions based on technical competencies only to flounder, either because the job is too big for them, or they are not given requisite authority over the resources required to get done the job at hand.

Would you, for example, stand for the radical idea that if you are to be held accountable for a piece of work, you get to decide who is in your team—regardless of the inconvenience to the broader organisation? Just because someone has nothing better to do, and is on the payroll, does it mean you must accept them on your team—and still be held accountable for the result?

Before leaping into planning the work, take the time to think through these questions:

- How many levels of work are there in your hierarchy, from the top boss to the frontline worker?

- What criteria do you use to determine the number of levels and the choice of people who fill them?

- In your organisation, who is accountable for what? And do they have the authority over the resources required to acquit their accountability?

- Is the boss accountable for the subordinates' work, or the other way round?

12. PREPARATION: Getting Ready to Perform

- How do you assign work within a functional silo and initiate work across a different silo, while always being clear about who is accountable for what, by when?

Architecting simplicity to navigate complexity

Surprisingly few senior executives think deeply about the questions above before embarking on their most hazardous journeys. Many will say that their work—the work of the big picture, the long horizon—is more important than addressing the topics of leadership, learning, culture, mindsets and behaviours, and accountability hierarchies. Perhaps they think only some of the topics apply to them, and their job is to hire people to deal with the rest.

Not reflecting on the ideas covered in this chapter is analogous to a conductor saying he is okay with not knowing how the strings work, because he knows the general principles of music, and the string section is paid good money not only to know their instruments, but how they best fit into the soundscape. You don't have to play the cello to have a deep understanding about its range, dynamics, timbre and contribution to the musical palette of a symphony. But you do need to know those attributes if you're to get the most from the cellist and understand what that sublime instrument can contribute to a richer musical experience.

Taking the time out to think about the domains outlined above takes resolve. The pressure to 'get stuff done' is always relentless, and mockery awaits anyone who dares suggest that 'pause for thought' is a good investment of time. Naysayers abound—from the cynics who talk of the 'fluff of culture' to the ignoramuses who protest about the 'trivial pursuit of operational excellence'. As Jung discovered, if you have fed your preference for either emotional or analytical perfection, then the opposite of your preference will form the lesser portion of your integrated view. Feed both.

It's a brave person who carves out a new path rather than continuing to amble down the beaten track. You need courage to explore a portion of yourself less developed than you are comfortable exposing in public. You must learn to give up habitual routines that have served you well, and instead, deliberately and bravely choose ignorance. Your voice of judgement will be rampant. How will you provide the psychological space for a new way of working to emerge?

Questions for PREPARATION

1. Why do you think learning could be a significant accelerator of innovation? What role does innovation play in the development of competitive advantage?

2. What mindset do you bring to your managerial leadership? How do you know?

3. Does your management hierarchy actively seek to match accountability with the authority over the resources required to acquit that accountability? How would you make sure?

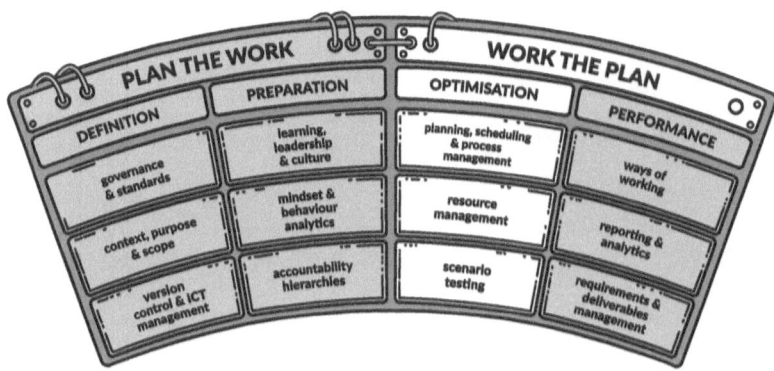

Figure 18: Work the plan: Optimisation

Chapter 13
OPTIMISATION: *Focusing your Efforts*

Good, better, best. Never let it rest.
'Til your good is better and your better is best.

St Jerome

NOBODY LIKES WASTE. Embedded deep in the development of our species is an understanding of the need to be frugal with our resources. If we are to ensure survival over the long term, we must conserve. And yet, after millennia, the evidence points to quite staggering amounts of waste in production, distribution and exchange.

We act as if our good earth has infinite resources, subconsciously privileging the human turn at the unfolding of history. It's as if we imagine ourselves as being once removed from nature's hierarchy, able to call the shots, for good or bad, without realising we are in fact intimately interwoven into the fabric of life itself.

Many organisations are so large and dominant in the markets they serve that they don't need to perform to any objective criteria of excellence. They merely need to better their competitors or use their powers to seek rent from their regulators. And then they fall asleep. Eventually, commercial, economic or political disruptors come along, and their once safe platform burns.

So, how do we stay sustainably competitive? What systematic practices in 'working the plan' might we adopt to remain ahead of the game? Before setting off to answer those questions, I would like to make the point, again, that while the classifications referred to in the diagram at the introduction to this Part 3 are useful, you should bear in mind that any system or framework is a more or less useful abstracted model of reality. It's the map, not the territory.

The whole is always more than the sum of its parts. For the best results, you must continuously strive to understand how the components interact with each other. Leverage—which is what we are seeking when talking about optimisation—more often than not resides in the connecting points and not in the nodes themselves. Information, the lifeblood of high performance, must flow freely between the people involved in planning and performing work.

Transparency, sharing and empowerment often rub up against ingrained habits of silo-based working patterns. There's a natural anxiety about having to rely on your subordinates' and peers' ability to hold and interpret information. Will they keep secrets about sensitive information, which if seen by outsiders could do you, your team or your organisation harm?

Paradoxically, however, if you want high performance to become routine, it will not come without sharing information and engaging the broadest possible pool of talent and experience to

13. OPTIMISATION: *Focusing your Efforts*

pursue the optimum path to the common goal. For an organisation to flourish, decision-making powers need to be at the lowest level of the organisation competent to wield them.

Ideas from different sources, from people of diverse backgrounds and temperaments, have a habit of building on each other. Finance has a perspective that's useful to marketing. Supply chain makes a contribution to HR. IT listens in to what Sales has to say about customer experience. An introvert will hear something an extrovert may not. Someone who is ordered would be better at bringing an idea to fruition than the person who dreamed it up in the first place. Being heard, at whatever level you participate in the management of the work, encourages a deeper level of participation, motivation and engagement. And in the process, it builds a more agile organisation.

Having the courage to overcome misgivings about letting go of the kind of control you've likely worked so hard to cultivate is no easy ask. It requires trust. We all have that voice in the head arguing, 'I would rather be the one to control the information and decisions if I'm to take ultimate accountability.' The paradox is, if you have chosen the right people in your team, having them take on accountability for their decisions leads to better outcomes all round. The right people have integrity, share your intention, have been selected for their competence and can demonstrate results.

It's one level of accountability to ask the right people to make recommendations, but then leave the decision-making in your hands. It's quite different, though, to give them skin in the game, and actually make the decision. That road, less travelled as it is, demands from them a deeper level of processing to understand the possible effects of their decisions. Hence, they are far more likely to exercise their discretionary powers more judiciously.

Empowered means engaged

In my experience, the vast majority of people, if appropriately selected for the team, not only rise to the challenge of being genuinely empowered, but relish the opportunity to demonstrate the contribution they can make. On the flipside, accountability without requisite authority leads to overloaded bosses, underwhelmed subordinates and inferior outcomes. Imagine a conductor having to provide a stroke of the baton for every note played by every musician.

'Working the plan', then, is all about how to marshal your resources to most productively achieve the goal you have set. High performance depends on comprehensively engaging the team in the processes of planning and scheduling the work, providing them with methods for doing so and ensuring they—both people and methods—are open to continuous improvement.

Planning should not be the exclusive domain of isolated planners or a planning department. Every managerial job has the mandatory components of planning and execution. Planners may be experienced in their ability to articulate a model of the plan in diagrams or tables. But to achieve consistent high performance, they must meaningfully engage with the people who can answer the question: 'What is the work?'

13. OPTIMISATION: *Focusing your Efforts*

In the Ensemble Way, optimisation has three components:

- Planning, scheduling and process management
- Resource management
- Scenario testing

The highly logical representations of planning and scheduling, or the mathematics of resource and scenario management may seem completely alien to you. Likewise, the kind of work involved in envisioning the future may not be your thinking preference, or suit your personality type. But, I have little doubt you will gain insights and benefits from stepping into the arena. We are all, after all, a part of one or more projects and to do what's best for the whole, the better your appreciation of the whole, the greater the contribution you're capable of making.

If you do happen to naturally lean towards the discipline and hard logic of planning, scheduling and resource management, and find some of what follows too simple for words, spend some time walking in the shoes of those who struggle with it. You work with such people all the time, and they could do with your help.

PLANNING, SCHEDULING AND PROCESS MANAGEMENT

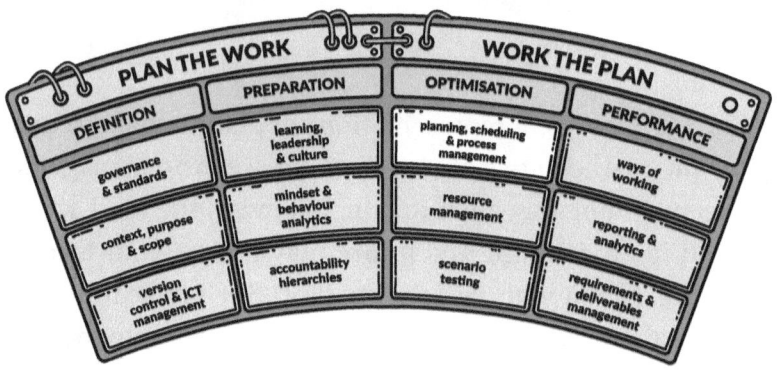

A process is simply a systematic series of actions directed to some end. Planning and scheduling are processes. Running your organisation is made up of many processes. Some may be explicit, documented in procedure manuals and able to be consistently repeated. Others may be tacit, held by individuals and teams who know from experience and common practice how to get things done. Processes are usually a combination of explicit documentation and tacit understandings.

The 2013 Sydney Opera House Enterprise Strategy illustrated this idea when it talked of its plans in these terms:

> This document outlines the rationale for our focus, what we will do, and the result we are seeking in relation to each of these elements in the short and medium term. Each element is supported by operational plans, including targets against which our performance and achievement of our objectives will be measured.

13. OPTIMISATION: *Focusing your Efforts*

When I begin a plan, I use a basic building block called the CPORT—context, purpose, outcomes, resources, timing—which we first encountered in Chapter 7. It's worth revisiting here, if only to demonstrate its universal value.

The CPORT (pronounced 'seaport', sometimes confusingly to the uninitiated) represents the least amount of information required to define work, regardless of its horizon. Leave any of the elements out and, other than through guesswork and inference, the person accountable for carrying out the work cannot know what the initiator is actually asking for. Ignoring any of these elements will be a cause of rework and waste.

The CPORT could be quite long, and describe horizons stretching out years, or could also be just an instruction about what to do tomorrow. People may rail against this simple discipline of fully describing a task, but without paying attention to planning, they'll be left wondering why projects run late, over budget and don't deliver all of what the 'customer' wants.

Context

What is the context within which the work is being specified? For the Sydney Opera House, it is the Enterprise Strategy with its express reference to both the short and medium term. The tradie doing the plumbing will be looking at a different context to the executive accountable for the building. However, each level of work nests progressively within the other, until the overarching context, articulated in the first part of the mission, is reached:

> The Sydney Opera House embodies beauty, inspiration and the liberating power of art and ideas. It is a masterpiece that belongs to all Australians.

Purpose

The purpose statement goes to the 'why' question. If you know why you're being asked to do a piece of work, you are better able to exercise judgement and discretion in how you go about getting it done. The why is contained in the second part of the Sydney Opera House mission.

> We will treasure and renew the Sydney Opera House for future generations of artists, audiences and visitors. Everything we do will engage and inspire people through its excellence, ambition and breadth. We will strengthen our central role in Australia's life and identity.

Outcomes

The outcomes can be classified in two parts—the quality of the work and its quantity. The quality may refer to elements such as building standards, technical specifications, regulatory requirements. Measuring outcomes by quality ensures compliance to a determined standard. As far as quantity is concerned, you simply ask, 'How many?' If one were to specify the luminaires for lighting the stage of the concert hall, the quantity part of the CPORT would tell us how many of which type are required.

Resources

This refers to the human, material, financial and information resources required to complete the desired work.

13. OPTIMISATION: Focusing your Efforts

Timing

This, of course, defines when the work must be completed.

To illustrate, let's assume you are the executive in charge of the building workstream of the Enterprise Strategy of the Sydney Opera House. Let's further assume you are fully briefed with the CPORT from the CEO. You know how your stream of work fits into the overall context of the rejuvenation of the Opera House, and why it's important.

You're also clear on the quality and quantity outcomes being demanded. You have been given a preliminary budget to procure the resources to conduct the work and you know not only the date by which your work on the building must be completed, but also any interim milestones. What, then, do you do from a planning point of view?

First the flight plan, then the schedule

The first step is to build a 'flight plan' to get you from the start to the completion of your assignment. This is a high-level, visually attractive document, used to simply communicate the major steps on the path to completion, as well as the key milestones along the way. It also serves to illustrate the critical dependencies, both within your stream and across different streams. For example, the structural modifications may have to wait for the earthworks to be completed, while the new sound system depends on your completing the new roof.

Flight plans

Understanding the flight plan is the equivalent of understanding the program of a season at the symphony. What pieces are going to form the repertoire? What musicians will be needed? What times are we going to run the performances? When will we schedule the interval and what refreshments will be served? What lighting do we need? How should the stage be set? How many people do we expect to attend? What security will we need? When will we open the concert hall doors? When will the final encore end? What time will everyone go home? How many staff of what type do we need on what rosters?

It's the 'big-picture' run-sheet that gets everyone on the same page. Even for the largest projects, the flight plan rarely requires more than 60 tasks, which are best laid out on a single page. When thinking about flight plans and schedules, it's useful to understand the concept of fractality—that is, self-similarity at different scales of focus.

Fractals are never-ending patterns. Look at any leaf, and you see in it the pattern of the tree: the petiole and veins have a shape and construction mimicking the trunk and branches of which it is a part. If you zoom out, you can see a basic shape and pattern of dependencies which resembles a similar pattern on zooming in. The flight plan is the zoomed-out version. Depending on the planning horizon, there may be more component flight plans and ever more detailed schedules as you zoom in. The flight plan provides a basic structure of the work to be done over the duration of the planning horizon. This is why it's important to make it visually attractive. People will be referring to the flight plan a lot. If it has inherent aesthetic appeal, it can also help inspire them to see where their daily effort fits in to the grand scheme.

Schedules

From the flight plan, we move to detailed scheduling. Now we break each component into progressive levels of detail, depending on the length of our planning horizon. As a rule of thumb, I would detail, as fully as possible, all work due to conclude at a milestone within the next 90 days. Anything beyond that can be articulated in a master schedule, at a lower level of granularity. This continuous decomposition of the work to higher and higher levels of resolution is what comprises the Work Breakdown Structure or WBS.

Committing to finite detail further than 90 days out is likely a fool's errand. Why? For me, the purpose of scheduling is to inform everyone working on the project about what they need to do, how much effort is involved in doing it and what the dependencies are. It is the highest level of resolution required to activate a person or a resource to start and complete a discrete packet of work. Through the analysis of these quantum packets of work and some statistical analysis of their variability, we can determine when we can reliably promise completion.

A schedule, for those working on a project, does what the musical score does for the orchestra. It tells us what notes need to be played, for how long and how loud, by which instrument, in what sequence. Indeed, if you think about it, a musical score is a schedule, providing the means by which perhaps a hundred musicians get to play in time and in tune, to the delight of the audience.

The big difference between the orchestral score and the project schedule is that the orchestra plays a composition developed in the mind of a lone genius. In projects, I have overwhelmingly found better results if the participants are deeply engaged in the process of planning and scheduling the work. It is the participants who have the detailed knowledge to fully articulate all the work required to deliver the scope on time and to budget—understanding all the interdependencies. And it is they who need to be engaged in determining how best to go about executing the plan.

Gather the team
Too often we fail to get the whole system in the room to nut out the optimum way to go about executing the work. Is it because managers and their workers do not see planning and scheduling as being real work? Are they anxious about spending the time involved in the difficult task of determining what work, done by whom, will come first, second and third, when they could rather just be getting on with it?

It's vital to have an idea up front of just what we're getting on with. It's a bold leader who is willing to stop the Gadarene rush to just do it and instead engage in a disciplined approach to the process of planning and scheduling the work; to share the context, purpose, outcomes, resourcing and timing; to build people and teams empowered to make decisions based on the knowledge gained from participating fully in the planning and scheduling processes.

In Part 4, we'll look at some of the social processes you

13. OPTIMISATION: Focusing your Efforts

may find helpful to engage the whole team in thinking before leaping.

Standard ways to schedule the dance

Some years ago, one of the senior members of my team was called on to develop a set of planning and scheduling standards for a global transformation project that involved simplifying and standardising all core functions of the business. This huge feat would support and enforce the redesign of their SAP business management software.

From the start, it was made clear that this was a business-led initiative with the technology playing a supporting role to the principles of simplification and standardisation.

These ideals made sense to all those involved in the project, and found expression in applying the Pareto principle—sifting out the 20% of processes that accounted for 80% of the work, then learning how to do those really, really well while letting the rest largely take care of themselves.

As part of the Project Management Office (PMO) for this transformational piece of work, we felt we could hardly lead the charge in this exercise to simplify and standardise all of the business if we didn't apply the same principles to our own work. After all, the PMO was accountable for delivering executable work plans for over 1,000,000 people-days of work, for almost 7,000 roles across 15 strategic business units that affected over 100 operations across Europe, Africa, Asia, Australia and North and South America.

The document ultimately produced ran to 68 pages of Arial 10 point, with many a technical diagram and 12 major headings that read:

1. Objectives
2. Introduction
3. Glossary of terms
4. Scheduling benchmarks and standards
5. Method and techniques
6. Scheduling and execution management processes
7. Tools
8. Scope and approach
9. Performance management processes
10. Workplan change management
11. Process discipline
12. Additional information for build to deploy planning

Now, admittedly, this document was hardly a thrilling read. But without it, we'd never have hit ten straight go-lives in a row that were on time, to scope, and at (or better than) budget.

The mechanics of the standards alone were insufficient to achieve this outcome. Indeed, as I've mentioned elsewhere, one of the most common mistakes made is to confuse a 'necessary condition' for sufficiency. To be sufficient, we had to talk about the compelling shared vision, the possibility the project represented for each and every member—and explore how that was going to be achieved. The support from the leadership—and for each other—had to be absolute.

13. OPTIMISATION: Focusing your Efforts

While there's no doubt that the standardisation of the approach around the use of Theory of Constraints (TOC) and its associated method of Critical Chain Project Management (CCPM) were necessary conditions of these repeated successes, they were by no means sufficient.

A fundamental part of getting our PMO system adopted by the whole project was a clear and shared understanding of what was being done, why it was necessary and what each and every participant in the project could expect as a result. A significant amount of time and money was spent on training all relevant stakeholders to the level of competence needed to be effective individuals in their teams. Everyone kept an eye and a steely resolve on the overall benefit of the project to the business at large.

Some questions on scheduling

Whether you live in a world where you have accountability for large, complex programs of work—whether you have responsibility for component parts of them or are an individual contributor—if you're committed to the most effective outcome of any planning activity, it's worthwhile contemplating the questions below.

- What time horizon are you planning to, and what degree of granularity for the planning and execution of work is required for that horizon?

- How do you create and represent the distinction between effort required and elapsed duration for any given task?

- How do you determine what skill types are required to complete any given packet of work, and how is this represented in the work instruction?

- When do you assign a particular person or team to get on with the task of completing any given packet of work, and how do you know that they have the skills that match the scope of the work?

- How do you represent the logic between different tasks; that is, how do you display which tasks are logical prerequisites of their successors?

- How do you represent and manage the uncertainty associated both with the time taken to complete an individual task and the cumulative effect of this uncertainty across all the tasks in the work you're planning and executing?

- How do you know how much of which type of resource you'll need at each stage of getting the work done?

- How do you recognise a resource overload and its consequence for successful completion of the work?

- How do you synchronise different streams of work to meet each other's needs at all major milestones?

Hopefully, from these questions, you have some fresh insights into the process of taming the stern taskmaster that is time. Ignore these challenges and the only real hope for your

13. OPTIMISATION: Focusing your Efforts

organisation's success is that your competitors are worse than you are. Such a hope is no way to build a sustainable business.

Remember the maxim, though, that more than half of a good answer is a powerful question. The questions above are as powerful as they come when what's at stake is a meaningful step change in performance, more satisfied customers and happier, more fulfilled people in your teams.

RESOURCE MANAGEMENT

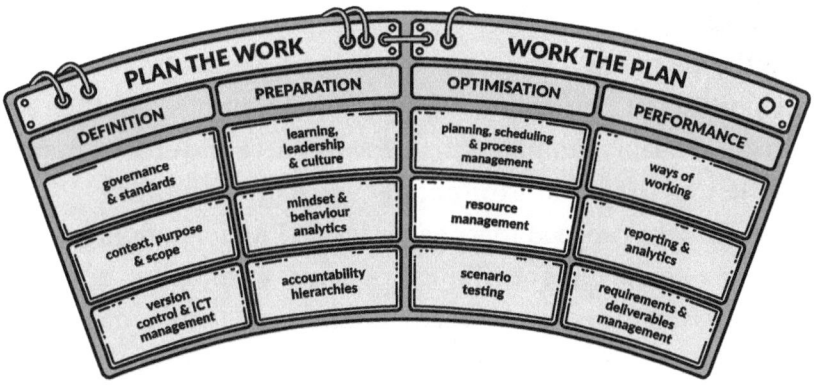

Resource management is the means by which you mobilise and demobilise your resources to achieve a defined piece of work. In most organisations I've worked with, there is quite some attention paid to the variety of positions that exist in the budget, staffing profiles, business-case documents, production routings and the like. These roles are filled whether for 'business as usual' or for projects.

The most common way they appear is as an entry in a

spreadsheet. They fit under the columns for 'resource type', 'name', 'cost' and 'cost centre', along with other columns—drifting away to the right—with intervals of days, weeks or months, depending on who will be using the data, and to what end. In many cases, some of the date columns will be blank for a while and then start to get filled, indicating that this particular resource (or the class of resource represented by a group of rows in the spreadsheet) ramps up over time.

Often each of the columns and rows is totalled providing a result in terms of units, dollars and time. Some organisations take a more complex or sophisticated approach and load this spreadsheet data into software applications. These, in turn, relate the resource data to other software applications such as accounting, procurement, scheduling, skill types and the like. You are probably familiar with these resource and cost exercises, whether on projects or for annual budget preparations.

Before we proceed to a deeper level of understanding about resource management, though, I have found that different people using the same words connect to the management of work in different ways. So while I'm not concerned that a client organisation use my exact language, it's important you understand, for the purposes of this book, how I'm using the following concepts:

Capability: The ability to perform or achieve certain actions or outcomes through a set of controllable and measurable faculties, features, functions, processes or services.

Resource: An asset capable of creating value through work,

13. OPTIMISATION: Focusing your Efforts

generally under the broad classification of human, material, financial and information.

Resource type: The classification of a resource using structured data as defined by the organisation's resource-type taxonomy.

Position: A role within an organisation that belongs to a node in its hierarchy that has, as a minimum, a manager, a start date, end date, capability and, often but not necessarily, associated cost and revenue.

Position assignment: The assigning of a resource to any given position, with matching capability, for no longer than the duration of the position and which, given the requisite authority, may cost and/or deliver revenue that could be more or less than that budgeted in the position.

Schedule: A sequence of tasks that includes, as a minimum, each task's description, predecessor(s), successor(s), resource type(s), effort by resource type and duration.

Schedule assignment: The assigning of a resource to a task in a schedule.

With these definitions clear in your mind, I would like to share a story that I think could have a consequence with as huge a productivity breakthrough for knowledge workers as the Toyota Production System had for manufacturing.

Being there isn't the same as doing it

The project I want to highlight was one that was going well. We had several successful go-lives behind us, each one setting new benchmarks within the industry. A colleague of mine was doing a piece of work for the upcoming release to see what level of resourcing it would need, then comparing that with the budgeted positions due to be submitted for funding approval by the board.

Essentially, he was comparing the total number of position-hours by resource type with the total number of scheduled-hours for that same resource type. I challenged him to put the dollars into his equation and to explore the question from a slightly different angle. Put simply, I was keen to have him answer the following: of all the money being invested in resourcing this release, how much of it was represented in the tasks in the schedule?

In his first cut of the numbers I was stunned to see that it was as low as 15%! After a second look, I figured there were many resources in the calculation that had project functions not represented in schedules. These included the project management office, solution delivery and the like.

'Okay,' I said, 'let's just take that class of resource that has nothing to do other than what is described on their schedules—the analysts.' I told him I wasn't particularly concerned about what type of analyst: finance, marketing, supply, HR or maintenance. The general principle would be that all analysts have all of their work, other than filling in a timesheet, articulated in the schedule.

13. OPTIMISATION: Focusing your Efforts

To my huge surprise, the schedule density—the ratio of the schedule-cost to the position-cost—turned out, over the year-long period of the release to be between 34% and 38% . By my rough calculation, using a very conservative blended rate for the difference between that number and the 80% loading I typically use for determining capacity limits, the dollar value lost in the ether was north of $100 million. So you can see, just being there *at work* isn't the same as doing the work!

This was a staggering revelation. I reasoned that even if one took into account the nature of the unevenness of the distribution of the work over time, as well as the inefficiencies that arose as a natural consequence of the geographical spread of the project, the number we were talking about was very large, and warranted deeper investigation. And remember, this was a program of work that had set new world-class benchmarks in terms of the time and cost required to successfully deliver release after release.

It brought to mind the idea I had encountered in manufacturing, when the great pioneers of the Toyota Production System asked, 'If it only takes a matter of minutes for a part to be produced at any given work centre, how come we have three to four months of stock on hand?'

Aggregation and the law of large numbers

Imagine for a moment the demand for structural engineers for our Sydney Opera House project. In one stream of work, the demand is eight hours on Monday, three hours on Tuesday, five hours on Wednesday, six hours on Thursday and then back to eight hours on Friday. In another stream of work, the same skill type is required, but the schedule shows no need for work on Monday, four hours on Tuesday, three hours on Wednesday, one hour on Thursday and nothing on Friday.

On average, one person could do all the work, as no day has more than eight hours of work in total. Often though, there will be two people on the job, as the manager for each stream will not be satisfied they will have the resource available when needed.

Such waste is the inevitable price we pay when the demand for the resource is potentially constrained by the supply, coupled to anxiety about the uncertainty of availability. This anxiety leads to just-in-case levels of resourcing.

Now, multiply our simple example by ten and add in the complicating factor from our schedules—the timing of the tasks were estimates, and sometimes the demand could be significantly more, and on other occasions equal to or less than those times articulated. Now add the complicating factor of dependencies between tasks and across workstreams. What to make of all this uncertainty?

If we were to resource each workstream to the level required to address the maximum demand on any given day, we would have vast numbers of people sitting idle much of the time, If, by contrast, we only resource up to a level of average demand, we would have periods of spikes in demand where the supply-side constraint causes an inevitable delay in completion of the work.

Fortunately, the laws of mathematics come to our rescue, and in particular the law of large numbers. In probability theory,

13. OPTIMISATION: Focusing your Efforts

the central limit theorem states:

> Given certain conditions, the arithmetic mean of a sufficiently large number of iterates of independent random variables, each with a well-defined expected value and well defined variance, will be approximately normally distributed, regardless of the underlying distribution.

In simple terms, applied to our example, the theorem says that no matter how varied the demand is for our engineers, on average, when all the tasks are taken together, the distribution of the demand will be in the shape of the classic bell curve. This fact makes the planning of supply to meet demand significantly easier than if each workstream and each resource working on it were treated as separate variables.

To take advantage of this power of aggregation, then, two necessary conditions must be met. The first is to have a signalling system correctly assigning resources to tasks according to a dynamic assessment of their priority. Such signalling is provided through the innovation of 'buffer management' in the Critical Chain Project Management methodology (see Chapter 9). The second necessary condition is the ability to match the 'demand for resources' articulated on the schedule with the 'supply of resources' articulated in the database of capabilities.

Practically capable of doing work

So, let's get practical. How do you better manage resources to take advantage of the power of two very fundamental principles:

aggregation and constraints?

It's relatively simple to get away without defining standards in a small group, knowing that Kelly will do this and Ian will do that. But as the complexity increases—and, let's face it, it gets complex quickly—you'll be better served by having a means of defining capability so a computer can read it. Structured data enables a matching of what is being called for from the work schedules to whom or what is available to be deployed to get that work done.

Over many years, I have found that getting the taxonomy of your resources right is one of the most important pieces of work you can do to set a solid foundation for a meaningful improvement in business performance.

For our purposes, I'd like to focus on how we get to a point where we can represent the resource capability in a standard way. That means data can be structured for a computer to gauge if a request is reasonable, given the resources you have at your disposal.

In Table 2, you'll see an example of an engineering environment that defines the following: what the domain is; the discipline within that domain; a specific skill within that discipline; a speciality, if there is one; the level of organisational hierarchy they belong to (front line, supervisor, manager and executive being the most common); and the organisation of which they are a part or, alternatively, what P&L they belong to.

In many ways, this definition is no different from creating a code for an item of stock in a warehouse. Understand the code and you know what the item is, where it belongs, how many of them are in stock, what we need to do to get more of them, and

13. OPTIMISATION: Focusing your Efforts

Domain	Discipline	Skill/Role	Speciality	Org level	Organisation
Answers the question: went to the school of?	This would be the major within the given discipline	Answers the question about the type of the discipline	Necessary if there is a highly specialised skill set needed for a task	If not frontline worker. Note: word 'specialist' often equivalent to frontline worker	What business unit or vendor the resource belongs to
Eng-	Elect-	Des-		Lead-	EPCM
Required	Optional	Optional	Optional	Optional	Optional

Table 2: An engineering environment defined

so on. Defining capability in this way can be seen as defining a stock code for knowledge workers. There's no reason, then, why it couldn't equally be used to define a piece of equipment, such as a crane, or materials such as electrical cable.

Once we have this idea nailed, we can assign these codes to roles within a project or the organisation, as well as to tasks in a schedule. If the same coding is used to define the capability of any given individual—who will in all likelihood have more than one capability—then we have satisfied the necessary and sufficient conditions of being able to establish a match between demand from our scheduling system and supply from our system of capability management. The implications are enormous. We can know, reliably, what can be done, by when and for how much—at any level of the enterprise.

Finding constraints and collaborating to optimise output

Let's return to the world of knowledge workers in large complex projects. We now know about the power of aggregation. But what signalling system do we need to ensure that in our quest for productivity improvement we are constantly looking to increase throughput and reduce costs without sacrificing quality or due-date performance?

To identify these, the planner must know their load versus capacity, which assumes minimum requisite standards for articulating schedules (load) and defining capabilities (capacity). Implementing these standards is a minimum necessary condition of getting any kind of step change in productivity improvement.

Your information system should be designed in such a way as to enable you to instantly report on all resource types where load versus capacity is greater than 80% over the next planning horizon. Why only 80%? As a rule of thumb, if demand is greater than 80% of supply, you increase the risk of turbulence. Demand doesn't come in a neat line at 80% of capacity—there will be peaks and troughs. Running at 80% of aggregate capacity allows for a degree of smoothing. Thus, if the load is shown as less than 80%, it means you have resource capacity available to do useful work. If not, you need to get more supply.

Once you have a good handle on the data, one way of tapping into existing capacity to solve the problem of resource bottlenecks is to query that data for anyone in the resource pool who has ever held a like position, and establish where they are now. If they are still in the resource pool, establish their current assignment and test if their position can be backfilled. In other words, can someone else, a non-constraint, be assigned to the constraint's existing role and thus free them to do *only that* which *only they* can do? (We call this the 'double-only' question.) After all, constraints are simply resources whose demand outstrips their supply. Finding ready supply within your existing resource pool is a fine way of maintaining the rate at which value is created.

If adding resources in the above manner is either not possible or not enough to close the capacity gap, you need to initiate your recruitment process. It's worth noting that backfilling is a lot easier than one thinks. The principle about constraints applies here. Where there is a constraint, by definition, non-constraints have capacity available. The productivity magic happens when non-constraints collaborate to support a focus on getting the constraint's priorities done at any given point in time.

The flipside of looking for the bottleneck is to identify unconstrained positions—for argument's sake, all resource types where load versus capacity is less than 50% over the planning horizon. List the names of all those people on the project whose assignment relates to the unconstrained positions. Ask if the unconstrained people have ever held a position or have a capability that could alleviate a current or future constrained position. If the answer is yes, then reassign that person to the constrained position. If no, the choice is either reskilling (training the person to do another job) or off-boarding (take the person off the project team).

These actions probably sound quite technical, and thinking through them is not everyone's cup of tea. But this is a big issue within the domain of resource management and optimisation. What I hope you get from thinking about it is that there's no substitute for the discipline of applying your standards for planning, scheduling and capabilities in a rigorous and proactive way. It is guaranteed to sustainably deliver continuous improvement in business performance.

At all levels of work, your people know what they have to do, and know that sufficient resource has been provided to get the work done on time and to quality. That goes a long way to fulfilling the criteria for *Just Work*, because you know what you have called for is both reasonable and possible, given the human and material resources you place at their disposal.

13. OPTIMISATION: Focusing your Efforts

SCENARIO TESTING

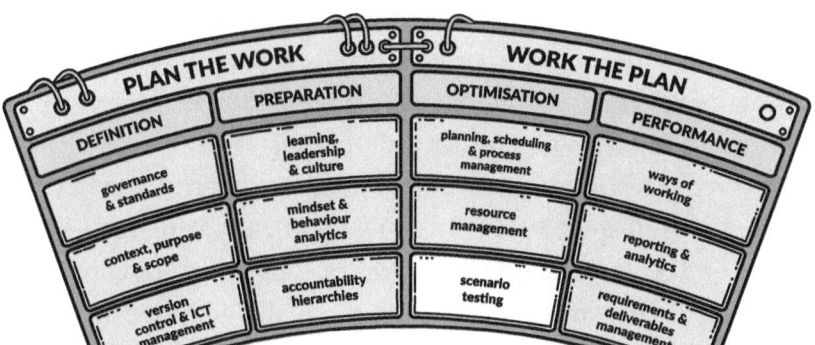

Classically, there are three levers one can pull when looking to optimise work: scope, cost and schedule. That is, you can determine what's included and excluded from the scope of work, how much resource you will provide to get the work done, and determine when it will be completed.

Let's have a look at two examples to illustrate these points from apparently different contexts—the Olympic Games, and the development of a new oil field.

First, the Olympics. The timing of the opening ceremony is set. So too are all the sports the athletes will compete for. We thus know what venues will be required, as well as when they'll need to be completed. Ideally, the host city runs a regional sports contest a year or so before the Olympics to ensure a time buffer is available to perfect the arrangements and iron out the bugs. Thus, provided the dates can be met for the planned events, there is no good reason to complete early. An optimum plan would have the last detail of the construction plan complete the day before the first event welcomes the athletes and spectators—just in time.

On the other hand, in the case of a new oil field, for every day the schedule is early, the project brings the owners millions of dollars of revenue. Applying additional resources to accelerate the schedule offers a handsome dividend.

Scenario testing is, thus, what you do to determine what will happen with respect to the overall goal under various schedules, scopes and costs. While smart, powerful computing could produce many scenarios—and we could test them all—what we are really concerned with is those few which qualify as plausible and relevant, including the best and worse cases.

Determining those scenarios is up to the project leadership team, as only they can assess what is reasonable and possible, given the resources at their disposal. With their teams, they can look at the feasibility and consequence of ramping resources up or down, changing the sequence of work, or determining what scope is included, rejected or left for later. Each of these scenarios will have their own costs, opportunity costs and risks, all of which have to be evaluated within the broader context of the organisation.

Scenario testing avoids the thinking trap that there's a single, silver-bullet answer to optimising the costs and benefits of the project. But having invested the time and effort to go through a few different plausible and relevant scenarios, the team becomes far more aware of what perils and opportunities may lie ahead.

13. OPTIMISATION: Focusing your Efforts

Agile and active is the way forward

The world will guarantee that things, inevitably, do not turn out as planned. But organisations that adopt this approach to planning will be the ones agile enough to adapt to whatever fortune may throw at them.

With the definition, preparation and optimisation complete, you're likely raring to find out how to get things done. For in the words of Bengali poet Rabindranath Tagore, 'You can't cross the sea merely by standing and staring at the water.'

So now, the orchestra is waiting in the green room in their tuxes and dresses, instruments warmed up and ready. The audience is filing in. You've checked the score and have the baton in hand.

It's performance time.

Questions for OPTIMISATION

1. How do you measure the demand you have for resources and the supply available to do the work? What's the difference worth?

2. What standards do you use for scheduling and resource management?

3. How do you go about testing the impact of plausible and relevant scenarios?

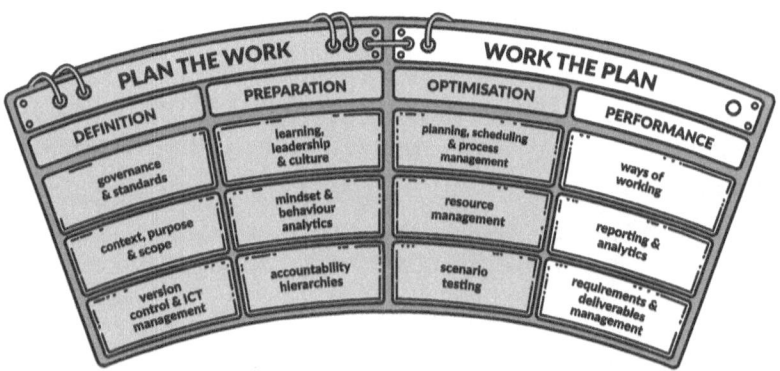

Figure 19: Work the plan: Performance

Chapter 14
PERFORMANCE: *Hitting All the High Notes*

A really great talent finds its happiness in execution.

Johann Wolfgang von Goethe

BEFORE LEAPING INTO DETAILS of execution management, it's important to first hold in mind the nature of the work being done. Not in terms of what type, but rather the time-horizon for which the manager in question is given discretion to use their judgement.

The barman at the Sydney Opera House will be interested in today's work, which includes receiving, counting and displaying deliveries of food and beverages before turning to serve patrons. On the other hand, The CEO of Sydney Opera House Trust, while resident in today's world, must envision a mental space that looks to the next decade and beyond, spending hundreds of millions of budgeted dollars on running the day-to-day while implementing the strategic program. The whole idea of execution management is something quite different for both of these characters; so, too, are the processes by which their work gets done.

To return to the massive SAP implementation (first introduced in Chapter 5), it was absolutely clear that this was not some continuous improvement exercise looking merely to enhance an existing system of management. It was a radical rewriting of the rule book. The hypothesis was that 80% of business benefits come from 20% of its processes. So why not apply maximum effort into doing those processes extremely well, in a simple and standard way?

The executive team understood the critical need to simplify processes. Besides reducing costs and maximising revenue, simplification and standardisation was the means by which the organisation would rein in risk. They understood how growth amplifies complexity geometrically. Different people, business units and functions doing their work in different ways, in different places around the globe, meant too much time spent reinventing the wheel, fixing failure and firefighting to effectively address root causes of underperformance.

The vision was realised by the unfettered will of the CEO and his leadership team to make this simplification a reality. More than five years after we started our involvement in the project, the successor CEO, giving his first round of interviews about the annual results drew attention to the work done to turn his predecessor's intentions into reality. He talked enthusiastically of the scale of the contribution the transformational program had made to a result well in excess of market expectations.

How did this big-picture intention articulated by the original CEO affect ways of working between the disparate parts of the organisation to deliver on the long-term growth of the

14. PERFORMANCE: *Hitting All the High Notes*

business? Such a bold and simple—even obvious—idea as simplification and standardisation of processes and data needed a similarly bold and simple way of executing work. Yet how to do it was far from obvious. If this transformation was going to be delivered on time and to budget, it would need an execution engine the likes of which the organisation had never seen.

For even when people were aligned with the goal of the project, it wasn't the case that senior executives of the operating divisions would roll over and do what this whole of enterprise initiative called on them to do. They would need facts to justify the deployment of their resources to the project. They would need a clear understanding of what demands were being made on their time by the overall business, as well as those of their own organisation, the results for which they were accountable. They needed to know how those demands would be communicated, and squared off against the realities of other priorities on the ground. They would need to know the principles informing the decision-making and how these decisions then got made.

Despite being an enterprise-wide project of major significance and the CEO's signature initiative, the competing demands on the divisional resources couldn't be ignored. The presidents had businesses to run, and were not given a free pass from the CEO on meeting their goals. One executive likened the feeling to changing the tyre while the car is in motion.

To add to the complexity, at least three releases could be running concurrently. Each business unit would be effected in different ways, depending upon which release cycle their unit was a part. While one release might be in the process of testing, another could be in the build phase and yet another in the early phases of conceptual and detailed design. Each had its rhythm, milestones and the scope of what needed to get done.

For the high-end parts of the solution design, it was often the case that solution architects and subject-matter experts were shared between the different projects making up the program of work. Being a global project, it had the added feature of including people from every corner of the world, with differing national, professional and business-unit cultures.

It was clear from the project's early days that success would depend on standard ways of working within the project and facing into the business. The hundreds of thousands of discrete packets of work would ultimately require more than 6,000 project positions. Each would need to be resourced according to the demand of the schedules we would have to create. Those schedules would be selected after running the few plausible and relevant scenarios needed to accommodate the inevitable competition between scope, cost and schedule.

For effective execution management, those of us accountable for the planning and performance of the work understood we would need the courage to step beyond anything we had in our filing system and reimagine a whole new way of working. We had to completely transform the processes by which the work was planned, scheduled and executed. Uncertainty and negative feedback were our friends, not the enemy. They allowed us to think deeply about the 'as well as' case rather than the 'instead of', if the given situation called for two seemingly contradictory approaches.

14. PERFORMANCE: *Hitting All the High Notes*

On many an occasion, we had to suspend the usual business rules, reconfigure the system of measurement and attend to the learning needs of those coming to grips with the new way of working. From the senior leadership of the steering committee down to the most humble developer, we had to provide an answer to the fundamental question of every single person on the project: 'What is the most important thing for me to do today to advance the goal of the project?' We were living and breathing the answer to the question, 'If success were guaranteed, what bold step would you take?' Except, success was not guaranteed.

In some ways, this section of the book has so far been talking about the scales and arpeggios of the musician. Constant practice is necessary to gain the fluency required to make music. The goal is not to get better and better at playing scales and arpeggios, but rather to use the mastery this practice creates to delight and inspire the audience. Ways of working is how we play the music.

WAYS OF WORKING

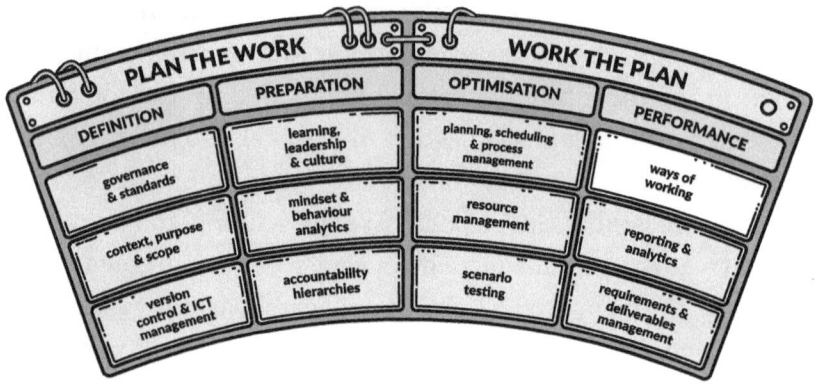

I am a great believer in the daily rhythm as the foundation of good operating discipline. However, the 'daily toolbox' meeting is the result of much longer planning cycles.

For any initiative, a Foundation Workshop (see Chapter 15) is necessary to provide all key stakeholder representatives an opportunity to come together to form the 'system in the room'. This provides the leadership of the project a crucial opportunity to hold a conversation around the topic of ways of working.

A necessary condition for enduring success is to give each of these people a voice, an opportunity to be heard, and to learn how different points of view need to be accommodated. Your project must also align with the vision and mission of the organisation as a whole and the set of values it practises.

To solve the problem of underachievement and cultivate high performance, it is of immense value to take the relatively short time necessary to do the work of building alignment. People who understand the purpose of the initiative, the prin-

14. PERFORMANCE: Hitting All the High Notes

ciples on which it is based and whose personal values are aligned to that of the project will deliver far more from head, heart and hand than those who have no such understanding.

Below are some of the principles used to guide the project I described earlier in this chapter. Articulating a set of principles to guide sense- and decision-making proved to be far more effective in leading and managing people than if we had resorted to the use of policies and procedures for every eventuality. Empowering people to make decisions is highly motivating, but empowerment shouldn't be in a vacuum. Governing principles are required to support sound reasoning.

Business case: Always ask if the decision helps or detracts from the overall business case. If it doesn't help, what could be done to make it so; if it turns out to be irrelevant, then why ask for the decision at all?

Adopt, don't adapt: Simplification and standardisation are predicated on the adoption by all, not adapting the solution to replicate complex legacy customisations.

Keep it simple: Reduce things to make them as simple as they can be, and no simpler.

Manage scope: Actively control scope creep and ensure that all required scope is accounted for.

Widespread, effective change management: Know the enormity of what you are asking people to give up and take on, and engage with the process to help minimise resistance while maximising support for the change.

Project governance and front-end loading: Make sure all the structures and processes of governance are in place and use them to ensure that planning is given its full weight in the overall management of the endeavour.

Process discipline: Measure and reward excellence in maintaining a disciplined approach to the planning and performance of work, including the timely contribution to all aspects of the system of management.

Armed with principles such as these, you can develop standing rules for meetings. The example below is simple, but powerful. For example, if people agree to abide by the rules before you start a workshop, it becomes easy for the facilitator or other participants to bring a maverick into line. Without such simple devices, maintaining focus is that much harder. As you can see from the example below, these rules need not be complex:

- The goal is to explore all perspectives.
- It is a big group and needs to be facilitated.
- Use the parking lot for questions which cannot be solved within the time and scope boundaries of this forum. Come back to it later rather than let it derail relevant conversations.
- Be open minded.
- Be on time.
- Be respectful.
- Switch off your phone. Using it is disrespectful of those in the room. If you have an emergency, please let us know, and exit the room when you have a call.

14. PERFORMANCE: *Hitting All the High Notes*

- Listen actively.
- Share your knowledge.
- Keep on track with the agenda—both in time and content.
- What needs to be achieved to make this a great meeting/workshop?

Running better meetings

Many people consider meetings the bane of their working lives. At best, a necessary evil; at worst, a sapper of both time and motivation. But with a little forethought it doesn't have to be that way. Below is a sample of a cycle of operational meetings for a typical project using TOC's Critical Chain method. Such a plan can help deliver the full promise of better ways to do better work by focusing on what really matters—at the right time when you can do something about it.

Daily toolbox meeting

Purpose: Set priorities for the day
Horizon: 1 day
Attendees: Everyone on the specific workstream
Agenda: Review of fever charts; Operating discipline reports; Task assignments; Task updates; Issue resolution or escalation; Help needed

Buffer management meeting

Purpose: Form a project-wide consensus on systemic bottlenecks; develop alternatives for resolution of the above; provide integration meeting and leadership team with alternatives for action

Horizon: This week and next

Attendees: Workstream leads; project controls; system integrator lead; project manager; project director

Agenda: Pipeline view; portfolio view; project control view (penetrating tasks); penetrating chain view; resource view (load versus capacity); constrained resource assignments; flow trend; escalated tasks; change control submissions

Integration meeting

Purpose: Identify issues critical to integration of all process streams and major project milestones

Horizon: The next major milestone

Attendees: Integration lead; solution delivery lead; OCM lead; system integrator lead; project manager; project director

Agenda: Buffer management meeting report and recommendations; pipeline view; resource portal (load versus capacity); flow trend; escalated tasks; help needed analysis

14. PERFORMANCE: *Hitting All the High Notes*

Leadership team meeting

Purpose: Consider alternatives developed from buffer management and integration team meeting and execute

Horizon: Whole of project

Attendees: Leadership team

Agenda: Buffer management meeting report; integration team meeting report and recommendations; pipeline view; resource portal (load versus capacity)

Although this list of meetings is specific to Critical Chain Project Management, rather than a definitive guide to all meetings, it does illustrate how you can set up a regular cadence of essential meetings to ensure decisions get made.

By thinking at the beginning of the initiative exactly what containers will be created for the different types of meeting—with their different purposes, frequency, attendees, content and horizon—a meaningful contribution is made to allaying the anxiety arising from people not knowing how to deal with any given issue. For whatever the need, there is a forum, it meets regularly, it is empowered to make decisions based on the best available data and, where necessary, the correct escalation mechanisms are in place.

There is an important and further aspect to consider about having a clearly constructed meeting cycle, and a steady cadence to the rhythm of work performance. With a set of agreed containers for communication at all levels—team, phase, release and program—you are able to work 'in flow' when it comes to completing your deliverables. Gaps in calendars should not be an opportunity to attend ad hoc, unstructured meetings, solving the crisis of someone else's bad planning. These gaps should be times to work uninterrupted on thought-intensive knowledge tasks, while remaining in sync with your team and the project or business as usual.

In the most productive teams I've worked with, such time for such work has been institutionalised. One leader of an organisation, headquartered in Singapore with operations around the globe, had the courage to designate Tuesday, Wednesday and Thursday mornings from 10am to 1pm 'flow-time'. This suited their interactions with the rest of the world, as Europe, Africa and the Americas were not yet at work and Australia and New Zealand could be dealt with before 10am. He promised no one would get in trouble if they declined to service a request during flow-time, and that he would do the work of briefing the senior executives from round the company as to what he was trying to achieve.

He talked of it as being the sacred hours of the day, when you had the right to get on, unhindered, with what you were tasked to do. People were encouraged to switch off any devices capable of interrupting their flow: mobile phones, instant messaging, emails and the like. A quiet, library-like atmosphere was encouraged, and simple rules of etiquette put in place to ensure those who didn't want any interruptions were left to get on with their work.

At first there were many sceptics who wondered if the team could be so disciplined, let alone be bold enough to 'just say

14. PERFORMANCE: *Hitting All the High Notes*

no' to some very senior executives making noisy and insistent demands on their time. But just as the Chairman of the Philharmonic doesn't interrupt the performance to ask about the plans for next season's concerts, so too should you orchestrate your workplace to allow you to complete your work with minimal distraction.

In our cycle of meetings, we should include the all-important time to reflect on what is not productive. Building the habit of learning by planning, doing, checking and acting creates a virtuous cycle of continuous improvement. Adopting productive work practices brings the possibility of significantly increasing the quantity of what we get done, the quality we produce and the joy we get from doing our best. Better ways of working lead to better results and the chance to shine.

REPORTING AND ANALYTICS

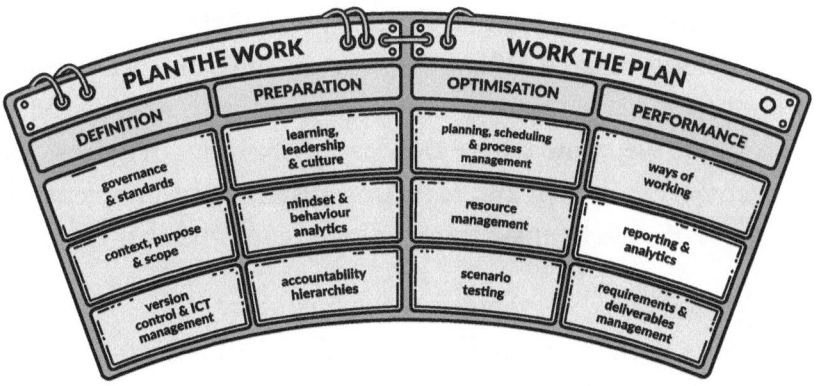

As powerful and valuable as correct measurement is, relying on measures to fully understand what is actually going on is much like reading a menu to understand the taste of a meal. Whatever we measure is an abstraction from the fullness of what is being measured, and we must be on the lookout to ensure we don't mistake the menu for the meal. Having said that, reporting on progress is fundamental to the delivery of high-performance outcomes. And the insights derived from good, solid data can make the difference between an initiative's success or failure. What, then, should we be measuring in the world of work?

The trouble with most measures I come across is their provenance. They almost always arise from a worldview grounded in a reductionist approach to managing complexity. Assuming the sum of the parts is equal to the whole is risky, yet it forms the very foundation of measures used in the vast majority of businesses whose core is in manufacturing, supply chains and projects. You need look no further than the old cost-accountant diehards of absorption costing and earned value to appreciate we haven't come far in terms of understanding how systems behave. When the primary measures we use are geared towards a mindset that erroneously equates activity with value, we know where the enemy of productivity resides.

Any measurement and reporting system worth implementing must be able to answer the following questions:

- What is the profitability of the business?
- What is the profitability of an individual business unit or project?
- Is a product or service attractive for us to make and sell?

14. PERFORMANCE: *Hitting All the High Notes*

- Is a customer attractive for us to do business with?
- Should we make a given product or supply a given service ourselves, or buy it from another source?
- Should we make a particular investment?

The question arises as to what measures to put in place to encourage behaviours that do what's best for the business? Put another way, how to get everyone in the enterprise to see the whole, and not just their silo? For more than 15 years, I've been using the measures developed under the TOC constraint-accounting methodology (Figure 20) and have found them as powerful as they are simple. The three fundamental measures are Throughput (T), Operating Expense (OE) and Investment (I):

Throughput (T) is the value of sales less the costs directly associated with those sales, for example commissions. Accounting professionals call this measure 'contribution margin'. It expressly excludes labour costs that are a fixed part of the payroll.

Operating expense (OE) is defined as the total cost of fixed labour and all overheads.

Investment (I) is all value locked into fixed and current assets, including raw material, work in process and finished goods not yet invoiced.

When you deduct Operating Expense from Throughput, you're left with profit. And the ratio of profit to investment will yield the return on investment. It's important to understand these simple definitions, as all businesses exist to deliver a return on investment (ROI), or at least they're supposed to in the free-enterprise system.

Thus, to improve return on investment, you have three levers. You can increase throughput, decrease operating expense or decrease investment. Since both operating expense and investment are far more limited in their scope for reduction than throughput is for its scope for amplification, the priority should almost always be on finding ways to increase throughput. This insight, incidentally, is what makes TOC potentially so much more powerful than methodologies, such as Lean, when they are used, mistakenly, simply to reduce costs.

Instrumentation

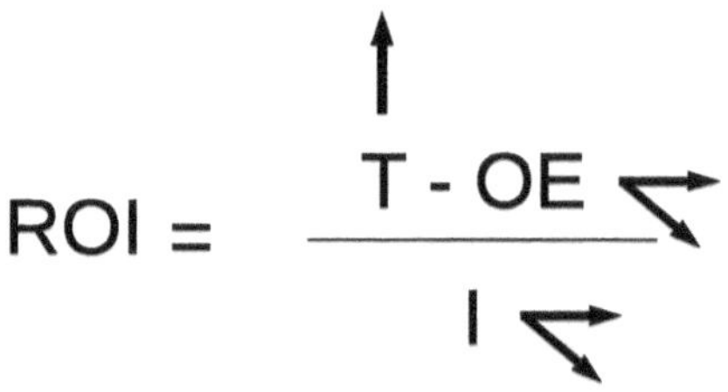

$$ROI = \frac{T - OE}{I}$$

T (Throughput) = sales minus variable costs
OE (Operating Expense) = labour plus overhead
I (Investment) = all money trapped in the system

Figure 20: Primary measures of the constraint accounting methodology

14. PERFORMANCE: *Hitting All the High Notes*

Due-date performance (DDP): A great way to improve throughput is to ensure you are always delivering to promise. Due-date performance is a measurement to tell everyone how reliable we are. Delivering people, parts and information to a work-front on time allows everyone to work in synch and minimise waste. Customers value reliability and often depend on superior due-date performance to maximise their profits. Often the value to the client of superior supplier reliability is such that as a consequence you can charge a premium for your products or services.

Lead-time (LT): Another great way to improve throughput is to deliver in shorter lead times than the market reasonably expects. In production environments, shorter lead times allow for less inventory held in the system, freeing up cash and providing the basis for competitive advantage. And with projects, a shorter lead time means a faster speed to market. The project's cost-burn stops, the benefits start flowing and—perhaps most importantly of all—the team can move on faster to the next big idea.

Quality (Q): Finally, in the pantheon of metrics, we must be sure to measure quality. The most useful way to do this is to understand how much rework is going on. If you can get it right the first time, people are not bogged down fixing errors, but are moving on to new value-adding work. Quality needs to be carefully thought through as an attribute of system design and not something to be inspected out. It is a verification, not a completion step.

From these six basic measures (T, OE, I, LT, DDP and Q), many more can be derived. But without these in place your value-creation engine is flying blind, without the instrumentation and control required to avoid the occasional crash. When you innovate, some crashes are inevitable. But who in their right mind would deliberately disable—or simply not install—the appropriate instruments that can help you set the right course and make adjustments as conditions change?

If you are going to have a serious go at improving return on investment, it's useful to report on some of the drivers of our core metrics to ensure people are focused on what matters. These metrics include:

Multitasking: How many open tasks have you got in front of you? The more open tasks in front of an individual, the higher the work in process and the more likely the flow of value will be log-jammed.

No updates: If assigned tasks are not updated in a timely fashion, it becomes very difficult to make sense of what is happening in the work environment. Effective decision-making is compromised.

Out-of-sequence work: Left to their own devices, people are notorious for cherry-picking the work they would like to do, or that work which will give them or their business unit an advantage (rather than the organisation as a whole). Doing work in the correct sequence is a prerequisite of coordinated efforts across functional silos and different workstreams, and must thus be measured to deliver synchronous flow.

14. PERFORMANCE: Hitting All the High Notes

Schedule assignments: When planning, the planner usually doesn't know the name of the person who is going to be called upon to do the work and thus uses a generic resource type. My recommendation is that two weeks out from the work having to be done, the assignee is selected and recorded in the system of record. Not knowing who is assigned to what piece of work means people arrive on any given day and get pulled frustratingly from pillar to post, or end up getting paid for performing the wrong work. Or perhaps worst of all, get paid for doing nothing, as no work is assigned to them.

Resource-load versus capacity: As the flow of value is dependent on constraints, it is important to understand load versus capacity—both at the level of generic interchangeable resource types, as well as at the level of individual-named task managers and participants. We can derive where a constraint is by understanding where the work in process sits; any build-up of work in process is a sure sign there is a bottleneck in front of it. It is, however, also valuable to find the constraint through analytical means—particularly as it can be done in a way that flags potential future bottlenecks in time to take remedial action.

Critical ratio: This metric records the rate at which work is being completed versus the rate at which the buffer of protective capacity is being consumed. It is an extraordinarily innovative way of knowing what is going to happen tomorrow rather than just recording what happened yesterday. As a lead indicator, it is invaluable in providing early warnings and enabling corrective action before it is too late. Lag indicators only tell you, after the fact that things have gone out of control.

Having such operational measures provides a sound basis for the analytics function. When putting them in place, ensure you measure trends—how they are doing over time. You don't necessarily have to achieve a given number to know you are improving. The trend can be your friend.

In our day, we have access to vast arrays of data which, when combined with machine learning and artificial intelligence, allow for powerful insights into performance. Of the thousands and even millions of transactions recorded every day in the designated system of record, the analysts can determine trends, and readily identify areas of high and low performance which would otherwise escape the human eye.

But, if the underpinning of this data is reductionist, don't be surprised if the behaviour it encourages is counter-productive. Be sure to provide those measures that encourage people at the local level to do what is best for the organisation as a whole.

14. PERFORMANCE: Hitting All the High Notes

REQUIREMENTS AND DELIVERABLES MANAGEMENT

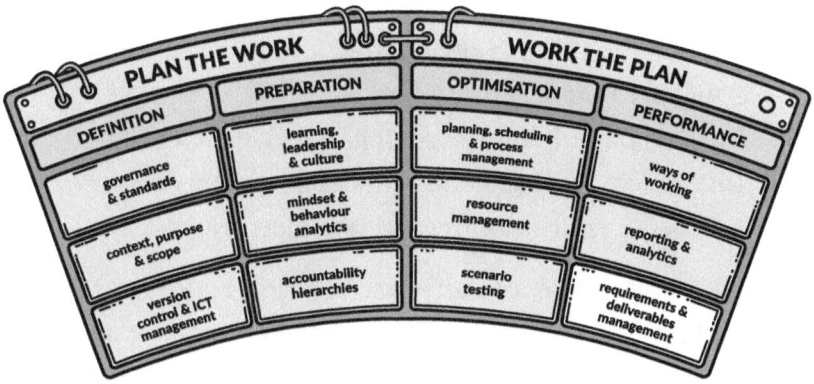

Why do we undertake the work we do in the world of projects? What need is being met? Seeing off a competitor? Satisfying a regulator? Turning an idea about an opportunity into a startup? Modernising a system of management for a productivity improvement? A typical sequence to turn an idea into value may look something like the list below:

- Someone has an idea that would be good for business, government, not-for-profit or academia
- Initial and supplementary approvals of time and money are granted and funds raised or made available
- A means is developed to govern any changes to scope, cost and schedule
- The costs, benefits and schedules are developed, and continuously refined
- User requirements are gathered and validated

- Functional specifications are developed
- Technical specifications are developed
- Deliverables are defined based on the requirements and specifications
- The business case is revalidated and its assumptions continuously monitored
- The design, build, test and deploy cycle are entered
- The project is closed out, with a learning review
- A benefits realisation review is undertaken

Whether you use an Agile or Waterfall approach to planning and performing the work, or indeed the many available variants of those concepts, the basic idea is pretty much the same. When some or all the steps above are left out, the result can be devastating for the outcome of the project. Performance suffers badly. We are so easily distracted by being buried in the doing of the work, or ashamed to admit the need for a rethink when, for whatever reason, the project is not going to plan that it is all too easy to allow momentum to defeat sound reason.

Hence, it is fundamental to the performance of successful projects that due consideration is given to how requirements and their deliverables are managed. Techniques such as the development of a requirements traceability matrix can be very powerful. It helps articulate dependencies between requirements and gives managers the opportunity to have clear visibility into what effect a change in one area will have on another. They can then make the trade-offs between time, scope and cost for any given change.

In addition, repetitive, successful performance comes about

14. PERFORMANCE: *Hitting All the High Notes*

when the schedule, deliverables and requirements are tied together. After all, a schedule is a means by which an instruction is given to do a sequence of work. This doesn't matter if it is articulated as a story point in an Agile endeavour or a bar on a Gantt chart in Waterfall. The principle is the same: the work is done to build a deliverable, which must function according to the need of a valid user requirement. The scheduling system should thus always articulate the end-to-end process—from conceptual design through to signoff by the functional owner or their delegated representative as meeting the original or suitably controlled changes to their requirements.

Finally, I can't overemphasise the need for robust change control of requirements and their associated deliverables. As the great pugilist Mike Tyson put it, 'Everyone has a plan until they get punched in the face.' Small, controlled course corrections, undertaken when the 'punch in the face' arrives, save thousands of miles of course correction required if the initial adjustment is ignored. A heading of only one degree off your target describes a bigger and bigger arc as the journey progresses. Far better to gently adjust the rudder as soon as the deviation is known.

Questions for PERFORMANCE

1. What meetings do you run? How often do you run them? Who attends? What's on the agenda? How do you capture and execute the action items arising?

2. What recurring issues are the topic of ad hoc conversations

which don't yet have a forum? How would you go about incorporating them into existing rhythms and routines or create a new forum?

3. What instrumentation and controls do you have on your value-creation engine? How well are they serving you?

4. Are you satisfied with the way you manage requirements and deliverables? How do you link requirements to specifications and deliverables?

Part 4
How to Change?

New Problems, New Thinking

The success of an intervention depends on the interior condition of the intervener.

Bill O'Brien

'WE CANNOT SOLVE our problems, said Einstein, 'with the same thinking we used when we created them.' And as our age is like no other before—in that we have the power to make unprecedented progress as a species, alongside our ability to create a mass extinction event—it seems legitimate to ask exactly how we generate new thinking, fit to solve today's problems.

We humans face massive challenges. In no particular order, we may wonder what might really reverse climate change and ecological devastation? How can we dramatically reduce poverty, war, terrorism, cybercrime, refugees, failed states, corruption, banking failures, debt crises, suicide? And of course technology comes along in the form of machine learning, artificial intelligence, advanced robotics, and we wonder what's going to happen to all the jobs this technology replaces, the social cohesion it shreds and the power it gives the authoritarian state? The list seems endless and can easily lead to despair or helpless indifference. If progress is to stand a chance, we must find new answers to these intense and persistent questions.

So how do we develop fresh thinking capable of generating real and effective innovations for our most difficult and deeply systemic challenges? By what means do we access a deeper sense of the direction of our path through the complexity of a life lived in this perilous age? In plumbing the depths of the source of our own innovation, how do we come to know how to make our fullest contribution? What compass helps us effectively navigate the work of making the world a better place for everyone?

From hell on earth to paradise city

With my rational engineer's mind, I used to follow a traditional rationalist approach. Proceed from A (hell on earth) to B (paradise city) in a linear, well-reasoned and logical manner. There was great appeal in creating the chain of cause and effect from the one to the other. While I was good enough at identifying necessary conditions for the journey from A to B, though, I repeatedly discovered my ideas were not sufficient when it came to the complexity bundled up with people. Was there a way, I wondered, to combine the benefits of the rational argument with the unpredictability of the emotional elements at play—to sense what was present and intuit connections? How best to cope with the power of free will? And, of course, free won't!

Almost a decade ago I discovered, in 'Theory U', a powerful way to think about these vexing questions. My hope is this framework for innovation, developed amongst others by MIT's Otto Scharmer, will encourage you to think and feel (if you don't already) that the universe actually wants to help. Rather than complaining there is nothing to be done, the truth is, when you listen in deeply and do what the world calls on you to do—that is, to follow your highest and most noble vision—help typically pops up everywhere. If this sounds a little esoteric, let me backtrack a little.

You may recall from the introduction that I first went to the National Productivity Institute in Pretoria in 1997 seeking advice on how I could improve productivity in the commercial refrigeration business I ran. I was given two books. In my left hand was placed *The Goal* by Eli Goldratt and, in the right, I was handed *The Fifth Discipline* by Peter Senge.

I had no idea then that these two books would contribute so significantly to the framework I have developed: the Ensemble Way. Writing this book some two decades on, I am reminded of a quote from T.S. Eliot, 'We shall not cease from exploration, and the end of all our exploring will be to arrive where we started and know the place for the first time.'

The productivity tide to practically lift all ships

At that time, Goldratt's Theory of Constraints, as outlined in *The Goal*, seemed more immediately practical and able to solve a particular and real problem I had. Due to a fortunate set of business circumstances, our company had secured an unprecedented order book, yet we had no idea how we could get it done in the time available without killing everyone through overwork.

The success of that first endeavour in South Africa, where we raised our margins by more than a third, taught me how the tide of productivity could raise all ships. Emboldened by this, at the very end of the last millennium, I emigrated to Sydney with my family to set up shop as a process consultant.

In 2006, six years on from starting my own company, offering consulting services based on these insights, I was happy to still be around doing what I love to do. But I couldn't figure out how to sustain the changes we were calling for over the long term. How to go beyond the immediate problem we were hired to solve, and make the process of improvement self-sustaining? As long as there was a sponsor within the client organisation who got what we were talking about, and they were prepared to use their fierce will to make the changes stick, we were good to go.

But the excitement my colleagues and I felt about the transformations we were trying to achieve didn't seem to be shared by our clients beyond what would be considered the norms of the existing culture's appetite for the new. And even with the sponsors who 'got it', we weren't sure if a real transformation would be sustained after our engagement.

Learning about fate and destiny

Back then, it was quite common for business people to subscribe to email digests. One fateful day, I received one from the American Production and Inventory Control Society (APICS). The thread I was following—about how to make transformational change endure—referenced Peter Senge's book *The Dance of Change*, a retrospective of ten years of his team's endeavours to implement the principles and practices first articulated in *The Fifth Discipline*, which itself explored ideas around organisations that learn.

As a keen follower of *The Fifth Discipline*, but a dilettante to be sure, I read the new volume, almost 600 pages, cover to cover. When I finally put it down, I recall thinking that this whole change management and transformation business was not for amateurs. For a few days, I let that idea germinate. About a week or so later, I found myself drawn to the business section of a large Sydney bookstore, wondering if Senge had written anything else since *The Dance of Change*.

At that moment, destiny came knocking at my door in the form of a book called *Presence*, co-authored by Senge with Otto Scharmer, Joe Jaworski and Betty Sue Flowers. I cracked the covers and found a quote that powerfully articulated what I had been sensing but hadn't yet been able to formulate. The metaphor of the machine, the Newtonian world of the clockwork universe, had been replaced by the metaphor of nature:

> It's common to say that trees come from seeds. But how could a tiny seed create a huge tree? Seeds do not contain the resources needed to grow a tree. These must come from the medium or environment within which the tree grows. But the seed does provide something that is crucial: a place where the whole of the tree starts to form. As resources such as water and nutrients are drawn in, the seed organizes the process that generates growth. In a sense, the seed is a gateway through which

the future possibility of the living tree emerges.

For the next few years, I went on a learning binge. I read everything I could about the theory. I went to classes in Boston with Otto Scharmer and later went on a solo nature retreat in Colorado under the guidance of Professor John P. Milton, whose work was referenced in the book.

The hero's journey—no highway option

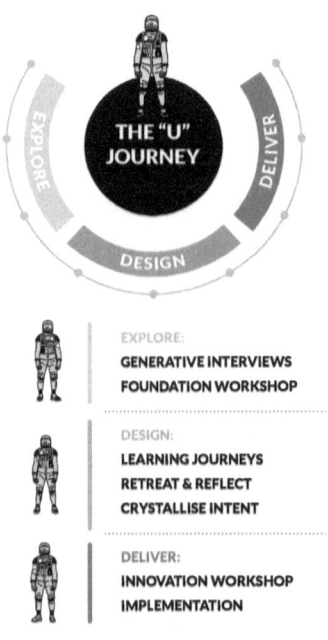

I would later realise these years of searching had been a classic hero's journey, the kind collected by the late Joseph Campbell, an American writer best known for his work in comparative mythology and religion. It's the basis for countless stories, both ancient and modern. It's the story of Gandalf going to Frodo to tell him it's his sacred duty to take the ring and put it in the fire on the mountain over there.

Even if you're not familiar with *The Lord of the Rings*, the scenario might seem familiar. 'No!' says Frodo in shock and panic, alarmed at the prospect of being singled out. 'Why me? I'm happy and comfortable here and it looks dark, dangerous and deathly over there. Surely, you've got the wrong guy ... and even if I am the right guy, which I'm not, can't you at least come back tomorrow, when I've had a chance to think it over? And, perhaps by then, you will have found someone else.'

I have come to understand we are all given the chance to be heroes of our own lives by serving something larger than ourselves. None of us can shake off our destiny without giving up something of what it means to be truly alive. For as Joseph Campbell put it, 'we do not look for the meaning of life, but rather seek the feeling of being alive.'

Theory U is at heart a contemporary rendering of the hero's journey. The 'U journey' operates at three distinct levels—as process, as a grammar of the social field and as a means of personal liberation. At its most basic, the U journey is a process map designed to help us come to understand who we are and to figure out what we are on earth to do. The process follows three waypoints on a U-shaped journey.

These fundamental movements are referred to by Brian Arthur of the Santa Fe Institute: 'Observe, observe, observe; retreat and reflect; act in an instant'. The observation motion is a descent to the bottom of the U, the 'retreat and reflect' is the stillness at the base of it, and the 'act in an instant' is the upward movement to the top.

The journey begins with the uncovering of common intent and listening to what others (and life) call on you to do. It demands an abandonment of the 'voice of judgement' that calls into question and raises your doubts about whether or not you are the one to take the journey—if you have what it takes.

When on the journey, something in your way of seeing shifts. Old patterns of thought are no longer adequate to satisfy your need to understand and, while you do not know where the quest will lead, you know you have no choice but to embark on the journey. You've embarked on that archetypal hero's journey mentioned above, known in one form or another in every culture since the dawn of consciousness. This is the 'explore' phase.

A second phase begins as you abandon cynicism and begin to sense what is really going on. You connect with people and places in empathic ways in which you learn not just the lessons of the mind, but also those of the heart. It is not a period of doing, so much as one of observing, observing and observing—all from the deepest sense of connection you have to the system as a whole. There is a penetrating vulnerability to this aspect of the U process. Cynicism is the cauterising shield to our naked emotions. Removing vulnerability by cauterising emotion may save you from your feelings. But who, in their right mind, would choose to live a life as an emotional corpse?

The middle part of the movement calls for a time to retreat and reflect. One needs to abandon the fear of death and mourn that which no longer serves you. Only by entering this field can that which wants to be born come into being. It cannot make an entrance if the old you is standing in the way.

Through a process of 'presencing', you summon from the deepest well of the source of your inspiration, the Grand Will of your destiny. In this time of profound retreat into self, best undertaken alone and in nature, fundamental questions are asked about who you are as your highest future Self. Why you are alive, now, in this time and place. What is your unique purpose? What are you on earth to do?

From this deep sense of inner knowing, the seeds of your future self are germinated—the microcosm of a future not yet fully articulated. A prototype, if you like, of the design of your life more fully and authentically lived. A landing strip for what is to follow. This part of the movement is an act of harnessing the full power of the vision you discover in the moments of presencing. This is the 'design' stage. Finally, you enter the 'deliver' stage where you make the vision manifest in the world—through deeds.

The concept of the U is fractal in its nature—there is similarity at different scales of focus. One could experience the movement through the U in some aspects in a matter of minutes, or take a period of many years to understand its full implications. You may, simultaneously or otherwise, move through the U collectively as a team.

Many people are reluctant to think too deeply about their job in these terms. Sure, they might ponder the deep questions in their 'personal life'—whether through meditation, gazing at the stars or uncorking a second bottle of Shiraz. But work—not so much. Yet when we get down to it, many of us have identified the wrong job, organisation or role as a prime cause of our unhappiness. We spend at least half our waking lives at 'work', after all. We needn't and shouldn't sleepwalk through it. What if we could really open our hearts, minds and will to the possibility of discovery and fulfilment? Wouldn't it be worth the journey?

A life vest, not a straitjacket

Like all process frameworks, Theory U should be held lightly, and not be turned into a straitjacket of dogmatic approaches to problem identification and solution. What is most important about Theory U is its ability to liberate those people using its constructs to experience the depths of their own sense of being and purpose. Were we to use a prescriptive and inflexible application of Theory U principles, it would defeat its purpose before we were out of the starting blocks.

In our age of instant communications, infinite distraction and alienation from nature, we often lose sight of our own being in the world and rarely pause sufficiently to experience that sacred still place at our source—the mystical root of our eternal present.

As the germinated seed takes root at the bottom of the U, the ultimate intention is to engage fully and confidently with a new way of being, filled with a purpose, to live a fuller, more courageous life. We'll look at each of the stages, and their practical application, in this final part of the book.

The U journey provides a means by which each of us can access that place of deep connection to all that ever was, all that is and all that ever will be—it's the residence of Jung's collective unconscious. It's a means to find, in your unique and individual way, an answer to what both ails and animates you.

Rather ironically, only in this place of intensely personal discovery can we realise that we are all connected. Through the act of changing what is most deeply personal, you have the deepest and most profound impact on the world at large.

I am reminded of the parable of a young man, much aggrieved by the state of the world with all its wars, conflict, poverty, corruption and vice. Determined to make things better, he set out to change the world. Sometime later, he scaled back his ambition and figured that if he couldn't change the world, he most certainly was capable of changing his country. Failing in this endeavour, too, he settled on his city. Then his suburb. Ultimately, not being able to change even his wife and children, he had no one left to change but himself. Succeeding in that mission, he changed the world.

Our world may not be a perfect place, but we can make it a better place, and learn to live within it, with all its joyful sorrow and sorrowful joy.

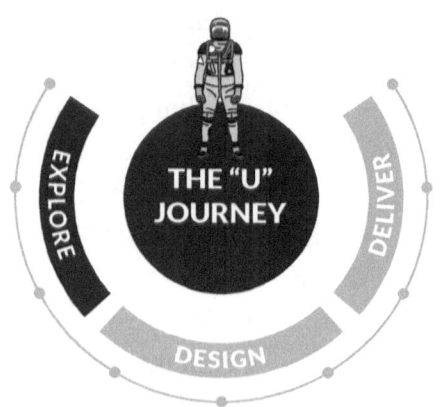

EXPLORE:
GENERATIVE INTERVIEWS
FOUNDATION WORKSHOP

DESIGN:
LEARNING JOURNEYS
RETREAT & REFLECT
CRYSTALLISE INTENT

DELIVER:
INNOVATION WORKSHOP
IMPLEMENTATION

Chapter 15
EXPLORE: *Mapping the Terrain*

> *If you want to build a ship, don't drum up people to collect wood and don't assign them tasks and work, but rather teach them to long for the endless immensity of the sea.*
>
> Antoine de Saint-Exupery

TRANSFORMATION IS TOUGH. According to no less an authority than Deming, it is simply not possible without what he called profound knowledge. That knowledge comprised four parts—'appreciation for a system', 'knowledge of variation', 'theory of knowledge' and the 'psychology of people society and change'. Thinking all the bases can be covered without a methodology is like thinking an orchestra could perform a symphony without ever having studied musical theory. Just how would the composer be able to convey his musical idea? By what means would the conductor engage with the musicians?

A key benefit of using a methodology to facilitate transformation is that we can learn from different instances of repeating the same basic process. Methodical practice reinforces learning and contributes to the building of actionable knowledge for future assignments and interventions.

Theory U is, among other things, a methodology for bringing about transformation. In my opinion, Otto Scharmer of MIT has done the most to develop the theoretical underpinnings of this framework, most clearly articulated in his book of the same name. His insights continue to act as a guide to my endeavours.

A powerful and compelling reason for using the U process as an underpinning of business transformation is because, more often than not, it works—not guaranteed, but it does work. By contrast, whenever I have tried to deliver a transformation in how teams plan and perform their work without going through the U process, it has failed.

GENERATIVE INTERVIEWS

EXPLORE:
GENERATIVE INTERVIEWS
FOUNDATION WORKSHOP

Many efforts to effect change in a system begin with conversations among people with a stake in that system. Yet such interactions often fail to penetrate to the depth needed to release latent forces for change. Generative interviews are a set of in-depth, one-on-one conversations with key stakeholders. These conversations provide the deep context for the next step of the transformation process: the Foundation Workshop.

The purpose of the generative interviews is to get the transformation process started by strengthening the connections of key stakeholders to the system—its current reality and its potential—to each other, and to the sources of their own commitments to effecting change.

15. EXPLORE: *Mapping the Terrain*

A few years ago, I was pitching for an assignment with a large national retailer in the throes of redefining their customer value proposition. The program of work derived from their strategy development included major transformational change in physical store layouts, supply-chain IT systems and the reconfiguration of their end-to-end distribution and replenishment network.

My proposal included a piece on running the generative interview process and called for a two-hour timeslot with the leader of the transformation program and all of her direct reports. When she first read my request, she told me categorically that two hours was far too much time to take out of these very busy people's days; we would have to cut it back. Holding my ground, I asked her how many hours she worked a year, and how many years the project was planned to run. She was a bit mystified by my question, but indulged me.

We concluded that on the basis of working, on average, at least 50 to 60 hours per week and the project being planned to run for at least three years, and taking into account holidays and the like, she would be dedicating at least 360,000 hours of her life to delivering what she hoped would be a successful project. On that basis, I noted, the generative interview represented about .0005% of the time she was likely to be working on bringing the project and its new value proposition to life.

I persevered and established she'd not yet had the opportunity for anyone in the team to devote even that small amount of time to listen deeply to her. Who, I asked, would allow her to talk through her thoughts and feelings about the desired transformation—the issues it was seeking to address, the major challenges and obstacles she expected to hit on the way? What was her vision for the end state, and the culture she wanted to build in getting there? Finally, I suggested it would be a powerful thing for her to articulate what she wanted to leave behind as her legacy. What was her answer to the big question of why she was doing it at all? What deeper purpose would sustain her over the long and difficult road to its ultimate completion?

There was a pregnant pause before she responded. I gave her time to dwell in that silence until she was ready to talk.

She remarked how, on reflection, it felt insane that she hadn't yet paused to put her thinking on these issues into words. She realised the opportunity to do so, with me as witness, was a gift she could give herself. It would strengthen her connection to what she thought the problem was and why she had taken on the challenge of solving it. She would have the opportunity to reflect on what she hoped to achieve for the team she was leading and how, if done well, it held out the possibility of leaving her organisation in much better competitive shape.

Keeping records

Whenever I do generative interviews, I record them and have the interviews transcribed. The participants are guaranteed anonymity but know I'll be using some of the material in the next step in the process—the Foundation Workshop. With the proviso that none of the quotes can be identified, these words—in the language and as a reflection of the culture of the people

15. EXPLORE: *Mapping the Terrain*

charged with changing a system—add remarkable power to every participant's understanding of the dynamics of their world, its current reality and its future potential.

The interviews are not only qualitative, but also help clarify any quantitative analysis done to support the case for value and benefits realisation. They provide the input to better understand the social system being examined, especially the group culture. They also give me a way, as intervener in my client's world, to deepen and enrich my relationships with them, including understanding and connecting with something of their personal stories. These stories invariably provide deep insight into worldviews, motives and ways of working.

The specific outcomes of the generative interviews include clarification of:

- the 'why'—the specific purpose of the Foundation Workshop—as the next step in the process

- the 'what'—challenges and concerns that must be addressed to release the full potential of the system

- the 'who'—key individuals who will be selected to participate in the Foundation Workshop

- the 'how'—design of the initial steps in the transformation process

In short, generative interviews raise the quality of thinking and relating within the system. The conversations are the first steps towards catalysing the transformation process.

Starting with ourselves

Recently I assigned one of my senior managers the task of running generative interviews and a Foundation Workshop within our own firm as we wrestled with how best to take our consulting and organisation to next practice. While the detail of the content is not relevant, what was remarkable for me as CEO was to come to understand just how much difference of opinion and anxiety there was about what we were about to embark on.

My firm is a boutique outfit specialising in anything and everything to do with the management of work. We don't span continents, nor do we have massive different strategic business units. We make a point of all being in the same room, physically if at all possible, but electronically if not, at least once a fortnight.

Thus it came as quite a surprise, not only to me but to all the participants, to find such divergent perspectives around what we were seeking to change, and what our business would look like once it was done.

How much then, I told my team, do we need to use this process to make ourselves aware of the impact of what we do. We need to challenge the assumption that our clients are able to put on our glasses and see what we see before we have put on theirs and taken the trouble to first come to know the world though their eyes.

15. EXPLORE: Mapping the Terrain

FOUNDATION WORKSHOP

The second part of the explore phase of the U Journey is the Foundation Workshop. As with a building, if the foundation is dodgy, the whole edifice will fall down.

EXPLORE:
GENERATIVE INTERVIEWS
FOUNDATION WORKSHOP

The philosophy behind the approach to the Foundation Workshop is Socratic in its nature. It is enquiry based and encourages anyone participating in it to articulate opposing viewpoints by asking and answering questions that, in turn, stimulate critical thinking. In the workshop, we use games, metaphor, storytelling and the Logical Thinking Process to illuminate ideas. Wherever possible, participants are encouraged to think, feel and act in ways that incorporate both the social and technical aspects of systems thinking as an indivisible whole.

Over the many years I have been running these foundation workshops, I have come to know the irreducible set of factors that go into making this aspect of the intervention successful. An ideal environment for the workshop is somewhere away from the demands of business as usual, and as close to nature as possible.

To get the best results, the environment should be conducive to deep thinking; the kind that comes from a relaxed and casual atmosphere where it is safe to express both fears and aspirations. When the workshop participants sleep over at the venue for its duration, something magical happens on the day you are neither arriving nor leaving, but going to sleep in the same bed you got out of that morning. This is a key reason why the workshop is held over three consecutive days, preferably soon after the generative interviews. This requirement for three days away is the one I have the most difficulty in persuading my sponsors about.

I make the point, as strongly as I can, that the three days are not about taking time off work but are an integral part of its proper planning. Planning both in terms of the processes to be adopted and the building of relationships between the people who will depend on each other through what will invariably be some pretty tough times.

There is a huge amount to get through in the Foundation Workshop. We use games to learn how Theory of Constraints takes the promise of systems thinking and makes it a reality. We take a deep dive into the outputs from the generative interviews and shift gear for the organisation to develop a clearly articulated goal, supported by a set of critical success factors and intermediate objectives.

Often, not even my arguments about the amount of work to be done over the course of the workshop wins the day, and I'm left having to dig deeper in the trench. I argue that it's significantly easier and makes for far more effective communication to take advantage of having a wide range of decision-makers and stakeholders in the Foundation Workshop—even if for three days straight. What, I ask, is the more productive way to plan your work?

Would it be better for everyone to scatter to the four corners

15. EXPLORE: *Mapping the Terrain*

of the organisation? Battle their way through emails? Try to set up meetings where key people are, invariably, absent? Would it be preferable to struggle to develop shared meaning and approaches to problems and opportunities through an atomised network, held together by the sticky tape and chewing gum of phone lines and the internet?

Or could we get real about what is being asked of the team, and declare the workshop as the place where all the important decisions are going to be made? The Foundation Workshop, as its name implies, is where alignment around the future vision gets built, where plans for the 'what' and 'how' of work execution are debated and resolved. Representatives of the whole system will be in the room, in real time, brought together by expert facilitation. Surely, I insist, we must ensure every voice has the chance to be heard and is given the opportunity to make a meaningful contribution.

I recall some years ago, the start of an assignment with an engineering company in the aviation business. The program of work brought together three distinct streams of work, none of which had much to do with the other besides drawing down on the same pool of experts.

The senior executive in charge of the engineering services of this company declared he was sick and tired of the fact that every time they had a new project, a new team was set up. A whole lot of people with the requisite skills were then sent on assignment, and were never seen again until the project was over. 'Exile to North Korea' is what he once called it.

For me, it was clear the change to new ways of working

would be transformative for the business. A whole new set of capabilities would be required to plan and execute work across multiple projects at a time; the organisational structure would have to be modified to properly match accountability with requisite authority; performance agreements would have to be rewritten to reflect a more collaborative way of working across functions; and habits of working the same way for years would have to be unlearned and new ways learned.

There was, though, a handbrake on change. It was the trump card the engineers played whenever faced with having to make changes to their ways of working: their statement—made in a menacing voice, whenever an aeroplane flew overhead—that were it not for them, working exactly the way they did, they might be able to guarantee every takeoff, but not necessarily every landing!

Plead as I might, I could not convince the executive to follow the process. He kept saying to me that all we needed was a couple of hours training in the Critical Chain techniques, perhaps a couple more hours to get the team familiar with the use of the software tool supporting these new techniques and, without a worry, 'she'll be right'.

Besides, he told me, this was a time of austerity and cutbacks in the industry. The 'optics' of a group of them going away for a three-day offsite wouldn't be good. So we were asked to 'please make do with what you've got'. I had to remind myself I was working with a multi-billion-dollar company where the value our project created was measured in tens, if not hundreds of millions of dollars.

15. EXPLORE: Mapping the Terrain

Around the same time this assignment started, we'd also begun a major transformation project in the replacement of an enterprise business management system for a Fortune 100 company. In this case, the executive sponsor understood very well the need for the Foundation Workshop. His aim was to bring together a team that had only recently been formed from different parts of their own vast business, as well as from the far corners of the business of their global IT partner. It was early days on the project, but already there had been some bitter exchanges about costs, risks and benefits.

The generative interviews had unearthed frustrations around issues such as the running of the project management office, accountability for master data, transparency around estimating cost and schedule for given amounts of scope. The list went on. The interviews also unearthed a deep desire on the part of the participants to work together as one team, regardless of which company they had come from. Each wanted the opportunity to learn and grow as individuals and in their teams for this once-in-a-lifetime project.

This Foundation Workshop, then, was run according to the three-day plan, and I was entrusted as the expert to deliver the outcome—an inspired and energised team, aligned behind the goal of delivering a sustainable competitive advantage by completing the project in the shortest time possible. It was remarkable and inspiring to witness the transformations occurring each day.

Developing a high-performing team requires new skills focused on personal mastery and team learning. You can't learn to swim by reading about it, or watching a YouTube clip. You have to get in the water. The sooner you do, the quicker you'll learn.

Practising through play, in the morning session, we ran a business game to introduce the power of systems thinking and its direct effect on the bottom line. One participant likened it to experiencing weightlessness in a zero-gravity simulator. Before you go for your moon shot, you must experience how a new approach—in this case Theory of Constraints, grounded in systems thinking—profoundly changes how you think, feel and act.

Why a game? Because learning happens faster, goes deeper—and sticks better—with an element of play. It helps us conquer our anxiety about appearing foolish and lets us admit we don't have all the answers. By creating a safe practice field to test new ideas—and compare results in real time—the game allows everyone to experience learning how to work in flow and judge the systemic implications of their decisions.

After the energy of the morning—and experiencing failure in the game's early rounds, followed by growing success in the later ones—the team gained a new sense of empathy for each other by trading ignorance and blame for profound knowledge and insight. The afternoon session of the first day provided a launch pad to develop a shared vision. Having conducted the generative interviews with the participants prior to the workshop, insights were gained to help tailor the afternoon session to the specific challenges and opportunities faced by the project.

With mental models expanded, what was holding them back came into focus. New creative ideas were developed to counter the disruption they all faced, which in turn inspired future work

15. *EXPLORE: Mapping the Terrain*

as a possibility to live into—not something to be feared.

Once the learning journey of the first day was completed, the team was equipped with a whole new and practical way of seeing how they could better do better work. There was palpable relief in every one of the participants as they properly understood the root causes of their disharmony. A renewed confidence in their own ability and trust in each other arose from understanding how the new knowledge contained in the organising principle of constraint-based management could be used to serve their vision. They understood how to effectively simplify the management of the complexity of what they had taken on. Without this new knowledge, and the opportunity to learn it together, as a team, they understood there was no way they could hope to succeed.

This awareness and understanding prepared the field for the tough conversations on Day 2, during which we shared selected output of the generative interviews. In the facilitation, I made sure everyone understood what it meant to listen empathically; to attempt to be in the shoes of the other, with an open heart. In fact, it moves beyond empathy, if what we understand by that term is the ability to feel what others feel. When we feel compelled to do something to help others who are struggling, or are in pain, it becomes compassion.

By Day 3, the team had coalesced into a single unit and motored through the preliminary planning, having got clear and excited about their vision of not only what they wanted to accomplish, but how they wanted to get there.

The Foundation Workshop was repeated every time a new

release was initiated and for every new business unit starting their transformation journey. Remarkably, people who participated in the workshop continued to reference the game weeks or months—even years—after the event. Specific moments became symbols to describe and anchor real-world situations.

Fail often to succeed sooner

In my years working with these processes—apart from what I gain from my time with the inspiring organisations I'm fortunate enough to find as clients—I've seen that you can often learn as much, if not more, from your failures as you can from your successes. While the business-system project went from strength to strength over several years, the engineering project fell apart after only a couple of months. The company continues to waste their pool of resources and the talents and passions of its people by assembling separate teams for each project.

In summary, the results you can expect at the completion of the explore phase of the U journey include a clear, shared goal and what that means for your organisation. In addition, you will have a high-level plan for the execution phases of the project, based on a common language around the principles of systems thinking. It will incorporate the Theory of Constraints and its approach to problem identification and solution, how to foster learning in organisations and what makes for productive and fair management hierarchies.

The participants will have had the chance to explore how the accountability hierarchy will be structured, both within the

15. EXPLORE: *Mapping the Terrain*

project itself and how the project interfaces with its sponsoring organisation and other critical stakeholders. There will be significantly improved levels of understanding and relationships between the workshop participants, which provide the basis for higher levels of team coherence and project performance.

In addition, time and again I've witnessed that, as a result of properly conducting the explore phase of these transformations, more work is done, on time, every time, in less time. There is less work 'in process' and more effective use of the people at the disposal of the project. There is a rational and transparent basis for decision-making, based on quantitative work management, through a single source of truth. There is visibility into the real constraints to goal achievement. There is a happier experience of working in a coordinated and synchronised way towards a common goal, with reduced multitasking and more flow. Communication is better and relationships stronger between people who have differing needs and perspectives. The opportunity is ripe to become fully engaged and turn a compelling and inspiring vision into a shared reality. More than just work indeed.

Questions for EXPLORE

1. Looking at the biggest challenge or opportunity on your plate, what would you say to an interviewer if she asked about the system's current reality, your vision for the future and the legacy you want to leave?

2. Recall a time when you were in a team that was completely aligned and working as one over a sustained period. How did that come about, how did it feel and how and why did it end?

3. What big idea do you have that can fundamentally change your business performance while enhancing your people's experience at work. What are you going to do to bring its value and potential into being?

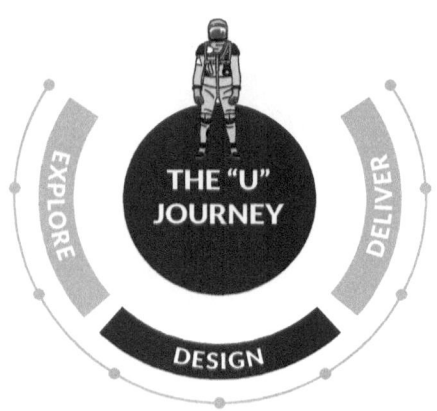

EXPLORE:
GENERATIVE INTERVIEWS
FOUNDATION WORKSHOP

**DESIGN:
LEARNING JOURNEYS
RETREAT & REFLECT
CRYSTALLISE INTENT**

DELIVER:
INNOVATION WORKSHOP
IMPLEMENTATION

Chapter 16

DESIGN: *Rewriting the Score*

Design is not just what it looks like and feels like. Design is how it works.

Steve Jobs

THE NEXT PHASE of a transformation project is the 'design' phase. Rationally, we know that everything not directly from nature and made by humans is designed. But what do we really mean by design? Often, we conflate it with the idea of making things beautiful because they give more pleasure and are thus perceived to be more valuable. There is nothing like excellent design to provide aesthetic arrest and prise attention away from our daily fare of poor products, clumsy processes and ill-fitting solutions.

A better way of looking at design, though, is to ask questions about the function, form and fit of whatever we're designing. What job does it do and how does it do it? How could how it looks and feels help it do that job better? Design doesn't have to be an object, though. It could be a phase of a project where we determine how a new process and supporting technology is going to work. It could mean developing a consistent way of providing burgers around the world (McDonalds) or putting '1,000 tunes in your pocket' (the iPod).

At the fundamental level, design means we have an intention of what we'd like to see in the world and set about doing the work of turning that into reality. So is the product or service able to solve the problem of the initial intent?

One of the errors made about the act of designing is the thought that it belongs exclusively to the creative class. I believe everyone has an innate ability to design, as we are all born into the world as both product of and active participant in creation and creativity. The trouble with the world of work I encounter, though, is that organisations lean too far towards the realm of facts and the figures—the privileging of truth over beauty and good.

Often, rather than seeing the whole person, what we actually see is a name in a row in a spreadsheet; a number in an adjacent column telling us what this 'resource' will cost; what skill the person brings in another column; and perhaps even what they will cost to retrench and how much money the enterprise will save by not having them there at all. This quantifying habit of the organisation rubs off onto the people working within it who feel that, if their job description doesn't include design, they are not up to design thinking.

One way to break old ways of thinking and get out of our habitual routines, habits of thought and deed is to expose ourselves to new and different ways of taking on our challenges. One of the real pleasures of my consulting practice is the opportunity to explore a wide variety of different workplaces on every continent across sectors as varied as mining, manufacturing, engineering, construction, aviation, banking, retail and business management technology.

In 2010, I attended the TED global conference in Oxford and was struck by a talk given by Matt Ridley, who famously describes himself as a rational optimist. He put forward the idea that through history, the engine of human progress and prosperity has been, and is, 'ideas having sex with each other'.

An effective way, then, for us to 'find a date' for our current stock of ideas is to go on a learning journey.

LEARNING JOURNEYS

In exploring innovative solutions to even our toughest challenges, it's important to actively create environments which counter the fear that so often punctures and deflates our ambition. The fear that the facts and figures don't stack up. The fear we don't know enough, or we'll make a mistake and be found out.

DESIGN:
- **LEARNING JOURNEYS**
- **RETREAT & REFLECT**
- **CRYSTALLISE INTENT**

Our rational minds can't escape the fact all new knowledge has arisen from the inquiring mind that has, until the point of discovery, been ignorant. Do we punish Galileo because he ignorantly peered into his telescope, not knowing whether or not he could prove the heliocentric hypothesis? Do we flog Einstein for the ignorance shown before imagining travelling on a beam of light and his theory of relativity was proven? And what is our attitude to both of them when physicist Richard Feynman, perhaps paraphrasing Niels Bohr, says: 'If you think you understand quantum mechanics, you don't understand quantum mechanics.'

It seems to me we must cultivate our ability to open up the part of the heart and mind that are comfortable with ambiguity, be aware and at ease with our ignorance, and be willing to enter the field of innovation with the possibility of failure, again and again.

If we look at nature, we see that trees have thousands of seeds. Yet very few of them make it to being a tree. In the world of business, the most successful investment companies will never rely on a single investment, but rather create a portfolio. For every outstanding success we have from the world of startups, there are at least ten failures.

In the first instance, the essence of learning journeys is a frame of mind allowing for many choices. Through a selection process designed to harness collective wisdom, your team chooses a few different plausible and relevant scenarios. These scenarios form the hypothesis from which you will, in due course, select the scenario with the highest future possibility for you, your team and your organisation. It will frame the broader implementation and transform what were once simply ideas into tangible new value and wealth.

Whenever we truly embrace the power of scientific method, we must be prepared to take a contrary view to how we usually go about testing our ideas. We must be willing to actively search for data that disconfirms even our most passionately held beliefs. Instead, for the most part, we tend to gather the evidence in support of our case so we can make an ever more ferocious

16. DESIGN: Rewriting the Score

argument as to the rightness of our position.

One assignment I led in the aviation industry had three separate workstreams, only coming together when they had to use the same set of data: one for regulatory compliance, one for a new supply-chain system and the third for the induction and decommissioning of aircraft into and out of service. From the ocean of data available, each sought information to bolster the case as to why, in the new world of information management, the data should be configured in a particular way to yield the results each group were looking for, and deemed more important than the other.

It took far too long and way too much wasted effort to demonstrate that if each had their own way, none would actually have the correct answers to their questions. To be sceptical about your own hypothesis—and willing to detach from the outcome the evidence points to—is a special quality requiring cultivation. At the heart of this quality is the courage to overcome a deep-seated fear of having to give something up without knowing what will replace it. But without that capability, no real learning can occur.

A good way to open up is to explore other industries and talk to people who can illuminate, with their experience, what you are trying to do. This is not at all like doing a benchmarking study, which I find to be of limited value. So often these studies are used as a shield against establishing what you and your organisation are truly capable of. Imagine the Wright brothers embarking on a benchmarking study of motor cars to establish how high they could fly!

That's not to say that the automotive industry cannot make a powerful contribution to the aviation industry. But first you have to decide if you're in the business of making things heavier than air fly, or if you're in the business of making a car better than all other cars participating in your study.

Imagination is the feedstock of innovation, and a benchmarking study is a safe refuge for those whose pleasure is taken in doing the limbo rather than the high jump. Daring to set the height so only a pole vault will get you over reveals a whole different level of possibility. Learning journeys can and should be practice fields for pole vaulting.

Visiting other enterprises isn't the only suggestion for our learning journeys. In a particular assignment with an engineering firm, we were at a loss as to how to approach the development of executable work plans for the design phase of a large infrastructure project. Should we have one massive plan covering everything and risk getting smothered in details that may never happen? Or should we break it down into the chunks that go together when being built, but which would lose us the overall integrated view? Should we organise by discipline and type of engineer: civil, mechanical, electrical and controls? Or should we organise by the physical area in which the infrastructure is to be built?

When we admitted none of us knew the answer, if indeed there was 'an answer', it was liberating. The discovery unleashed a creative storm of possible ways we could arrive at a solution to meet or exceed the goal of the project.

In this case, as is common with many others, we teamed a

16. DESIGN: *Rewriting the Score*

pair of consultants with a pair from the client organisation. Our teams were given some coaching on whom to speak to, how to approach them in a spirit of inquiry and not alienate them with biased advocacy for our preferred options. We talked through what kind of questions would likely reveal the social, process and technical difficulties we were all trying to better understand (and overcome), and agreed on the process of debriefing immediately after the interviews, to deepen our understanding of what we had just heard.

We paid careful attention to both the rationale for each suggested scenario and the emotional payload each carried. I recall a debrief from the project-controls people getting very heated about how one scenario solving the problem for coordinating work between engineers by following their natural flow of work, had the very negative effect of breaching the standards used for reporting to the client. By trying out ideas in our practice field of the learning journey and making a conscious effort to both see the problem and to feel the pain, we were able to create a new way of working that satisfied the requirements of both sides of the conflict.

RETREAT AND REFLECT

DESIGN:
LEARNING JOURNEYS
RETREAT & REFLECT
CRYSTALLISE INTENT

There comes a time when the head and the heart are brimming with experiences and insights gained on the learning journeys. Some of the scenarios have wilted on the vine as others have taken powerful shape and embody the full value of the idea that kicked off the whole journey. It is now time to retreat and reflect from all of this seeing and sensing, to go to a place where there is no fear of judgement, no inner voice of the cynic, and no dread of letting your old self die so that the new you can be born.

I have found this inner place best approached as a sacred quest, undertaken in nature, together with a like-minded group. At the beginning, before the solo immersion, the group shares thoughts, feelings and expectations through a process of facilitated deep dialogue. I recommend a bare minimum of two days and a night of alone or 'all-one' time in nature, before re-emerging to join the group—each of whom has undertaken a similar solo retreat into nature. The reconnecting after this 'bottom of the U' experience is a very special time of being relaxed, deeply present and alive to what life calls on you to do. Sharing the whole experience of coming to know about outer, inner and true nature is a powerful way of mobilising the will to transform the seed of an idea into a mighty life purpose.

We in the west have lost the rituals of our more 'primitive' forebears. As a naturalised Australian, I'm keenly aware that

16. DESIGN: Rewriting the Score

the country's original landowners continue to practice retreats into nature, and I look to their tradition for inspiration.

My first experience of such a retreat was on a Sacred Passage, held with John P. Milton, in the Sangre de Cristo Mountains of Colorado. John has been a Professor of Ecology at the University of Illinois, a Woodrow Wilson Scholar at the Smithsonian and an advisor to Richard Nixon's White House. In addition, John is a highly accomplished spiritual teacher dedicated to helping others open an authentic connection with outer, inner and true nature.

Deep in nature, I have found it possible to be at one with the universe and discovered the freedom to ask afresh the deepest questions of my Being: Who is my Self? And what is my Work? Not my small 's' self, governed by instincts and things, but my large 'S' self that, in the words of philosopher Martin Buber, quits 'defined' for 'destined' being. Or as spiritual teacher Marianne Williamson puts it, 'Self-awareness is not self-centeredness, and spirituality is not narcissism. "Know thyself" is not a narcissistic pursuit.'

Some of my clients think I'm joking when I talk about retreating into nature. How can that help with their business problem, they wonder? Am I going to go all 'woo-woo' on them? The simple fact is that to achieve a deep connection with our purpose, we need to step away from our desk, our office and everything we associate with our daily work. Only then, I believe, can we really get a sense of perspective.

After all, every one of the most systemic changes we have seen in the world started with an idea in one person's mind.

MORE THAN JUST WORK

The most deeply personal is also the most profoundly systemic. Let me share with you an episode of my own solo experience during my Sacred Passage.

* * *

I CLIMB ONTO A LOG, an inverted Y that angles away from the bank, descending into the creek from the dense sun-dappled greens and browns of the riverine foliage. It's a perfect size—large enough to stand on, but not so large it cannot flex to my movement. It reminds me when, as a boy, I would dare myself to see how much my bouncing could amplify the school's diving board without falling off. As I rejoice in my dance of the shimmering stream, the log amplifies and resonates to my bounce in my whirling dervish celebration of nature's delights. All the while, the stream calls after me, beckons me in, tempts me with a promise of transcendence beyond mere joy.

I walk the log to the end, particularly aware of my balance and movement, supported by the tiny connection of clutching a leaf to the left and a twig to the right. My fairy wheel stabilisers let me make it all the way along to the perfect Y at the end of the log, which then bows down to the riverbed. I place my left leg on one part of the Y and my right on the other. There, directly below, is a natural rock pool: a quiet, slow flowing part of the stream, long enough and deep enough to fit my whole body, head and face under water. I worry that my feet will be frozen motionless and that I'll struggle to get out again, but the lure of the place is too strong, and on the count of three, I put my best foot forward.

16. DESIGN: *Rewriting the Score*

Before I can change my mind, I lower myself quickly into the water until my feet touch the smooth rocks of the riverbed. Still gasping from the shock, I submerge my head. My body tightens in the cold's grip, but I'm disciplined and with my head under water slowly count to 20. I become one with the flow of water. Now I hear a different sound as my ears tune in to the vibrations mediated through the molecular form of the water itself. I feel waves of energy pass through and around me, charging every cell in my being with vitality as primal as the stream itself. For a brief moment, I cut through to beautiful clarity and spaciousness; everything is connected, everything comes from Source. I am one in the Stream and one with Source itself.

My head breaks the surface, my lungs expanding as I suck in air, and the immediate spell is broken. But my mind is still charged as I haul myself out and towel off, shivering in the sun...

...Right next to my tent is a flat piece of rock that lends itself to lying on and gazing at the heavens in the extraordinary clear sky. I see the constellations in all their glory, as they have appeared to every generation before me. Here, away from the light-pollution plague of the industrialised world, I can clearly make out the trail of the Milky Way and my mind boggles at the vastness of what lies there and beyond.

My awareness is habitually drawn to objects in front of me—aromas I smell, sounds I hear, textures I feel and the flavours I taste. Now, though, I'm fully conscious of the reality of a 'rising' earth, with the 'setting' sun as the illusion. I try to imagine an objective reality within this boundless network of dark and shadow from which the stars radiate their essence. I spend time and effort bringing the focus of my awareness to the gaps between the stars and leave to peripheral vision the shining shimmering phenomena themselves.

A deep sense emerges from within me that there is immeasurably more darkness than light, and I let rest in me for some time an awakening of what might lie in that gargantuan, unmanifest part of the heavens. After some indeterminate time, in the deep still presence of the unmanifest, I notice a planet, probably Venus, making its slow way across the infinite dome of the night sky. I cast my mind back, and then further back and further back still. The ancient questions of the self-aware mind begin to emerge: Where am I from? How did I get here? What is my purpose?

To me, it's one of nature's rich paradoxes that we are blessed with just enough intelligence and consciousness to understand how unimaginably vast our universe is—only to realise our own total insignificance within it. The grains of sand I rub between my fingers and casually let fall back to the ground seems of more consequence to me than I am to the unfathomable depths of the deep space I witness. And yet, I am all I know; or at the very least, I am what I know best.

If it were not for me, a product of consciousness and one who uses consciousness as an instrument of navigation through these unanswered questions, would any of what I perceive even exist? And what does it matter about the size of it all, when on every day of my Sacred Passage I have marvelled at the sheer beauty of all being—irreducible and all connected. There is on the one hand a seemingly total and meaningless irrelevance to my life on this infinitesimal morsel of Big Bang's memory; and, on the other, a direct and profound connection to the infinite depths of Source.

* * *

CRYSTALLISE INTENT

DESIGN:

LEARNING JOURNEYS
RETREAT & REFLECT
CRYSTALLISE INTENT

The essence of design thinking is to consider how the user of a design will interact with what is made, be it a product or a service. The best designers have a mindset that puts their talents at the service of their customer experience. Having completed the learning journey, you will have stared into the deep mystery of your problem domain, camped by it, and explored how others have defined and solved problems useful for what you're looking to remedy. You will have developed ideas and solution scenarios for what you might do next.

The goal of the retreat into nature, in practical terms, is to gain clarity around what to do with what you have learned—both the personal growth of your interior space and what you have dreamed possible to make manifest in the world.

After the retreat, you emerge with a heightened sense of what the world calls on you to do. The vision is rendered richer, the Grand Will is harnessed, and the leap into your highest future self is primed for lift-off. What you do next has the possibility of greatness.

It's hard to imagine you doing your best work without a love for what you do. To create a thing of beauty, there is no gaming the outcome through cynical manipulation or hiding away from the scary parts. Your users or customers will be onto you in a flash. Where form meets function, you are the architect of possibility, and you need to take time to crystallise your intention. What is your mission now? What does the world call on you to do? Where should you be placing your attention?

There are numerous practical ways you can crystallise intention: journaling, reading, attending relevant training, getting a coach, meditation and so on. When I came off my first Sacred Passage it took me several weeks to write down what happened and enter conversations with people I identified as being able to bring the product of my new insights into the world. I recall my guide to the Sacred Passage, John P. Milton, telling me as I exited the solo period of the retreat: 'Many seeds were planted during your alone time in nature, and not all of them will germinate at once.' All things have their gestation period.

Some of my earliest ideas didn't get past first base, but here I am, having written this book and encouraging you to fully engage with your life—at the deepest level. For what could make a life better lived than knowing yourself, discovering your bliss and pursuing it with all that your unique gifts of head, heart and hand can muster.

It is impossible to imagine a world in which I am fully actualised, where the work I do is only for myself. That's not to say I need be the world's greatest altruist; not at all. But if I'm to be the hero of my life, I must be so in service to something

16. DESIGN: Rewriting the Score

bigger than myself. The thought is powerfully and succinctly captured in *Pirkei Avot,* or *Ethics of the Fathers*: 'If I am not for me, who is? If I am only for me, what am I? If not now, when?'

With that thought echoing in our minds, it's time to see how we move into a higher plane of excellence through the 'deliver' phase.

Questions for DESIGN

1. What three biggest fears get in the way of your seeing, feeling and acting in new ways?

2. What role does nature play in your creative being?

3. Why, if at all, is it important to you to stand in the shoes of those who would use your new product or service?

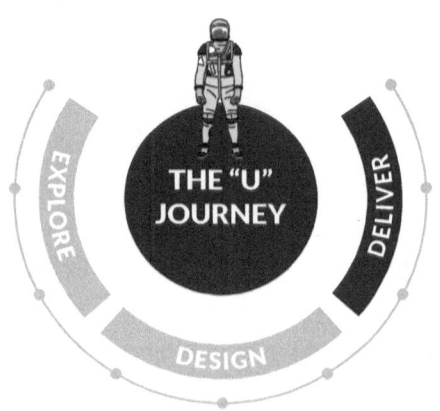

EXPLORE:
GENERATIVE INTERVIEWS
FOUNDATION WORKSHOP

DESIGN:
LEARNING JOURNEYS
RETREAT & REFLECT
CRYSTALLISE INTENT

DELIVER:
INNOVATION WORKSHOP
IMPLEMENTATION

Chapter 17
DELIVER: *Tuning the Innovation Engine*

> *The improvement of understanding is for two ends: first, our own increase of knowledge; secondly, to enable us to deliver that knowledge to others.*
>
> John Locke

THE SYSTEMS OF MANAGEMENT we put in place to transform our ways of working are no more immune to the laws of entropy than any other phenomenon in the natural world. Perhaps even more so. For while organisms continue to thrive as long as the sun keeps shining, those responsible for creating change in organisations often forget they, too, need a constant source of energy to prevent falling apart. While sustaining change initiatives is hard, getting them started can be even harder. At the opposite end of the spectrum from organisational entropy lies inertia.

Significant change initiatives have a very poor track record of delivering sustainable outcomes, as evidenced by Harvard's John Kotter who, in a study of one hundred top management-driven 'corporate transformation' efforts, concluded that half did not survive the initial phase. While he found a few that were 'very successful'—and a few 'utter failures'—the vast majority lay 'somewhere in the middle, with a distinct tilt towards the lower end of the scale'.

If ever we are to come to know how to repeatedly and reliably deliver the outcomes that our best-laid plans call for, we need to better understand why this is the case.

I'm not so foolhardy as to claim to know how to create a capability within any organisation that has at its core an innovation engine able to evolve and adapt at the pace called for by changes in the external environment. I do know, however, that knowing how to build such a capability must lie at the core of any organisation seeking to stay in the game for the long run.

Establishing a valid theory in the domain of social systems is devilishly difficult compared with the exact sciences. For the exact sciences, we can set up controlled experiments and consider the results of our hypothesis under different conditions. In social systems, we can never return to the starting point with all factors reset to the same values and run the 'experiment' again with different settings.

Even if you were to state the problem as a constant and put it as simply as, for example: 'What makes for a successful implementation of the Theory of Constraints?', every implementation is going to yield a different answer. Why? Because every time you are out in the field trying to do it, one or more of the following factors will have an influence: learning takes place which changes the going-in positions of the players; the mix of the players is different which changes the team dynamic; a change in leadership brings a different view of the problem and how to deliver a solution; the external environment changes, responding in a different way to the first time round; and so much more in the category of uncontrolled variables. So, what is to be done?

The dance of change

In his book *The Dance of Change*—a retrospective on ten years of effort to build learning organisations—Peter Senge had a very significant insight that is worth quoting at some length:

> In practice, most learning initiatives do not reflect any deep understanding of nature's growth dynamics. In effect, they deal only with the growth processes, and not with the limiting processes. Developing learning capabilities in the context of working groups and real business goals can lead to powerful reinforcing growth processes. This has been the focus of most of the 'learning organisation work' for the past twenty years. Activating the self-energizing commitment and energy of people around changes they deeply care about has been the key to the many successes that have been achieved.
>
> But, nothing in nature grows in the absence of limiting processes. And, we have given these limiting processes much too little attention. This is why so many learning initiatives, like so many other change initiatives, ultimately fail to sustain momentum. Sustaining any profound change process requires a fundamental

shift in thinking. We need to understand the nature of growth processes (forces that aid our efforts) and how to catalyze them. But we also need to understand the forces and challenges that impede progress, and to develop strategies for dealing with these challenges. We need to appreciate the 'dance of change', the inevitable interplay between growth processes and limiting processes.

What are these limiting factors? We would all be familiar with some or all of the following reasons, identified by Senge and given from within an organisation as to why so often—despite a perceived need for change—the rate at which that change can take root and flourish is constrained:

- There's not enough time.
- There's not enough money.
- There's not enough help, and we don't know what we're doing.
- It's irrelevant.
- The leadership is not walking the talk, so why should I?
- I'm not sure if I'm able.
- Can these people be trusted?
- Can I trust myself?
- Why is it taking so long?
- I don't want to be part of a new religion.
- What they're doing is a complete mystery to me, and I'm anxious about showing my ignorance.
- Who's in charge?

17. DELIVER: *Tuning the Innovation Engine*

- The old guard won't give up the power.
- We've seen this all before.
- Where is all this leading?

I've chosen to work with 'Theory U' as an approach to sustaining transformative change within an organisational setting because it has at its core the primacy of the individual as actor within a social system. Change is not driven from the top. In fact, the whole metaphor of 'driving change' is unhelpful. Successful change doesn't come from the driver's seat alone. If it does, you end up with a lot of backseat drivers, or disgruntled passengers. People are not machines, and mechanical metaphors invite mechanical responses.

At the heart of the method is an invitation for everyone involved in the initiative to examine their own connection to its purpose such that they become intrinsically motivated by a compelling shared vision of the future. In a way, the learning then comes from this emerging future rather than an extrapolation of the past. Personal commitment simply can't happen by edict, no matter how charismatic the leader.

Once participants become active players in the dialogue around the 'why', 'what', 'to what' and 'how' questions of the change, their collective will and energy dwarfs whatever the heroic leader can muster. The role of the leader is to hold open the space for all those involved in the initiative to actively engage with all the questions about limits to growth; to camp by the problem with the tribe; to retreat and reflect on what is being said, felt and done; and when the wise knowing comes, to act in an instant with boldness and courage.

The 'deliver' phase of the 'U' process, as I've adapted in my consulting practice, comprises two significant parts: the Innovation Workshop and implementation. Before going into a brief description of each, recall that this process should not be treated like a detailed map, to be followed step by step. Rather treat it like a compass that can help point the way, leaving the detailed exploration of the path to you.

I am reminded of reading once that whenever the Knights of the Round Table met in the forest, when it came time to leave, they would never exit via a well-defined path, but would often choose the most dense and darkest part of the forest as their way out. It was said that for a Knight of the Round Table it was unworthy of their valour and chivalric code to go where others had made their path for them. While the U process acts as compass, every path is different by virtue not only of the path, but by the interior condition of the person walking it.

INNOVATION WORKSHOP

DELIVER:
INNOVATION WORKSHOP
IMPLEMENTATION

Following the design phase comes 'delivery'. The first part, the Innovation Workshop, should take place not long after the period spent crystallising intent. The key players in the process will by now have a real sense of clarity around their unique gifts as contributors to the collective effort and feel deeply connected to the purpose of the transformation.

A while back, I had an assignment with a company who

17. DELIVER: *Tuning the Innovation Engine*

routinely released a hundred or more new consumer products into the market each year. They had an excellent engineering and design capability to develop their own products from scratch. They also adapted selected products designed and engineered overseas that they thought might fill specific niches in the Australian market. By the time we arrived at the Innovation Workshop, relations between the different functional teams were strong and the degree of mutual trust provided a safe environment to challenge ideas without playing the person.

To a large degree each knew that the other's intent was focused on doing what was best for the business as a whole, even if it meant their own numbers would suffer. During the workshop, I remember a deep conversation that teased out how to best fix the performance management system so that design would not keep throwing work over the fence to an already overloaded engineering function. Government R&D grants gave significant tax concessions for the design work to be accounted for in a particular way. Without thinking through the implications, senior management determined that the same set of measures would be used as performance metrics for the design team.

This performance management system was diagnosed as the root cause of the behaviour experienced by the engineering function and its creation of some fairly serious tensions between them and the design team. By this stage of the project, many of the people, and particularly the leadership, had come to understand new concepts about social fields, the difference between dialogue and debate, how to practice personal mastery and engage in deeper and richer team learning.

Significant work still needed to be done, though, to set up the workshop in a way that would enable generative conversations to be held. Prior to the workshop, participants were asked to complete an industry-standard psychological profile assessment to provide insights into preferred ways of thinking and acting, and what role that might play in helping better the performance of their teams. It was a way to progress the idea that the best and highest performing teams respect the idea of having a minimum requisite variety in them, finding a balance between those whose primary strength resides in one of 'detailed analysis', 'robust process', 'big-picture thinking' or 'interpersonal relationships'.

To reinforce this idea of bringing different strengths and characteristics to the business on an ongoing basis, four people—each with high scores in one of the areas—were asked to be guardian of that way of thinking at any future meetings. With the permission of the whole group, they were encouraged to red flag any occasion when insufficient attention was being paid to the need for a different way of turning up to a given situation.

The workshop was run in a residential format, over two consecutive days, with 23 people in the room. (The number of participants can range from 12 to over 100.) An essential element of the workshop was to include the key leaders of the team. It was made clear from the outset that all decisions regarding future ways of working would be decided at the workshop; if you weren't willing to make the necessary arrangements to attend you would forfeit your right to have a say in how your future might unfold. Given the highly reflective and relational

17. DELIVER: *Tuning the Innovation Engine*

nature of the activities, we chose an environment away from the demands of business as usual and as close to nature as possible. Everyone appreciated the importance of the environment for the workshop being conducive to deep thinking and the expression of personal concerns and aspirations.

The senior executive and sponsor was highly supportive in investing what was required to secure a venue in an area with sufficient space and facilities for one-on-one and small-group informal conversations, taking quite some care to ensure that the main meeting area was sheltered from distractions such as noise, passage and other functions. Many of the activities included drawing, listening to music, watching videos, engaging in deep dialogue and quiet contemplation.

As always when these workshops work well, it was a source of great pleasure to see the growing empowerment of the team. They became awake to the idea that, as each decision arose, they didn't have to go anywhere or reference anyone outside of the room to get a yes or a no. This was their system and they alone were accountable to make sure it worked for them, within the context of the business goal.

The Innovation Workshop invites participants to define what is truly reasonable and possible given the human and material resources available. It offers a framework for innovation in the context of the planning and performance of the work that will deliver the desired strategic outcomes. These outcomes are always constrained by the timeframes and budgets called for by the business, usually as a product of the business case.

We humans tend to forget what the terrain looked like at

the beginning of the journey, but are only too happy to complain about how much there is yet to do. It's like the kids on a road trip nagging their parents, 'Are we there yet?' So it's very important to acknowledge the success of the prior phases through storytelling, and reviewing early interviews, allowing everyone to celebrate their progress from that first step at the beginning of the transformation. There may still be much to do. But if we can see how far we've already travelled, that progress can act as fuel to sustain the rest of the journey.

That journey includes developing approaches to Organisational Change Management—from organisational design, competency frameworks and workforce transition through to training needs analysis, learning and performance system support and overall leadership capacity building.

Properly managed, the period of and around the Innovation Workshop is a time of high energy and expectation, and the leadership team is encouraged to continuously imagine and reimagine how the changes to the new way of working will impact people's lives in a positive way. There is a strong will to continuously build on individual and collective strengths, deliver great team experiences and provide the organisation as a whole with its pathway to sustainable growth and prosperity.

The Innovation Workshop creates an accelerated learning environment and a vibrant vision for the organisation's future of highest potential It acts as a stimulant for the planning required to achieve it.

17. DELIVER: Tuning the Innovation Engine

IMPLEMENTATION

DELIVER:
INNOVATION WORKSHOP
IMPLEMENTATION

Implementation demands a profound understanding of how people, process and technology come together to create results that give high levels of personal satisfaction and extraordinary business outcomes. During this phase, we further develop then execute the plans from the Innovation Workshop, making controlled adjustments where the situation requires.

I've found it useful to establish a coaching and mentoring initiative during implementation. If change is to be sustained, one needs to develop muscle memory in each of the people who have stewardship over the long-term progress of the new way of working.

The leadership team must become the relentless architects of the possibility their people live into. They must develop the capacity to be trusted advisors, offering an empathic sounding board, reducing the anxiety associated with learning new ways, making mistakes along the way, and being sympathetic as their charges explore and discover the difference between right and wrong—what works and what doesn't. If the new systems are successfully implemented, they will provide a solid platform for the growth of a self-sustaining culture of continuous improvement.

A brief story to illustrate. On a significant business initiative in a financial institution using new technology to transform business capabilities, we were about a month out from 'Go Live' and the senior business sponsor was concerned about how the value articulated in the business case would be fully realised. I had told her of my experience of new technology systems going through some predictable phases after the euphoria and adrenaline rush of the Go Live. Whatever happens, there is always a slump as the system is stabilised, bugs are fixed, data errors are corrected and people become generally familiar with how the new system operates.

Following on from this phase, the road splits in two—call it the high and low road scenarios. Without any further intervention, take the low road and soon the business sees what has been delivered as 'just a transaction system'. As frustration mounts during the stabilisation phase, people get into poor practices with regard to operating discipline, with the consequence that those who were hoping to rely on the system for the benefits promised fail to see them realised.

In due course, it descends into workarounds, localised fixes and the seeds of the next big project have already been sown. All that investment of time and money not only makes things worse for the people using the system, but once again reinforces the general perception that big transformation projects cannot deliver on their promise.

I outlined to the executive an alternative approach that proactively planned to deal with the slump post-Go Live, but in a way that put the trajectory for the users onto the high road. For a relatively modest investment, a team was assembled to buddy up with those using the new system to help them adopt it.

We were able to show that the system didn't merely provide

17. DELIVER: *Tuning the Innovation Engine*

the mechanism for doing this particular operator's transactions, but was part of a seamless process from the origination of a deal through to the ongoing delight of the customer. With practice, people gained deeper and deeper mastery of how the system worked, not only within their own area but for the overall goal of the business unit. Like our floor-sweeper at NASA, they could feel as if their job was to 'put people on the moon'.

As the plans laid down in the Innovation Workshop become facts on the ground, it is vital for leadership to approach the work of Organisational Change Management with high levels of intellect, compassion and courage. Built into the process should be regular opportunities to reflect on staying true to the core of all that is good in your culture, while stimulating progress towards the envisioned future.

Everyone involved should feel a sense of ownership and full responsibility for the new way of working. A significant multiplier effect can be gained if your senior team cascades their understanding into the rest of the organisation, sharing the practical application of what they have learned on their leadership journey along with everything that animates their desire to go further in testing the limits of what is reasonable and possible.

If the earlier phases are about architecting the future of the business, the implementation phase relates to building it on a solid foundation. As each day passes, confidence grows that this change will deliver the desired results. Outcomes include increasing personal mastery, building teams that learn to collaborate effectively and growing profound knowledge of systemic thinking and systematic approaches.

Done right and done well, implementation continues the evolution of your business into one that nurtures and cultivates an environment fit for being a whole human at work, fully actualised, in right relationship with others, creating value for oneself and the organisation of which one is an integral part. Or put more simply: a better way to do better work for better results.

Questions for DELIVER

1. What are the three top limits to the growth of your people, working in their teams for the goal of the business?

2. How do you encourage all your people to bring head, heart and hand to bear on delivering the promise of your biggest and most important initiatives?

3. What three things are you not doing that would make the biggest difference to getting the most from your most important initiatives?

EPILOGUE
Transcending the Game

> *I do not know what I may appear to the world, but to myself I seem to have been only like a boy playing on the seashore, and diverting myself in now and then finding a smoother pebble or a prettier shell than ordinary, whilst the great ocean of truth lay all undiscovered before me.*
>
> Sir Isaac Newton

IN 2015, I HAD THE IDEA to write about what I know of the world of work. Now, two years later, I've just finished polishing the fifth draft with my editor before handing it over for typesetting. It's been quite a journey of discovery for me. If you've accompanied me this far, I thank you and hope you've made some progress along your own path.

As we part company, I feel I should say something strong and powerful, like 'Remember these five points and you'll turn into a superstar and your business will thrive.' Finding and selling a simple and repeatable formula for success, however—even if it were possible—has never been my intention or my forte. I would rather confess to the Socratic idea that all I know is that I know nothing. But who would subscribe to the ideas of someone who confesses to knowing nothing?

I understand the desire for a degree of certainty in our lives. To a greater or lesser extent, we'd like to think our lived experience isn't an infinite variety of random events, without connection, cause or predictability. We love the elegant solutions that bring simple understanding to complex phenomena. We know anxiety attends uncertainty, and the human mind forever looks to make simplifying sense out of the unfathomable mystery of being alive. We feel continuously compelled to tame both the uncertainty and its attendant anxiety.

Indeed, ever since the first human started to think, we have collectively tried to order our understanding of the universe's mystery, including our place in it, by marching away from the ignorance and fear of the superstitious mind to the enlightened realms afforded by reason, compassion and wisdom. Not in a straight line, to be sure. But our species has made undeniable progress in our understanding of the nature of nature. I hope that in writing this book, I have usefully put my shoulder to the wheel of advancing our learning and growth. As inconsequential as that contribution might be, all the same, I felt obliged to make it.

I set out on this journey knowing I wanted to write about the Theory of Constraints, organisational learning and management hierarchies as well as other areas such as the unavoidable importance of technology in our world—and, most importantly, the purpose of work itself. I scribbled a bunch of these topics on scraps of paper, screwed them into balls and put them in an empty Maltesers box. I took myself off to a country retreat with my laptop, the box and no other distractions. I would pick

EPILOGUE: *Transcending the Game*

a paper ball and proceed to get my thoughts down in whatever order the topics came out. Some time later, when I showed the resulting draft to a small group of friends and family, I was encouraged enough to continue with the project. Many of them, though, felt that while the first draft included some useful pointers and interesting stories, they weren't sure how the whole thing hung together. Or, as the two people who would edit the manuscript with me said: 'What's the theme?'

In a word, the theme of *More Than Just Work* is courage. Courage to explore the deep, and sometimes scary question of who we are, discover why we're here and cleave to those inalienable truths when it might sometimes be easier to ignore them. It takes courage to pursue one's truth to the exclusion of every soft-option temptation to veer off course. The courage to repeatedly go into the dark parts of the forest, and leave familiar comforts for the uncertain frontier of primal experience.

It's the courage to discern what matters to us; to our idea of a civil, even enlightened, world. And let die what doesn't—again and again. I believe there are enough brave souls on this good earth who share these ideals, and who will apply the best of what they have to offer to ensure our species surmounts the coming challenges, especially of technology and the whole future of work—including artificial intelligence and the encroaching automation of jobs, both blue-collar and white, the erosion of civil liberties and our remarkable system of free enterprise. Further, I believe we together most certainly are capable of finding ways to better collaborate with the next generation of machines themselves as a means of solving some of the biggest challenges of our times.

This book offers a framework for thinking about work to help address the great tests and experiments ahead of us. It celebrates the power of having the courage to risk looking ignorant and foolish in pursuit of knowledge and wisdom, becoming comfortable with the notion that ideas are often wrong, don't work or have no audience. And, even if no one's listening, to continue.

Every idea in the book should create a feeling of encouragement (the 'courage' word again) to find and lead the life that is a personal grace. A grace that acknowledges we have beaten the immense and mysterious odds of never having made it onto this good earth in the first place.

More Than Just Work is about finding the wherewithal to act from the deepest and most profound source of connection to all of nature, and to be in ever-present service to it. Not an esoteric connection, but one grounded in the world of our everyday toil; connecting the practice of our talents to our desire to heal the world and make it a better place—safer, more sustainable, kinder, more connected, inclusive and trusting. Within the book's pages is the idea of the Hero who, as the individual acting from a sense of purpose transcendent of the locus of self, abides in the powerful questions: 'How can I serve the greater whole? What does the universe call on me to do?'

If you allow me to stretch my musical metaphor one last time, what I have tried to do in writing this book is provide you with some composition tools for your own hero's journey. If I have succeeded at all, it's because you now know more about how some of the instruments work, and how each might be

EPILOGUE: *Transcending the Game*

more fully expressed in relation to the whole.

My hope is that I have made you think in new ways, that you feel empowered and excited to learn more from the source works which have been the bedrock of my own inspiration, and that you will have the knowledge and faith to leap into your destined future—the one calling you to courageously will it into being.

APPENDICES
The Thinking Process

THE THINKING PROCESS was developed by Eli Goldratt as a series of tools that complement his Theory of Constraints. Personally, I think of the process as an invitation to the kind of 'slow thinking' espoused by Nobel laureate Daniel Kahneman in *Thinking, Fast and Slow*—the reason-based kind that our emotions so often like to circumvent, often to our later regret.

The trees that follow are simplified samples that aim to give you a taste of what the output of logical thinking looks like. The trees are based on Eli Goldratt's insights but have since been developed further by Bill Dettmer.

For (a lot) more detail on logic trees, I refer to you to his excellent book, *The Logical Thinking Process*.

Appendix A: Sample Goal Tree

> A Goal Tree is a graphical representation of a system's goal, critical success factors and the necessary conditions for achieving them. These elements are arrayed in a logically connected hierarchy, with the goal at the top, the success factors immediately below it, and the supporting conditions below them.
>
> (Dettmer, 68)

You read the Goal Tree from the top down: In order to… {____} we must… {____} and so on.

Goal Trees are a practical and highly effective way of gaining consensus among the system's team around the core goal—and how to go about achieving it. They help you focus on what really brings the most leverage as well as not overlook certain aspects that you may have been taking for granted. In retrospect, the Goal Tree can seem so obvious that people forget how hard it was to focus on what really matters for the system as a whole, rather than on the smaller needs of the various silos within the organisation.

APPENDICES: *The Thinking Process*

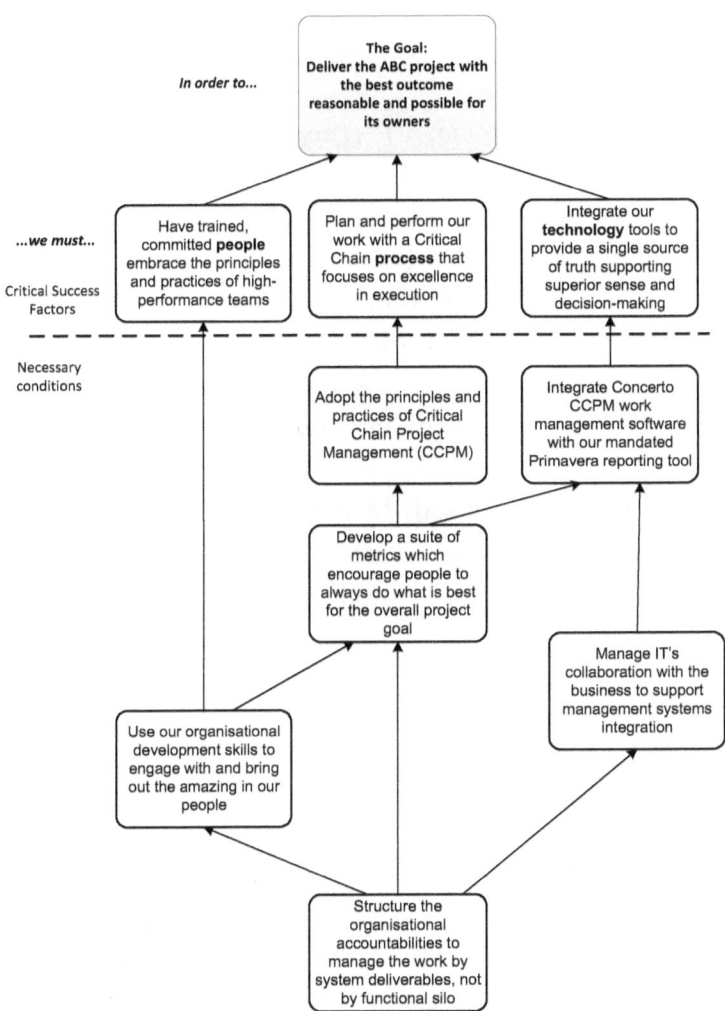

Appendix B: The Current Reality Tree

As its name suggests, the Current Reality Tree shows you how your system is functioning (or not) today. It aims to drill down to root causes, as well as pointing out any undesirable effects as a result of the behaviour of the current system.

The ellipse shape shows how several causes combine to create an effect. The absence of any one of these would cancel the effect.

The bowtie shape (with MAG) indicates a 'magnitudinal effect', that is, two or more causes combine to produce an effect. Take one of the causes away and the effect would still be there—just to a lesser extent.

APPENDICES: *The Thinking Process*

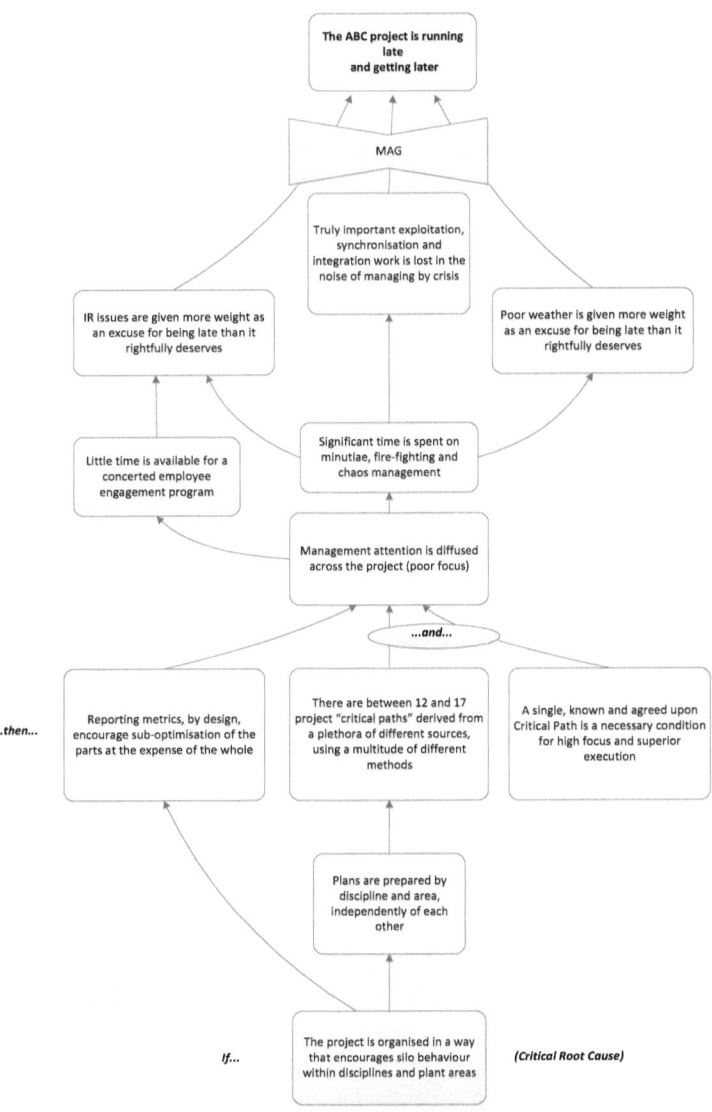

Appendix C: The Evaporating Cloud

This diagram needs a little introduction. The core idea is that you want to achieve an objective that has two conflicting options. This presents a dilemma, since you can't do both.

The Evaporating Cloud is so named because it evaporates the contradiction and creates clarity.

To read the diagram, then, you start with the objective (the far-left box). Read the top half first:

> In order to **deliver the best outcome**, I must **adopt innovative solutions** because…

You then move to the assumptions on the top left ('The project is already behind schedule…' etc.).

Now look at the necessary condition to achieve the first option:

> In order to **adopt innovative solutions**, I must **integrate CCPM into the project** because…

Then move to the assumptions above ('CCPM is the highest leverage innovation…' etc.).

Although you read it from left to right, the arrows flow from right to left because they show the logic of the necessary conditions.

* * *

Now we look at the lower half of the diagram and read it in the same way, referring of course to the other assumptions for each box.

The two boxes on the right are connected with a jagged arrow. This shows our conflict: you can't both integrate and ignore CCPM in this case.

The conflict is broken by questioning all the assumptions. By surfacing every reason we can think of (positive or negative), we find the underlying causes of the problem. Often, there's an injection we can then make that makes the decision clear.

APPENDICES: *The Thinking Process*

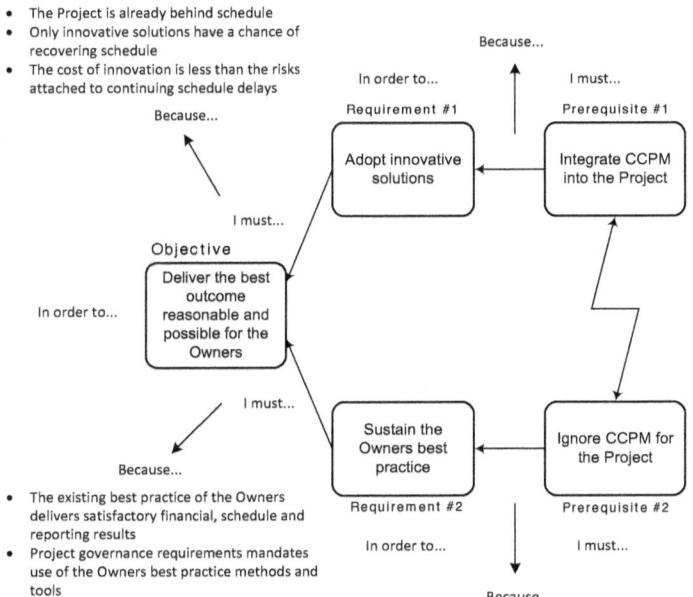

- CCPM is the highest leverage innovation available to the Owners
- CCPM lends itself, by design, to the need to manage by system deliverable across functional boundaries
- Proven commercial software is available in the form of Concerto to rapidly integrate CCPM into the project
- The Owners can develop the capability to get the benefit from CCPM

- The Project is already behind schedule
- Only innovative solutions have a chance of recovering schedule
- The cost of innovation is less than the risks attached to continuing schedule delays

- The existing best practice of the Owners delivers satisfactory financial, schedule and reporting results
- Project governance requirements mandates use of the Owners best practice methods and tools

- CCPM is not in the existing solution set of the Owners
- CCPM cannot comply with the mandated governance requirements
- There is not sufficient time and/or money to do both the Owners best practice and CCPM
- There is a valid way to manage by system deliverables without using CCPM, within the timeframe demanded by the project

415

Appendix D: The Future Reality Tree

The Future Reality Tree is designed to show you what will happen after you make changes to the status quo.

Like the other trees, it is based on sufficiency-type logic. Looking at the bottom of the tree, you can imagine the effects (desirable and, sometimes, undesirable) that your injections into the system will have.

Taken together, I have found the logic trees to enable stakeholders to see the map of the terrain in front of them, even very large transformational projects. I believe they are an essential part of your toolkit that will enable you to dig deep into the real issues holding you back and define ways together that will chart a course to remarkable results.

APPENDICES: *The Thinking Process*

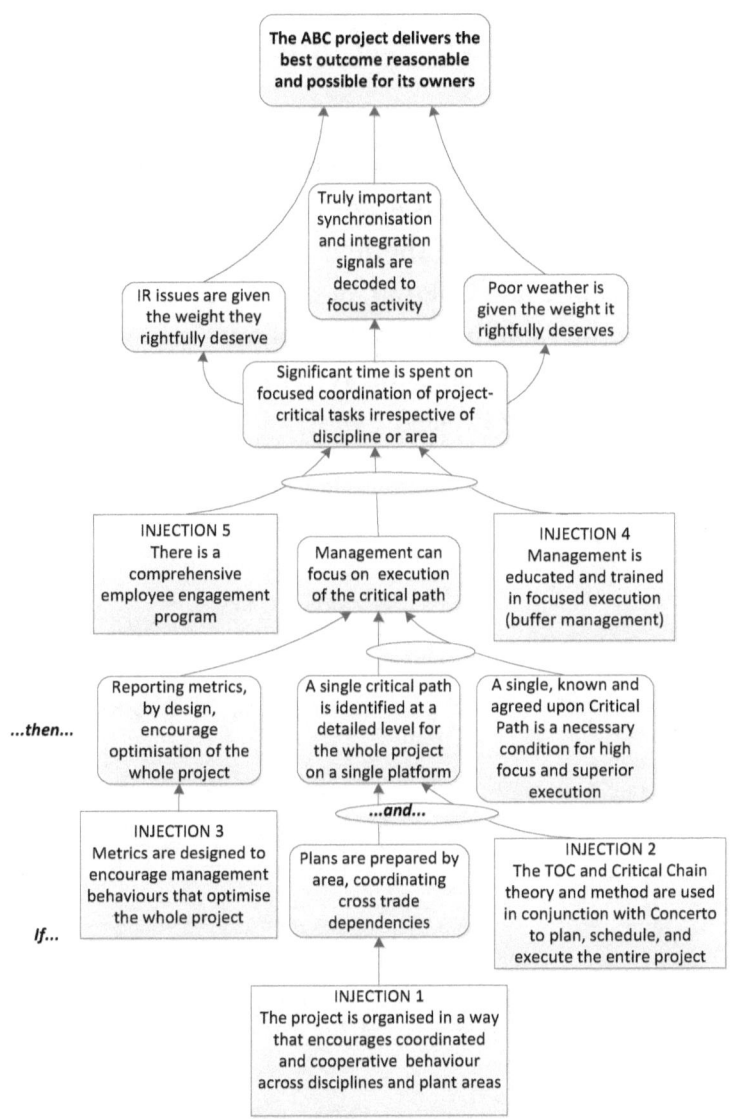

Appendix E: Logic Checks

Along with the ideas of the Logical Thinking Process comes a way to validate the logic. Had you been around at the time of Aristotle and gone to his academy, you would have learned about the codification of the logical fallacies. A comparison between Aristotle and Goldratt, developed by Bill Dettmer, can be found in the table below. What follows is how these logic checks can be found using the system of symbols adopted in the Logical Thinking Process.

Aristotle's Logical Fallacies	Goldratt's Categories of Legitimate Reservation
Material Fallacies (sophistical refutations)	
Improper application of the general rule (inclusion)	(no corresponding category)
Improper application of a special rule (extension)	(no corresponding category)
Irrelevant conclusion (six subordinate cases)	Causality existence, cause-effect reversal, tautology
Circular argument	Tautology
False cause	Causality existence, additional cause, predicted effect
Many questions	Additional cause
Non sequitur	Causality existence
Verbal Fallacies	
Equivocation	Clarity
Amphiboly	Clarity
Accent	Clarity
Composition	Entity existence
Division	Entity existence
Formal Fallacies	
Denial of the antecedent	(no corresponding category)
Affirmation of the consequent	(no corresponding category)

APPENDICES: *The Thinking Process*

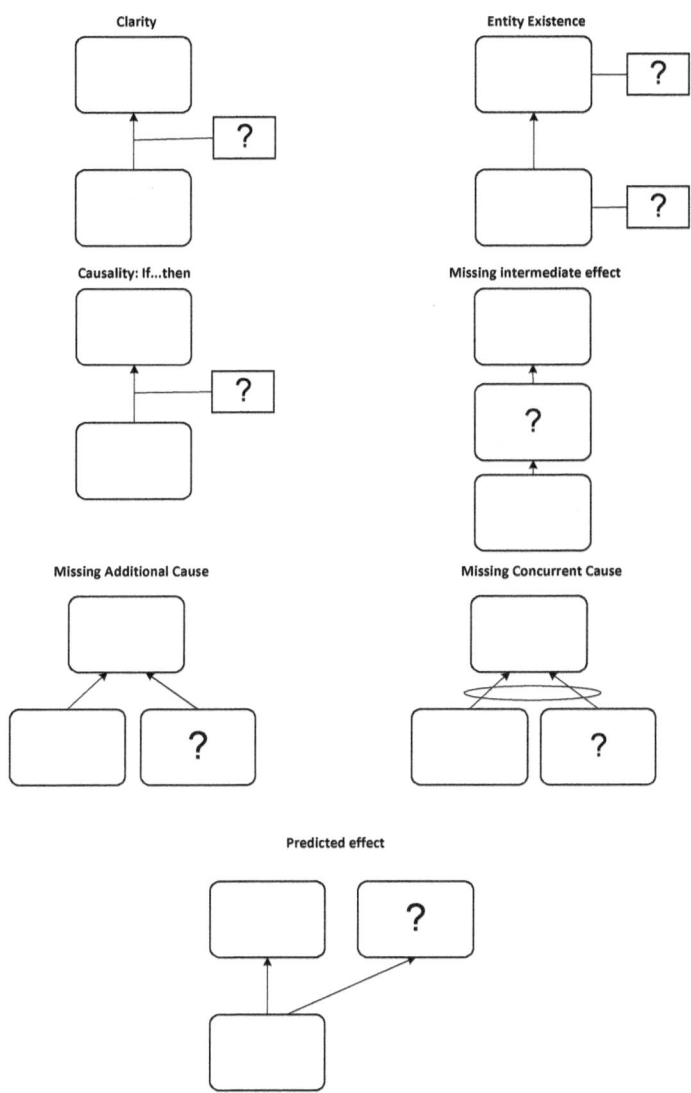

Bibliography

Berry, Thomas, *The Sacred Universe: Earth, Spirituality, and Religion in the Twenty-First Century* (2009), Columbia University Press.

Bohm, David, *On Dialogue* (1996), Routledge.

Campbell, Joseph, *The Hero with a Thousand Faces* (1949), 3rd edition (2012), New World Library.

———. *Pathways to Bliss* (2004), New World Library.

Caspari, John A., *Management Dynamics* (2004), John Wiley & Sons.

Collins, Jim, *Good to Great: Why Some Companies Make the Leap … and Others Don't* (2001), Random House.

Covey, Stephen R., *The 7 Habits of Highly Effective People* (1989), Simon and Schuster.

Darwin, Charles, *The Origin of Species* (1859), ed. John Murray, Penguin Classics (1985).

Dettmer, H. William, *The Logical Thinking Process: A Systems Approach to Complex Problem Solving* (2007), ASQ Quality Press.

Frankl, Viktor E., *Man's Search for Meaning* (1946), new edition (2004), Rider.

Fussell, Chris and Charles Goodyear, *Mission: How Leaders Build a Team of Teams* (2017), Macmillan.

Gardner, Howard, *Changing Minds: The Art and Science of Changing Our Own and Other People's Minds* (2006), Harvard Business School Press.

Goldratt, Eliyahu M. (& Jeff Cox), *The Goal: A Process of Ongoing Improvement* (1984), North River Press; 2nd rev. edition (1992).

Goldratt, Eliyahu M., *Critical Chain* (1997), Gower Publishing.

———. *It's Not Luck* (1994), Gower Publishing.

Greenleaf, Robert K., *Servant Leadership: A Journey into the Nature of Legitimate Power & Greatness* (1997), Paulist Press.

Hamel, Gary, with Bill Breen, *The Future of Management* (2007), Harvard Business School Press.

Isaacs, William, *Dialogue: The Art of Thinking Together* (2008), Crown Publishing.

Isaacson, Walter, *The Innovators* (2014), Simon and Schuster UK.

Jaworski, Joseph, *Synchronicity: The Inner Path of Leadership* (2011), Berrett-Koehler Publishers.

Jaques, Elliott, *Requisite Organization: A Total System for Effective Managerial Organization and Managerial Leadership for the 21st Century* (1998), Cason Hall.

Jaques, Elliott, Stephen D. Clement, and Ronnie Lessem, *Executive Leadership: A Practical Guide to Managing Complexity* (1994), Wiley.

Jung, Carl Gustav, *The Archetypes and the Collective Unconscious* (2nd edition, 1991), Routledge.

Jung, Carl Gustav and Aniela Jaffe, *Memories, Dreams and Reflections* (Vintage Books edition 1989), Random House.

Kahneman, Daniel, *Thinking, Fast and Slow* (2012), Penguin.

Kegan, Robert, Lisa Laskow Lahey, *An Everyone Culture: Becoming a Deliberately Developmental Organization* (2016), Harvard Business Review Press.

Kotter, John P., and Dan S. Cohen, *The Heart of Change: Real Life Stories of How People Change Their Organizations* (2002), Harvard Business School Press.

Lao-Tzu, *Tao Te Ching*, trans. Stephen Addiss and Stanley Lombardo (2007), Shambhala Publications.

Leach, Lawrence P., *Critical Chain Project Management* (2005), Artech House.

Macdonald, Ian, Catherine Burke and Karl Stewart, *Systems Leadership: Creating Positive Organisations* (2012), Gower Publishing.

McChrystal, Stanley, David Silverman, Tantum Collins and Chris Fussell, *Team of Teams: New Rules of Engagement for a Complex World* (2015), Penguin.

McCullough, David, *The Wright Brothers* (2015), Simon & Schuster.

Milton, John P., *Sky Above, Earth Below: Spiritual Practice in Nature* (2006), Sentient Publications.

Peterson, Jordan B., *Maps of Meaning: The Architecture of Belief* (2002), Routledge.

———. *12 Rules for Life: An Antidote to Chaos* (2018), Penguin.

Pink, Daniel, *Drive: The Surprising Truth about What Motivates Us* (2010), Canongate Books.

Porter, Michael E., *Competitive Advantage: Creating and Sustaining Superior Performance* (2004), Free Press.

Scharmer, C. Otto. *Theory U: Learning from the Future as it Emerges* (2009), Berrett-Koehler Publishers.

Schein, Edgar H., *Organizational Culture and Leadership* (2010), John Wiley & Sons.

Schragenheim, Eli, *Management Dilemmas: The Theory of Constraints Approach to Problem Identification and Solutions* (1998), CRC Press.

Schragenheim, Eli, H. William Dettmer, and J. Wayne Patterson. *Supply Chain Management at Warp Speed: Integrating the System from End to End* (2009), Taylor & Francis.

Senge, Peter, et al., *The Dance of Change: The Challenges to Sustaining Momentum in a Learning Organization* (1999), Crown Publishing.

———. *The Fifth Discipline: The Art and Practice of the Learning Organization,* 2nd revised edition (2006), Random House Business.

———. *The Fifth Discipline Fieldbook: Strategies and Tools for Building a Learning Organization* (1994), Doubleday.

Senge, Peter, C., Otto Scharmer, Joseph Jaworski and Betty Sue Flowers, *Presence: Exploring Profound Change in People, Organizations and Society* (2005), Nicholas Brealey Publishing.

Siegel, Daniel J., *Mindsight: The New Science of Personal Transformation* (2010), Bantam Books.

Wilber, Ken, *A Brief History of Everything* (2001), Shambhala.

Thanks and acknowledgements

WHEN YOU'VE BEEN AROUND as long as I have, you come to realise that there are an awful lot of people you are grateful to. To all of you, especially my more than just work-mates, thanks!

But, in terms of getting this book done, there is a very special debt of gratitude to Angus Grundy, my editor. It is absolutely fair to say that not only is the book better than it ever could have been without him, I really wonder if it would have been completed without his patience, wisdom and encouragement.

Thanks also to Ben Hourigan, whose mastery of the ancient art of typesetting and the modern world of Indie Publishing have proved invaluable to getting this book to you in the shape it's in.

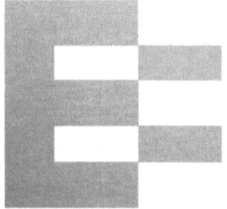

Ensemble
Consulting
Group

—

Let's Redefine What's Possible

—

EnsembleConsultingGroup.com

www.ingramcontent.com/pod-product-compliance
Lightning Source LLC
Chambersburg PA
CBHW020313010526
44107CB00054B/1820